C-3254 CAREER EXAMINATION SERIES

This is your
PASSBOOK for...

Supervising Painter

Test Preparation Study Guide
Questions & Answers

COPYRIGHT NOTICE

This book is SOLELY intended for, is sold ONLY to, and its use is RESTRICTED to individual, bona fide applicants or candidates who qualify by virtue of having seriously filed applications for appropriate license, certificate, professional and/or promotional advancement, higher school matriculation, scholarship, or other legitimate requirements of education and/or governmental authorities.

This book is NOT intended for use, class instruction, tutoring, training, duplication, copying, reprinting, excerption, or adaptation, etc., by:

1) Other publishers
2) Proprietors and/or Instructors of "Coaching" and/or Preparatory Courses
3) Personnel and/or Training Divisions of commercial, industrial, and governmental organizations
4) Schools, colleges, or universities and/or their departments and staffs, including teachers and other personnel
5) Testing Agencies or Bureaus
6) Study groups which seek by the purchase of a single volume to copy and/or duplicate and/or adapt this material for use by the group as a whole without having purchased individual volumes for each of the members of the group
7) Et al.

Such persons would be in violation of appropriate Federal and State statutes.

PROVISION OF LICENSING AGREEMENTS – Recognized educational, commercial, industrial, and governmental institutions and organizations, and others legitimately engaged in educational pursuits, including training, testing, and measurement activities, may address request for a licensing agreement to the copyright owners, who will determine whether, and under what conditions, including fees and charges, the materials in this book may be used them. In other words, a licensing facility exists for the legitimate use of the material in this book on other than an individual basis. However, it is asseverated and affirmed here that the material in this book CANNOT be used without the receipt of the express permission of such a licensing agreement from the Publishers. Inquiries re licensing should be addressed to the company, attention rights and permissions department.

All rights reserved, including the right of reproduction in whole or in part, in any form or by any means, electronic or mechanical, including photocopying, recording, or by any information storage and retrieval system, without permission in writing from the Publisher.

Copyright © 2024 by
National Learning Corporation

212 Michael Drive, Syosset, NY 11791
(516) 921-8888 • www.passbooks.com
E-mail: info@passbooks.com

PUBLISHED IN THE UNITED STATES OF AMERICA

PASSBOOK® SERIES

THE *PASSBOOK® SERIES* has been created to prepare applicants and candidates for the ultimate academic battlefield – the examination room.

At some time in our lives, each and every one of us may be required to take an examination – for validation, matriculation, admission, qualification, registration, certification, or licensure.

Based on the assumption that every applicant or candidate has met the basic formal educational standards, has taken the required number of courses, and read the necessary texts, the *PASSBOOK® SERIES* furnishes the one special preparation which may assure passing with confidence, instead of failing with insecurity. Examination questions – together with answers – are furnished as the basic vehicle for study so that the mysteries of the examination and its compounding difficulties may be eliminated or diminished by a sure method.

This book is meant to help you pass your examination provided that you qualify and are serious in your objective.

The entire field is reviewed through the huge store of content information which is succinctly presented through a provocative and challenging approach – the question-and-answer method.

A climate of success is established by furnishing the correct answers at the end of each test.

You soon learn to recognize types of questions, forms of questions, and patterns of questioning. You may even begin to anticipate expected outcomes.

You perceive that many questions are repeated or adapted so that you can gain acute insights, which may enable you to score many sure points.

You learn how to confront new questions, or types of questions, and to attack them confidently and work out the correct answers.

You note objectives and emphases, and recognize pitfalls and dangers, so that you may make positive educational adjustments.

Moreover, you are kept fully informed in relation to new concepts, methods, practices, and directions in the field.

You discover that you are actually taking the examination all the time: you are preparing for the examination by "taking" an examination, not by reading extraneous and/or supererogatory textbooks.

In short, this PASSBOOK®, used directedly, should be an important factor in helping you to pass your test.

SUPERVISING PAINTER

WHAT THE JOB INVOLVES:
Supervising Painters, under general supervision, supervise, direct and are responsible for the work of painters and other assigned personnel in inside and outside painting of a general nature including all coats, filling, priming, matching colors and mixing paints; assign and lay out work for painters; inspect and check work progress in all stages of completion; examine the work of contractors, evaluate adherence to contract specifications and direct changes to conform to the contract; select proper type of ladder, scaffold, or platform for any particular job; take off quantities from plans and specifications; requisition required materials and equipment; keep records and make reports. Perform related work.

SCOPE OF THE EXAMINATION:
The written test will be of the multiple-choice type and may include questions on supervisory techniques and procedures; safe working practices; proper painting procedures and related tools and equipment; paint failures; relevant trades; preparing reports, ordering materials and maintaining records; estimating time, cost and materials; proper employee conduct; and other related areas.

HOW TO TAKE A TEST

I. YOU MUST PASS AN EXAMINATION

A. *WHAT EVERY CANDIDATE SHOULD KNOW*

Examination applicants often ask us for help in preparing for the written test. What can I study in advance? What kinds of questions will be asked? How will the test be given? How will the papers be graded?

As an applicant for a civil service examination, you may be wondering about some of these things. Our purpose here is to suggest effective methods of advance study and to describe civil service examinations.

Your chances for success on this examination can be increased if you know how to prepare. Those "pre-examination jitters" can be reduced if you know what to expect. You can even experience an adventure in good citizenship if you know why civil service exams are given.

B. *WHY ARE CIVIL SERVICE EXAMINATIONS GIVEN?*

Civil service examinations are important to you in two ways. As a citizen, you want public jobs filled by employees who know how to do their work. As a job seeker, you want a fair chance to compete for that job on an equal footing with other candidates. The best-known means of accomplishing this two-fold goal is the competitive examination.

Exams are widely publicized throughout the nation. They may be administered for jobs in federal, state, city, municipal, town or village governments or agencies.

Any citizen may apply, with some limitations, such as the age or residence of applicants. Your experience and education may be reviewed to see whether you meet the requirements for the particular examination. When these requirements exist, they are reasonable and applied consistently to all applicants. Thus, a competitive examination may cause you some uneasiness now, but it is your privilege and safeguard.

C. *HOW ARE CIVIL SERVICE EXAMS DEVELOPED?*

Examinations are carefully written by trained technicians who are specialists in the field known as "psychological measurement," in consultation with recognized authorities in the field of work that the test will cover. These experts recommend the subject matter areas or skills to be tested; only those knowledges or skills important to your success on the job are included. The most reliable books and source materials available are used as references. Together, the experts and technicians judge the difficulty level of the questions.

Test technicians know how to phrase questions so that the problem is clearly stated. Their ethics do not permit "trick" or "catch" questions. Questions may have been tried out on sample groups, or subjected to statistical analysis, to determine their usefulness.

Written tests are often used in combination with performance tests, ratings of training and experience, and oral interviews. All of these measures combine to form the best-known means of finding the right person for the right job.

II. HOW TO PASS THE WRITTEN TEST

A. NATURE OF THE EXAMINATION

To prepare intelligently for civil service examinations, you should know how they differ from school examinations you have taken. In school you were assigned certain definite pages to read or subjects to cover. The examination questions were quite detailed and usually emphasized memory. Civil service exams, on the other hand, try to discover your present ability to perform the duties of a position, plus your potentiality to learn these duties. In other words, a civil service exam attempts to predict how successful you will be. Questions cover such a broad area that they cannot be as minute and detailed as school exam questions.

In the public service similar kinds of work, or positions, are grouped together in one "class." This process is known as *position-classification*. All the positions in a class are paid according to the salary range for that class. One class title covers all of these positions, and they are all tested by the same examination.

B. FOUR BASIC STEPS

1) Study the announcement

How, then, can you know what subjects to study? Our best answer is: "Learn as much as possible about the class of positions for which you've applied." The exam will test the knowledge, skills and abilities needed to do the work.

Your most valuable source of information about the position you want is the official exam announcement. This announcement lists the training and experience qualifications. Check these standards and apply only if you come reasonably close to meeting them.

The brief description of the position in the examination announcement offers some clues to the subjects which will be tested. Think about the job itself. Review the duties in your mind. Can you perform them, or are there some in which you are rusty? Fill in the blank spots in your preparation.

Many jurisdictions preview the written test in the exam announcement by including a section called "Knowledge and Abilities Required," "Scope of the Examination," or some similar heading. Here you will find out specifically what fields will be tested.

2) Review your own background

Once you learn in general what the position is all about, and what you need to know to do the work, ask yourself which subjects you already know fairly well and which need improvement. You may wonder whether to concentrate on improving your strong areas or on building some background in your fields of weakness. When the announcement has specified "some knowledge" or "considerable knowledge," or has used adjectives like "beginning principles of..." or "advanced ... methods," you can get a clue as to the number and difficulty of questions to be asked in any given field. More questions, and hence broader coverage, would be included for those subjects which are more important in the work. Now weigh your strengths and weaknesses against the job requirements and prepare accordingly.

3) Determine the level of the position

Another way to tell how intensively you should prepare is to understand the level of the job for which you are applying. Is it the entering level? In other words, is this the position in which beginners in a field of work are hired? Or is it an intermediate or advanced level? Sometimes this is indicated by such words as "Junior" or "Senior" in the class title. Other jurisdictions use Roman numerals to designate the level – Clerk I, Clerk II, for example. The word "Supervisor" sometimes appears in the title. If the level is not indicated by the title, check the description of duties. Will you be working under very close supervision, or will you have responsibility for independent decisions in this work?

4) Choose appropriate study materials

Now that you know the subjects to be examined and the relative amount of each subject to be covered, you can choose suitable study materials. For beginning level jobs, or even advanced ones, if you have a pronounced weakness in some aspect of your training, read a modern, standard textbook in that field. Be sure it is up to date and has general coverage. Such books are normally available at your library, and the librarian will be glad to help you locate one. For entry-level positions, questions of appropriate difficulty are chosen -- neither highly advanced questions, nor those too simple. Such questions require careful thought but not advanced training.

If the position for which you are applying is technical or advanced, you will read more advanced, specialized material. If you are already familiar with the basic principles of your field, elementary textbooks would waste your time. Concentrate on advanced textbooks and technical periodicals. Think through the concepts and review difficult problems in your field.

These are all general sources. You can get more ideas on your own initiative, following these leads. For example, training manuals and publications of the government agency which employs workers in your field can be useful, particularly for technical and professional positions. A letter or visit to the government department involved may result in more specific study suggestions, and certainly will provide you with a more definite idea of the exact nature of the position you are seeking.

III. KINDS OF TESTS

Tests are used for purposes other than measuring knowledge and ability to perform specified duties. For some positions, it is equally important to test ability to make adjustments to new situations or to profit from training. In others, basic mental abilities not dependent on information are essential. Questions which test these things may not appear as pertinent to the duties of the position as those which test for knowledge and information. Yet they are often highly important parts of a fair examination. For very general questions, it is almost impossible to help you direct your study efforts. What we can do is to point out some of the more common of these general abilities needed in public service positions and describe some typical questions.

1) General information

Broad, general information has been found useful for predicting job success in some kinds of work. This is tested in a variety of ways, from vocabulary lists to questions about current events. Basic background in some field of work, such as sociology or economics, may be sampled in a group of questions. Often these are principles which have become familiar to most persons through exposure rather than through formal training. It is difficult to advise you how to study for these questions; being alert to the world around you is our best suggestion.

2) Verbal ability

An example of an ability needed in many positions is verbal or language ability. Verbal ability is, in brief, the ability to use and understand words. Vocabulary and grammar tests are typical measures of this ability. Reading comprehension or paragraph interpretation questions are common in many kinds of civil service tests. You are given a paragraph of written material and asked to find its central meaning.

3) Numerical ability

Number skills can be tested by the familiar arithmetic problem, by checking paired lists of numbers to see which are alike and which are different, or by interpreting charts and graphs. In the latter test, a graph may be printed in the test booklet which you are asked to use as the basis for answering questions.

4) Observation

A popular test for law-enforcement positions is the observation test. A picture is shown to you for several minutes, then taken away. Questions about the picture test your ability to observe both details and larger elements.

5) Following directions

In many positions in the public service, the employee must be able to carry out written instructions dependably and accurately. You may be given a chart with several columns, each column listing a variety of information. The questions require you to carry out directions involving the information given in the chart.

6) Skills and aptitudes

Performance tests effectively measure some manual skills and aptitudes. When the skill is one in which you are trained, such as typing or shorthand, you can practice. These tests are often very much like those given in business school or high school courses. For many of the other skills and aptitudes, however, no short-time preparation can be made. Skills and abilities natural to you or that you have developed throughout your lifetime are being tested.

Many of the general questions just described provide all the data needed to answer the questions and ask you to use your reasoning ability to find the answers. Your best preparation for these tests, as well as for tests of facts and ideas, is to be at your physical and mental best. You, no doubt, have your own methods of getting into an exam-taking mood and keeping "in shape." The next section lists some ideas on this subject.

IV. KINDS OF QUESTIONS

Only rarely is the "essay" question, which you answer in narrative form, used in civil service tests. Civil service tests are usually of the short-answer type. Full instructions for answering these questions will be given to you at the examination. But in case this is your first experience with short-answer questions and separate answer sheets, here is what you need to know:

1) Multiple-choice Questions

Most popular of the short-answer questions is the "multiple choice" or "best answer" question. It can be used, for example, to test for factual knowledge, ability to solve problems or judgment in meeting situations found at work.

A multiple-choice question is normally one of three types—
- It can begin with an incomplete statement followed by several possible endings. You are to find the one ending which *best* completes the statement, although some of the others may not be entirely wrong.
- It can also be a complete statement in the form of a question which is answered by choosing one of the statements listed.

- It can be in the form of a problem – again you select the best answer.

Here is an example of a multiple-choice question with a discussion which should give you some clues as to the method for choosing the right answer:

When an employee has a complaint about his assignment, the action which will *best* help him overcome his difficulty is to
- A. discuss his difficulty with his coworkers
- B. take the problem to the head of the organization
- C. take the problem to the person who gave him the assignment
- D. say nothing to anyone about his complaint

In answering this question, you should study each of the choices to find which is best. Consider choice "A" – Certainly an employee may discuss his complaint with fellow employees, but no change or improvement can result, and the complaint remains unresolved. Choice "B" is a poor choice since the head of the organization probably does not know what assignment you have been given, and taking your problem to him is known as "going over the head" of the supervisor. The supervisor, or person who made the assignment, is the person who can clarify it or correct any injustice. Choice "C" is, therefore, correct. To say nothing, as in choice "D," is unwise. Supervisors have and interest in knowing the problems employees are facing, and the employee is seeking a solution to his problem.

2) True/False Questions

The "true/false" or "right/wrong" form of question is sometimes used. Here a complete statement is given. Your job is to decide whether the statement is right or wrong.

SAMPLE: A roaming cell-phone call to a nearby city costs less than a non-roaming call to a distant city.

This statement is wrong, or false, since roaming calls are more expensive.

This is not a complete list of all possible question forms, although most of the others are variations of these common types. You will always get complete directions for answering questions. Be sure you understand *how* to mark your answers – ask questions until you do.

V. RECORDING YOUR ANSWERS

Computer terminals are used more and more today for many different kinds of exams.
For an examination with very few applicants, you may be told to record your answers in the test booklet itself. Separate answer sheets are much more common. If this separate answer sheet is to be scored by machine – and this is often the case – it is highly important that you mark your answers correctly in order to get credit.

An electronic scoring machine is often used in civil service offices because of the speed with which papers can be scored. Machine-scored answer sheets must be marked with a pencil, which will be given to you. This pencil has a high graphite content which responds to the electronic scoring machine. As a matter of fact, stray dots may register as answers, so do not let your pencil rest on the answer sheet while you are pondering the correct answer. Also, if your pencil lead breaks or is otherwise defective, ask for another.

Since the answer sheet will be dropped in a slot in the scoring machine, be careful not to bend the corners or get the paper crumpled.

The answer sheet normally has five vertical columns of numbers, with 30 numbers to a column. These numbers correspond to the question numbers in your test booklet. After each number, going across the page are four or five pairs of dotted lines. These short dotted lines have small letters or numbers above them. The first two pairs may also have a "T" or "F" above the letters. This indicates that the first two pairs only are to be used if the questions are of the true-false type. If the questions are multiple choice, disregard the "T" and "F" and pay attention only to the small letters or numbers.

Answer your questions in the manner of the sample that follows:

32. The largest city in the United States is
 A. Washington, D.C.
 B. New York City
 C. Chicago
 D. Detroit
 E. San Francisco

1) Choose the answer you think is best. (New York City is the largest, so "B" is correct.)
2) Find the row of dotted lines numbered the same as the question you are answering. (Find row number 32)
3) Find the pair of dotted lines corresponding to the answer. (Find the pair of lines under the mark "B.")
4) Make a solid black mark between the dotted lines.

VI. BEFORE THE TEST

Common sense will help you find procedures to follow to get ready for an examination. Too many of us, however, overlook these sensible measures. Indeed, nervousness and fatigue have been found to be the most serious reasons why applicants fail to do their best on civil service tests. Here is a list of reminders:

- Begin your preparation early – Don't wait until the last minute to go scurrying around for books and materials or to find out what the position is all about.
- Prepare continuously – An hour a night for a week is better than an all-night cram session. This has been definitely established. What is more, a night a week for a month will return better dividends than crowding your study into a shorter period of time.
- Locate the place of the exam – You have been sent a notice telling you when and where to report for the examination. If the location is in a different town or otherwise unfamiliar to you, it would be well to inquire the best route and learn something about the building.
- Relax the night before the test – Allow your mind to rest. Do not study at all that night. Plan some mild recreation or diversion; then go to bed early and get a good night's sleep.
- Get up early enough to make a leisurely trip to the place for the test – This way unforeseen events, traffic snarls, unfamiliar buildings, etc. will not upset you.
- Dress comfortably – A written test is not a fashion show. You will be known by number and not by name, so wear something comfortable.

- Leave excess paraphernalia at home – Shopping bags and odd bundles will get in your way. You need bring only the items mentioned in the official notice you received; usually everything you need is provided. Do not bring reference books to the exam. They will only confuse those last minutes and be taken away from you when in the test room.
- Arrive somewhat ahead of time – If because of transportation schedules you must get there very early, bring a newspaper or magazine to take your mind off yourself while waiting.
- Locate the examination room – When you have found the proper room, you will be directed to the seat or part of the room where you will sit. Sometimes you are given a sheet of instructions to read while you are waiting. Do not fill out any forms until you are told to do so; just read them and be prepared.
- Relax and prepare to listen to the instructions
- If you have any physical problem that may keep you from doing your best, be sure to tell the test administrator. If you are sick or in poor health, you really cannot do your best on the exam. You can come back and take the test some other time.

VII. AT THE TEST

The day of the test is here and you have the test booklet in your hand. The temptation to get going is very strong. Caution! There is more to success than knowing the right answers. You must know how to identify your papers and understand variations in the type of short-answer question used in this particular examination. Follow these suggestions for maximum results from your efforts:

1) Cooperate with the monitor

The test administrator has a duty to create a situation in which you can be as much at ease as possible. He will give instructions, tell you when to begin, check to see that you are marking your answer sheet correctly, and so on. He is not there to guard you, although he will see that your competitors do not take unfair advantage. He wants to help you do your best.

2) Listen to all instructions

Don't jump the gun! Wait until you understand all directions. In most civil service tests you get more time than you need to answer the questions. So don't be in a hurry. Read each word of instructions until you clearly understand the meaning. Study the examples, listen to all announcements and follow directions. Ask questions if you do not understand what to do.

3) Identify your papers

Civil service exams are usually identified by number only. You will be assigned a number; you must not put your name on your test papers. Be sure to copy your number correctly. Since more than one exam may be given, copy your exact examination title.

4) Plan your time

Unless you are told that a test is a "speed" or "rate of work" test, speed itself is usually not important. Time enough to answer all the questions will be provided, but this does not mean that you have all day. An overall time limit has been set. Divide the total time (in minutes) by the number of questions to determine the approximate time you have for each question.

5) Do not linger over difficult questions

If you come across a difficult question, mark it with a paper clip (useful to have along) and come back to it when you have been through the booklet. One caution if you do this – be sure to skip a number on your answer sheet as well. Check often to be sure that you have not lost your place and that you are marking in the row numbered the same as the question you are answering.

6) Read the questions

Be sure you know what the question asks! Many capable people are unsuccessful because they failed to *read* the questions correctly.

7) Answer all questions

Unless you have been instructed that a penalty will be deducted for incorrect answers, it is better to guess than to omit a question.

8) Speed tests

It is often better NOT to guess on speed tests. It has been found that on timed tests people are tempted to spend the last few seconds before time is called in marking answers at random – without even reading them – in the hope of picking up a few extra points. To discourage this practice, the instructions may warn you that your score will be "corrected" for guessing. That is, a penalty will be applied. The incorrect answers will be deducted from the correct ones, or some other penalty formula will be used.

9) Review your answers

If you finish before time is called, go back to the questions you guessed or omitted to give them further thought. Review other answers if you have time.

10) Return your test materials

If you are ready to leave before others have finished or time is called, take ALL your materials to the monitor and leave quietly. Never take any test material with you. The monitor can discover whose papers are not complete, and taking a test booklet may be grounds for disqualification.

VIII. EXAMINATION TECHNIQUES

1) Read the general instructions carefully. These are usually printed on the first page of the exam booklet. As a rule, these instructions refer to the timing of the examination; the fact that you should not start work until the signal and must stop work at a signal, etc. If there are any *special* instructions, such as a choice of questions to be answered, make sure that you note this instruction carefully.

2) When you are ready to start work on the examination, that is as soon as the signal has been given, read the instructions to each question booklet, underline any key words or phrases, such as *least*, *best*, *outline*, *describe* and the like. In this way you will tend to answer as requested rather than discover on reviewing your paper that you *listed without describing*, that you selected the *worst* choice rather than the *best* choice, etc.

3) If the examination is of the objective or multiple-choice type – that is, each question will also give a series of possible answers: A, B, C or D, and you are called upon to select the best answer and write the letter next to that answer on your answer paper – it is advisable to start answering each question in turn. There may be anywhere from 50 to 100 such questions in the three or four hours allotted and you can see how much time would be taken if you read through all the questions before beginning to answer any. Furthermore, if you come across a question or group of questions which you know would be difficult to answer, it would undoubtedly affect your handling of all the other questions.

4) If the examination is of the essay type and contains but a few questions, it is a moot point as to whether you should read all the questions before starting to answer any one. Of course, if you are given a choice – say five out of seven and the like – then it is essential to read all the questions so you can eliminate the two that are most difficult. If, however, you are asked to answer all the questions, there may be danger in trying to answer the easiest one first because you may find that you will spend too much time on it. The best technique is to answer the first question, then proceed to the second, etc.

5) Time your answers. Before the exam begins, write down the time it started, then add the time allowed for the examination and write down the time it must be completed, then divide the time available somewhat as follows:
    - If 3-1/2 hours are allowed, that would be 210 minutes. If you have 80 objective-type questions, that would be an average of 2-1/2 minutes per question. Allow yourself no more than 2 minutes per question, or a total of 160 minutes, which will permit about 50 minutes to review.
    - If for the time allotment of 210 minutes there are 7 essay questions to answer, that would average about 30 minutes a question. Give yourself only 25 minutes per question so that you have about 35 minutes to review.

6) The most important instruction is to *read each question* and make sure you know what is wanted. The second most important instruction is to *time yourself properly* so that you answer every question. The third most important instruction is to *answer every question*. Guess if you have to but include something for each question. Remember that you will receive no credit for a blank and will probably receive some credit if you write something in answer to an essay question. If you guess a letter – say "B" for a multiple-choice question – you may have guessed right. If you leave a blank as an answer to a multiple-choice question, the examiners may respect your feelings but it will not add a point to your score. Some exams may penalize you for wrong answers, so in such cases *only*, you may not want to guess unless you have some basis for your answer.

7) Suggestions
    a. Objective-type questions
        1. Examine the question booklet for proper sequence of pages and questions
        2. Read all instructions carefully
        3. Skip any question which seems too difficult; return to it after all other questions have been answered
        4. Apportion your time properly; do not spend too much time on any single question or group of questions

5. Note and underline key words – *all, most, fewest, least, best, worst, same, opposite*, etc.
6. Pay particular attention to negatives
7. Note unusual option, e.g., unduly long, short, complex, different or similar in content to the body of the question
8. Observe the use of "hedging" words – *probably, may, most likely*, etc.
9. Make sure that your answer is put next to the same number as the question
10. Do not second-guess unless you have good reason to believe the second answer is definitely more correct
11. Cross out original answer if you decide another answer is more accurate; do not erase until you are ready to hand your paper in
12. Answer all questions; guess unless instructed otherwise
13. Leave time for review

  b. Essay questions
1. Read each question carefully
2. Determine exactly what is wanted. Underline key words or phrases.
3. Decide on outline or paragraph answer
4. Include many different points and elements unless asked to develop any one or two points or elements
5. Show impartiality by giving pros and cons unless directed to select one side only
6. Make and write down any assumptions you find necessary to answer the questions
7. Watch your English, grammar, punctuation and choice of words
8. Time your answers; don't crowd material

8) Answering the essay question

Most essay questions can be answered by framing the specific response around several key words or ideas. Here are a few such key words or ideas:

M's: manpower, materials, methods, money, management
P's: purpose, program, policy, plan, procedure, practice, problems, pitfalls, personnel, public relations

  a. Six basic steps in handling problems:
1. Preliminary plan and background development
2. Collect information, data and facts
3. Analyze and interpret information, data and facts
4. Analyze and develop solutions as well as make recommendations
5. Prepare report and sell recommendations
6. Install recommendations and follow up effectiveness

  b. Pitfalls to avoid
1. *Taking things for granted* – A statement of the situation does not necessarily imply that each of the elements is necessarily true; for example, a complaint may be invalid and biased so that all that can be taken for granted is that a complaint has been registered

2. *Considering only one side of a situation* – Wherever possible, indicate several alternatives and then point out the reasons you selected the best one
3. *Failing to indicate follow up* – Whenever your answer indicates action on your part, make certain that you will take proper follow-up action to see how successful your recommendations, procedures or actions turn out to be
4. *Taking too long in answering any single question* – Remember to time your answers properly

IX. AFTER THE TEST

Scoring procedures differ in detail among civil service jurisdictions although the general principles are the same. Whether the papers are hand-scored or graded by machine we have described, they are nearly always graded by number. That is, the person who marks the paper knows only the number – never the name – of the applicant. Not until all the papers have been graded will they be matched with names. If other tests, such as training and experience or oral interview ratings have been given, scores will be combined. Different parts of the examination usually have different weights. For example, the written test might count 60 percent of the final grade, and a rating of training and experience 40 percent. In many jurisdictions, veterans will have a certain number of points added to their grades.

After the final grade has been determined, the names are placed in grade order and an eligible list is established. There are various methods for resolving ties between those who get the same final grade – probably the most common is to place first the name of the person whose application was received first. Job offers are made from the eligible list in the order the names appear on it. You will be notified of your grade and your rank as soon as all these computations have been made. This will be done as rapidly as possible.

People who are found to meet the requirements in the announcement are called "eligibles." Their names are put on a list of eligible candidates. An eligible's chances of getting a job depend on how high he stands on this list and how fast agencies are filling jobs from the list.

When a job is to be filled from a list of eligibles, the agency asks for the names of people on the list of eligibles for that job. When the civil service commission receives this request, it sends to the agency the names of the three people highest on this list. Or, if the job to be filled has specialized requirements, the office sends the agency the names of the top three persons who meet these requirements from the general list.

The appointing officer makes a choice from among the three people whose names were sent to him. If the selected person accepts the appointment, the names of the others are put back on the list to be considered for future openings.

That is the rule in hiring from all kinds of eligible lists, whether they are for typist, carpenter, chemist, or something else. For every vacancy, the appointing officer has his choice of any one of the top three eligibles on the list. This explains why the person whose name is on top of the list sometimes does not get an appointment when some of the persons lower on the list do. If the appointing officer chooses the second or third eligible, the No. 1 eligible does not get a job at once, but stays on the list until he is appointed or the list is terminated.

X. HOW TO PASS THE INTERVIEW TEST

The examination for which you applied requires an oral interview test. You have already taken the written test and you are now being called for the interview test – the final part of the formal examination.

You may think that it is not possible to prepare for an interview test and that there are no procedures to follow during an interview. Our purpose is to point out some things you can do in advance that will help you and some good rules to follow and pitfalls to avoid while you are being interviewed.

What is an interview supposed to test?

The written examination is designed to test the technical knowledge and competence of the candidate; the oral is designed to evaluate intangible qualities, not readily measured otherwise, and to establish a list showing the relative fitness of each candidate – as measured against his competitors – for the position sought. Scoring is not on the basis of "right" and "wrong," but on a sliding scale of values ranging from "not passable" to "outstanding." As a matter of fact, it is possible to achieve a relatively low score without a single "incorrect" answer because of evident weakness in the qualities being measured.

Occasionally, an examination may consist entirely of an oral test – either an individual or a group oral. In such cases, information is sought concerning the technical knowledges and abilities of the candidate, since there has been no written examination for this purpose. More commonly, however, an oral test is used to supplement a written examination.

Who conducts interviews?

The composition of oral boards varies among different jurisdictions. In nearly all, a representative of the personnel department serves as chairman. One of the members of the board may be a representative of the department in which the candidate would work. In some cases, "outside experts" are used, and, frequently, a businessman or some other representative of the general public is asked to serve. Labor and management or other special groups may be represented. The aim is to secure the services of experts in the appropriate field.

However the board is composed, it is a good idea (and not at all improper or unethical) to ascertain in advance of the interview who the members are and what groups they represent. When you are introduced to them, you will have some idea of their backgrounds and interests, and at least you will not stutter and stammer over their names.

What should be done before the interview?

While knowledge about the board members is useful and takes some of the surprise element out of the interview, there is other preparation which is more substantive. It *is* possible to prepare for an oral interview – in several ways:

1) Keep a copy of your application and review it carefully before the interview

This may be the only document before the oral board, and the starting point of the interview. Know what education and experience you have listed there, and the sequence and dates of all of it. Sometimes the board will ask you to review the highlights of your experience for them; you should not have to hem and haw doing it.

2) Study the class specification and the examination announcement

Usually, the oral board has one or both of these to guide them. The qualities, characteristics or knowledges required by the position sought are stated in these documents. They offer valuable clues as to the nature of the oral interview. For example, if the job involves supervisory responsibilities, the announcement will usually indicate that knowledge of modern supervisory methods and the qualifications of the candidate as a supervisor will be tested. If so, you can expect such questions, frequently in the form of a hypothetical situation which you are expected to solve. NEVER go into an oral without knowledge of the duties and responsibilities of the job you seek.

3) Think through each qualification required

Try to visualize the kind of questions you would ask if you were a board member. How well could you answer them? Try especially to appraise your own knowledge and background in each area, *measured against the job sought*, and identify any areas in which you are weak. Be critical and realistic – do not flatter yourself.

4) Do some general reading in areas in which you feel you may be weak

For example, if the job involves supervision and your past experience has NOT, some general reading in supervisory methods and practices, particularly in the field of human relations, might be useful. Do NOT study agency procedures or detailed manuals. The oral board will be testing your understanding and capacity, not your memory.

5) Get a good night's sleep and watch your general health and mental attitude

You will want a clear head at the interview. Take care of a cold or any other minor ailment, and of course, no hangovers.

What should be done on the day of the interview?

Now comes the day of the interview itself. Give yourself plenty of time to get there. Plan to arrive somewhat ahead of the scheduled time, particularly if your appointment is in the fore part of the day. If a previous candidate fails to appear, the board might be ready for you a bit early. By early afternoon an oral board is almost invariably behind schedule if there are many candidates, and you may have to wait. Take along a book or magazine to read, or your application to review, but leave any extraneous material in the waiting room when you go in for your interview. In any event, relax and compose yourself.

The matter of dress is important. The board is forming impressions about you – from your experience, your manners, your attitude, and your appearance. Give your personal appearance careful attention. Dress your best, but not your flashiest. Choose conservative, appropriate clothing, and be sure it is immaculate. This is a business interview, and your appearance should indicate that you regard it as such. Besides, being well groomed and properly dressed will help boost your confidence.

Sooner or later, someone will call your name and escort you into the interview room. *This is it.* From here on you are on your own. It is too late for any more preparation. But remember, you asked for this opportunity to prove your fitness, and you are here because your request was granted.

What happens when you go in?

The usual sequence of events will be as follows: The clerk (who is often the board stenographer) will introduce you to the chairman of the oral board, who will introduce you to the other members of the board. Acknowledge the introductions before you sit down. Do not be surprised if you find a microphone facing you or a stenotypist sitting by. Oral interviews are usually recorded in the event of an appeal or other review.

Usually the chairman of the board will open the interview by reviewing the highlights of your education and work experience from your application – primarily for the benefit of the other members of the board, as well as to get the material into the record. Do not interrupt or comment unless there is an error or significant misinterpretation; if that is the case, do not hesitate. But do not quibble about insignificant matters. Also, he will usually ask you some question about your education, experience or your present job – partly to get you to start talking and to establish the interviewing "rapport." He may start the actual questioning, or turn it over to one of the other members. Frequently, each member undertakes the questioning on a particular area, one in which he is perhaps most competent, so you can expect each member to participate in the examination. Because time is limited, you may also expect some rather abrupt switches in the direction the questioning takes, so do not be upset by it. Normally, a board member will not pursue a single line of questioning unless he discovers a particular strength or weakness.

After each member has participated, the chairman will usually ask whether any member has any further questions, then will ask you if you have anything you wish to add. Unless you are expecting this question, it may floor you. Worse, it may start you off on an extended, extemporaneous speech. The board is not usually seeking more information. The question is principally to offer you a last opportunity to present further qualifications or to indicate that you have nothing to add. So, if you feel that a significant qualification or characteristic has been overlooked, it is proper to point it out in a sentence or so. Do not compliment the board on the thoroughness of their examination – they have been sketchy, and you know it. If you wish, merely say, "No thank you, I have nothing further to add." This is a point where you can "talk yourself out" of a good impression or fail to present an important bit of information. Remember, *you close the interview yourself*.

The chairman will then say, "That is all, Mr. _____, thank you." Do not be startled; the interview is over, and quicker than you think. Thank him, gather your belongings and take your leave. Save your sigh of relief for the other side of the door.

How to put your best foot forward

Throughout this entire process, you may feel that the board individually and collectively is trying to pierce your defenses, seek out your hidden weaknesses and embarrass and confuse you. Actually, this is not true. They are obliged to make an appraisal of your qualifications for the job you are seeking, and they want to see you in your best light. Remember, they must interview all candidates and a non-cooperative candidate may become a failure in spite of their best efforts to bring out his qualifications. Here are 15 suggestions that will help you:

1) Be natural – Keep your attitude confident, not cocky

If you are not confident that you can do the job, do not expect the board to be. Do not apologize for your weaknesses, try to bring out your strong points. The board is interested in a positive, not negative, presentation. Cockiness will antagonize any board member and make him wonder if you are covering up a weakness by a false show of strength.

2) Get comfortable, but don't lounge or sprawl

Sit erectly but not stiffly. A careless posture may lead the board to conclude that you are careless in other things, or at least that you are not impressed by the importance of the occasion. Either conclusion is natural, even if incorrect. Do not fuss with your clothing, a pencil or an ashtray. Your hands may occasionally be useful to emphasize a point; do not let them become a point of distraction.

3) Do not wisecrack or make small talk

This is a serious situation, and your attitude should show that you consider it as such. Further, the time of the board is limited – they do not want to waste it, and neither should you.

4) Do not exaggerate your experience or abilities
In the first place, from information in the application or other interviews and sources, the board may know more about you than you think. Secondly, you probably will not get away with it. An experienced board is rather adept at spotting such a situation, so do not take the chance.

5) If you know a board member, do not make a point of it, yet do not hide it
Certainly you are not fooling him, and probably not the other members of the board. Do not try to take advantage of your acquaintanceship – it will probably do you little good.

6) Do not dominate the interview
Let the board do that. They will give you the clues – do not assume that you have to do all the talking. Realize that the board has a number of questions to ask you, and do not try to take up all the interview time by showing off your extensive knowledge of the answer to the first one.

7) Be attentive
You only have 20 minutes or so, and you should keep your attention at its sharpest throughout. When a member is addressing a problem or question to you, give him your undivided attention. Address your reply principally to him, but do not exclude the other board members.

8) Do not interrupt
A board member may be stating a problem for you to analyze. He will ask you a question when the time comes. Let him state the problem, and wait for the question.

9) Make sure you understand the question
Do not try to answer until you are sure what the question is. If it is not clear, restate it in your own words or ask the board member to clarify it for you. However, do not haggle about minor elements.

10) Reply promptly but not hastily
A common entry on oral board rating sheets is "candidate responded readily," or "candidate hesitated in replies." Respond as promptly and quickly as you can, but do not jump to a hasty, ill-considered answer.

11) Do not be peremptory in your answers
A brief answer is proper – but do not fire your answer back. That is a losing game from your point of view. The board member can probably ask questions much faster than you can answer them.

12) Do not try to create the answer you think the board member wants
He is interested in what kind of mind you have and how it works – not in playing games. Furthermore, he can usually spot this practice and will actually grade you down on it.

13) Do not switch sides in your reply merely to agree with a board member
Frequently, a member will take a contrary position merely to draw you out and to see if you are willing and able to defend your point of view. Do not start a debate, yet do not surrender a good position. If a position is worth taking, it is worth defending.

14) Do not be afraid to admit an error in judgment if you are shown to be wrong

The board knows that you are forced to reply without any opportunity for careful consideration. Your answer may be demonstrably wrong. If so, admit it and get on with the interview.

15) Do not dwell at length on your present job

The opening question may relate to your present assignment. Answer the question but do not go into an extended discussion. You are being examined for a *new* job, not your present one. As a matter of fact, try to phrase ALL your answers in terms of the job for which you are being examined.

Basis of Rating

Probably you will forget most of these "do's" and "don'ts" when you walk into the oral interview room. Even remembering them all will not ensure you a passing grade. Perhaps you did not have the qualifications in the first place. But remembering them will help you to put your best foot forward, without treading on the toes of the board members.

Rumor and popular opinion to the contrary notwithstanding, an oral board wants you to make the best appearance possible. They know you are under pressure – but they also want to see how you respond to it as a guide to what your reaction would be under the pressures of the job you seek. They will be influenced by the degree of poise you display, the personal traits you show and the manner in which you respond.

ABOUT THIS BOOK

This book contains tests divided into Examination Sections. Go through each test, answering every question in the margin. We have also attached a sample answer sheet at the back of the book that can be removed and used. At the end of each test look at the answer key and check your answers. On the ones you got wrong, look at the right answer choice and learn. Do not fill in the answers first. Do not memorize the questions and answers, but understand the answer and principles involved. On your test, the questions will likely be different from the samples. Questions are changed and new ones added. If you understand these past questions you should have success with any changes that arise. Tests may consist of several types of questions. We have additional books on each subject should more study be advisable or necessary for you. Finally, the more you study, the better prepared you will be. This book is intended to be the last thing you study before you walk into the examination room. Prior study of relevant texts is also recommended. NLC publishes some of these in our Fundamental Series. Knowledge and good sense are important factors in passing your exam. Good luck also helps. So now study this Passbook, absorb the material contained within and take that knowledge into the examination. Then do your best to pass that exam.

EXAMINATION SECTION

EXAMINATION SECTION
TEST 1

DIRECTIONS: Each question or incomplete statement is followed by several suggested answers or completions. Select the one that BEST answers the question or completes the statement. *PRINT THE LETTER OF THE CORRECT ANSWER IN THE SPACE AT THE RIGHT.*

1. A brush which has been used in lacquer should be cleaned by washing it in   1.____

   A. cold water
   B. wood alcohol
   C. lacquer thinner
   D. linseed oil

2. In a paint shop, brushes that are in frequent use can be kept in good condition by suspending them in a *brushkeeper* filled with   2.____

   A. spar varnish
   B. a mixture of raw linseed oil and turpentine
   C. yellow soap solution
   D. a mixture of water and alcohol

3. The primary colors are red, blue, and yellow, and the secondary colors are   3.____

   A. brown, orange, and violet
   B. orange, violet, and green
   C. violet, green, and brown
   D. green, brown, and orange

4. Before we repaint a wood surface on which the old paint film has developed some wrinkling, we should subject the surface to a   4.____

   A. thorough scraping
   B. light shellacking
   C. wash-down with dilute muriatic acid
   D. rubbing down of the wrinkles with fairly coarse sandpaper

5. The combination of any of the various colors with white is called a   5.____

   A. shade   B. tone   C. tint   D. hue

6. The BEST method to make sure that all foreign material, including tight mill scale, is removed from structural steel shapes before painting them is   6.____

   A. chipping
   B. scraping
   C. wire brushing
   D. sandblasting

7. When wood is being painted, the turpentine in the paint performs a number of services, but it does NOT   7.____

   A. help the paint to penetrate into the pores of the wood
   B. promote drying
   C. help the paint to spread and brush out more evenly and smoothly
   D. prevent mildewing of the finished paint surface

8. Excessive moisture on the surface being painted would MOST likely result in

   A. alligatoring B. blistering
   C. cracking D. sagging

9. Before painting a new concrete floor or wall that has not had a chance to dry for several months, it should be treated with

   A. a solution of zinc sulphate
   B. a solution of sodium chloride
   C. strong soap and water
   D. turpentine or benzine

10. When hard, dry putty must be removed from a wood window frame in order to put in a new pane of glass, the BEST tool with which to do this job is a

    A. screwdriver B. putty knife
    C. wide wood chisel D. pocket knife

11. When a pane of window glass is being replaced, the glass may be found to be too large for the wood opening.
    In such a case,

    A. the wood should be cut to fit the glass
    B. the glass should be cut to fit the opening
    C. both the wood and the glass should be cut to obtain a fit
    D. the glass should be discarded

12. The first or shop coat for iron and steel is GENERALLY a(n) _____ paint.

    A. red lead B. iron oxide
    C. white lead D. zinc white

13. When a wood sash is being reglazed, the NEXT step after securing the new window glass in place with glazier's points is to

    A. give the sash a coating of linseed oil
    B. putty the window on the outside
    C. enamel the window
    D. paint the putty

14. Galvanized sheet metal that has weathered to a dull no-gloss appearance

    A. should not be painted
    B. should be washed down with a strong acid solution before being painted
    C. may be painted without special pre-treatment
    D. should be flame-cleaned with a torch and painted while still warm

15. All of the following are white pigments EXCEPT

    A. lithopone B. zinc oxide
    C. lead chromate D. titanium dioxide

16. Those materials which are added to a paint vehicle to regulate its consistency and thus increase its spreading power and facilitate its application are called

    A. driers B. thinners C. extenders D. oxidents

17. A paint that is characterized by its ability to dry to an especially smooth, hard, glossy or semi-glossy finish is called a(n)   17.____

    A. primer   B. sealer   C. glaze   D. enamel

18. Of the following materials, the one that is NOT used as a thinner in paints is   18.____

    A. acetone   B. water   C. resin   D. ether

19. Driers are necessary ingredients in _____ paints.   19.____

    A. oil   B. water   C. latex   D. cement

20. The ability of a paint to obscure the color of the underlying surface is called its   20.____

    A. adhesion   B. hiding power
    C. coverage   D. gloss

KEY (CORRECT ANSWERS)

1.	C	11.	B
2.	B	12.	A
3.	B	13.	B
4.	D	14.	C
5.	C	15.	C
6.	D	16.	B
7.	D	17.	D
8.	B	18.	C
9.	A	19.	A
10.	C	20.	B

TEST 2

DIRECTIONS: Each question or incomplete statement is followed by several suggested answers or completions. Select the one that BEST answers the question or completes the statement. *PRINT THE LETTER OF THE CORRECT ANSWER IN THE SPACE AT THE RIGHT.*

1. When structural steel is to receive several coats of paint, the colors of the different coats are made different from each other so that

   A. there will be a better bond between the coats
   B. a more decorative effect will be achieved
   C. the chances of electrolysis developing between the various coats will be reduced
   D. it can be easily seen whether or not all the steel has been covered by each coat

2. If any woodwork which is to be painted or varnished has been dampened by condensation or rainy weather, it would be good practice to

   A. wipe all the woodwork as dry as possible with dry rags and proceed with the work
   B. wait at least one week before proceeding with the work
   C. apply a gasoline blowtorch to the wet wood to dry it as the work proceeds
   D. wait until at least two clear, warm, sunny days have elapsed before starting the work

3. In applying varnish to woodwork, care should be taken that the varnish is

   A. *flowed* on with light, full strokes
   B. well-brushed out with short, heavy brush strokes
   C. *flowed* on with short, heavy strokes
   D. well-brushed out with light, full strokes

4. In applying varnish to woodwork, it is good practice to apply the varnish

   A. only when the air temperature is at least 60° F and to allow about two days for drying between coats
   B. at any temperature above freezing, and to allow about two days for drying between coats
   C. only when the air temperature is at least 60° F, and to allow about two or three hours for drying between coats
   D. at any temperature above freezing, and to allow about two or three hours for drying between coats

5. When galvanized metal surfaces are to be repainted, all the loose and scaling paint should FIRST be removed by using

   A. heavy scrapers   B. hammer and chisel
   C. putty knives   D. coarse steel wool

6. When containers of paint are opened, their contents should be thoroughly mixed so as to evenly distribute the pigment throughout the vehicle by a procedure known as

   A. boxing   B. bulking   C. kneading   D. parging

7. When a concrete floor is to be repainted, it must first be thoroughly cleaned, and the FIRST step in the cleaning process is to

   A. thoroughly scrub the floor with soap powder in water
   B. mop the floor with a mild solution of muriatic acid
   C. rinse the floor with pure benzine
   D. wipe the floor with carbon tetrachloride

8. The process of binding the ends of scaffold ropes with cord to prevent them from unraveling is called

   A. braiding   B. anchoring   C. whipping   D. splicing

9. Of the following painting materials, the one that dries and produces a coating or film solely by the evaporation of the solvent and not by the action of the oxygen in the air on the vehicle is

   A. enamel   B. lacquer   C. varnish   D. oil paint

10. Of the following factors, the one that a painter will find to be of the LEAST importance in getting a good paint job is the

    A. quality of the paint used
    B. skill with which the paint is applied
    C. prior preparation of the surface to be painted
    D. condition of the brushes and other tools used for the job

11. A gang foreman in charge of a paint job on exposed steelwork of an elevated structure would be open to criticism if he suspended all paint work whenever

    A. the weather became damp or rainy
    B. a strong wind was blowing on the surface of the steel
    C. the temperature rose above 90°F
    D. the temperature fell near the freezing point

12. When the gang foreman feels that conditions at a job site call for thinning any of the paint materials with which he has been supplied, the BEST thing for him to do is to

    A. immediately proceed with such thinning for the entire job without checking with his superior, since he must take the responsibility for exercising his own judgment in such cases
    B. let the job proceed with the paint materials *as is* unless he is notified to do otherwise by his superior
    C. check with his foreman as to whether he should modify any of the paint materials, and, if thinning is permitted, he should thin only one day's supply since job conditions may change
    D. thin only one day's supply of paint and proceed with the work without bothering his superior, since only one day's work and paint are involved and job conditions may change

13. When held at a slight distance, alternating blue and yellow lines of equal width, drawn close and parallel, will appear as

    A. dark yellow
    B. light blue
    C. gray
    D. blue-green
    E. green

14. To subdue a bright color and still retain its harmony in a scheme, it is BEST to add a little of

    A. black
    B. an adjacent color
    C. white
    D. its complement
    E. a darker tone of the same color

15. Which of these colors is neutral?

    A. Blue   B. Gray   C. Green   D. Red   E. Yellow

16. The color harmony formed by adjacent colors in the color wheel is known as

    A. complementary   B. triadic   C. analogous
    D. monochromatic   E. sliding

17. The best color for the walls of a kitchen with a northern exposure is

    A. blue   B. green   C. violet   D. rose   E. yellow

18. In mixing colors, which of the following will NOT make orange more gray? Adding

    A. a small amount of gray
    B. a small amount of blue
    C. a darker shade of orange
    D. small amounts of black and white
    E. small amounts of red and yellow

19. The pair which does NOT consist of complementary colors is

    A. blue-orange   B. yellow-violet
    C. red-green   D. gray-white

20. Of the following, the one that is a primary color is

    A. orange   B. purple   C. green   D. red

KEY (CORRECT ANSWERS)

1. D
2. D
3. A
4. A
5. D

6. A
7. A
8. C
9. B
10. A

11. C
12. C
13. E
14. D
15. B

16. C
17. E
18. E
19. D
20. D

EXAMINATION SECTION
TEST 1

DIRECTIONS: Each question or incomplete statement is followed by several suggested answers or completions. Select the one that BEST answers the question or completes the statement. *PRINT THE LETTER OF THE CORRECT ANSWER IN THE SPACE AT THE RIGHT.*

1. Creosote stain

    A. is a poor preservative
    B. is an excellent primer for any paint
    C. will usually bleed through most paints
    D. should be well-weathered before paint is applied over it

    1._____

2. *Checking* of a paint coat is *most likely* to occur if

    A. the top coat is too soft
    B. the undercoat is too soft
    C. there is too much drying time between coats
    D. water is present under the paint

    2._____

3. Of the following woods, the one that will retain paint the LONGEST assuming similar conditions of weathering is

    A. Douglas fir B. hemlock
    C. redwood   D. spruce

    3._____

4. Of the following types of fabric rollers, the one that should NOT be used to apply latex paint is a _____ roller.

    A. lambs wool B. dynel
    C. mohair   D. dacron

    4._____

5. A zinc chromate priming paint would *most likely* be used on

    A. concrete   B. metal   C. plaster   D. wood

    5._____

6. Normal paint deterioration on the exterior wood of a building is usually MOST severe on the side facing

    A. east   B. north   C. south   D. west

    6._____

7. A 2" brush should have bristles that are *most nearly* _____ long.

    A. 1"   B. 2"   C. 3"   D. 4"

    7._____

8. Discolored streaks are often formed on painted surfaces which are below unpainted metal parts of a building.
   Of the following metals, the one that will cause the LEAST discoloration of a painted surface is

    A. copper   B. iron   C. steel   D. aluminum

    8._____

9. Of the following, the difference between glazing compound and putty is that glazing compound

   A. is applied directly to unprimed wood
   B. is used only on metal sash
   C. should be painted before it is dry
   D. does not dry hard throughout

10. Of the following materials, the one that is NOT considered a thinner for some type of paint is

   A. linseed oil   B. resin
   C. turpentine   D. water

11. Skinning would probably be MOST troublesome when the paint is a

   A. gloss enamel   B. varnish paint
   C. latex paint   D. stain

12. Of the following pigments, the one that is LEAST likely to be used in a ready-mixed paint is

   A. aluminum   B. iron oxide
   C. lithopone   D. red lead

13. Extenders added to paints are of LEAST value in

   A. adjusting the consistency of the paint
   B. adding to the hiding power of the paint
   C. controlling the gloss of the paint
   D. increasing the durability of the paint

14. The type of paint that is BEST for application to a new concrete interior wall is

   A. enamel   B. latex
   C. oil-base   D. varnish

15. In comparing spray painting to applying paint with a brush on woodwork, it is CORRECT to say that spray painting

   A. requires a cleaner surface
   B. is always less time-consuming
   C. generally gives better results
   D. requires more skill

16. Of the following woods, the one that is LEAST likely to be used for exterior building surfaces is

   A. cedar   B. oak   C. pine   D. spruce

17. Stages in the normal deterioration of paint on exterior woodwork include chalking, checking, and flatting.
    The ORDER in which these stages usually take place is

   A. chalking, checking, flatting
   B. chalking, flatting, checking
   C. flatting, checking, chalking
   D. flatting, chalking, checking

18. Wrinkling of paint on exterior woodwork is LIKELY to be caused by

    A. damp weather
    B. the presence of oily dirt on the surface before painting
    C. a sharp drop in temperature after the paint is applied
    D. too much thinning of the paint

19. The height of the nap on a roller used in painting chain-link fences should be *most nearly*

    A. 1/4"   B. 3/8"   C. 3/4"   D. 1 1/4"

20. In three-coat work on exterior woodwork, the FEWEST number of gallons of paint will be required for the

    A. priming coat
    B. second coat (first coat of finish paint)
    C. third coat
    D. coat with the deepest color

21. Under favorable conditions, the drying time between coats of a linseed oil exterior paint should be AT LEAST ____ hours.

    A. 12   B. 24   C. 48   D. 96

22. An oak floor is to be filled, stained, and varnished. The proper SEQUENCE is

    A. fill, stain, varnish
    B. varnish, stain, fill, varnish
    C. stain, fill, varnish
    D. stain, varnish, fill, varnish

23. When varnishing a floor, POOR results will be obtained if

    A. several smooth, thin coats of varnish are used
    B. varnish is first brushed across the grain and then leveled off with the grain
    C. very fine sandpaper or steel wool is used between coats
    D. any coat is applied on top of a coat that is not thoroughly dry

24. When painting of exterior woodwork must be done in near-freezing weather,

    A. the paint should be thinned with linseed oil
    B. driers should be added to the paint
    C. the paint should be warmed before use
    D. the drying time between coats should be reduced

25. The total thickness of a two-coat system used for exterior woodwork, as compared to the total coating thickness of three-coat work, should be

    A. about the same
    B. greater
    C. less
    D. either greater or less depending on the type of pigment

26. When new softwood steps are to be painted, the BEST protection and appearance will be provided by

    A. many thick coats   B. many thin coats
    C. two or three thick coats D. two or three thin coats

27. A second coat of paint should be applied ONLY when the first

   A. no longer appears to be wet
   B. is tacky to the touch
   C. is dry to the touch
   D. can be sandpapered without gumming

28. The BEST way to thin varnish with turpentine is to add the turpentine _____ while stirring the varnish _____.

   A. quickly; vigorously
   B. quickly; gently
   C. gradually; vigorously
   D. gradually; gently

29. The bristles of a 3-inch brush are 4 inches long. The depth to which the bristles should be dipped when picking up paint is *usually* _____ inch(es).

   A. 1
   B. 2
   C. 3
   D. 4

30. The BEST way to apply the first coat of an oil paint to exterior wood siding is to

   A. empty the brush in one long horizontal stroke, then work the paint in with short vertical strokes
   B. use short vertical, overlapping strokes until brush is empty, then work in with long horizontal strokes
   C. use short, light strokes, flowing the paint on with the least possible brushing
   D. apply the paint in spots, brush out each spot into its neighbor, and then smooth the entire strip with long, gentle strokes

31. A pan-type roller is to be used to apply latex paint to plaster.
    The statement that gives the MOST complete description of the proper way to load the roller is:

   A. Roll it no deeper than the thickness of the cover in the shallow section of a half-filled tray
   B. Roll it no deeper than the thickness of the cover in the shallow section of a half-filled tray, then roll it over the corrugations on the exposed bottom of the tray
   C. Roll it from one end of a well-filled tray to the other
   D. Place it in the deepest portion of the tray so that the cover can soak up an ample paint supply

32. A paneled door is to be painted white.
    The parts of the door which should be painted FIRST are the

   A. moulded edges of the panels
   B. panels
   C. horizontal crossboards
   D. vertical sideboards

33. Of the following, the component of an oleo-resinous varnish that is NOT found in a spirit varnish is

   A. resin
   B. volatile solvent
   C. drying oil
   D. shellac

34. Mercuric chloride (also known as bichloride of mercury and corrosive sublimate) is added to paint to PREVENT

    A. bleeding
    B. fading
    C. flatting
    D. mildewing

35. Boiled linseed oil differs from raw linseed oil PRINCIPALLY in that it

    A. has been heated to high temperatures
    B. has had solvent added to it
    C. has had air blown through it
    D. is acid refined

36. A white lead paint becomes too thick in cold weather.
    The BEST way of restoring the paint to its proper consistency is to add

    A. alcohol
    B. drier
    C. linseed oil
    D. turpentine

37. Refined lac dissolved in denatured alcohol is called

    A. lacquer   B. sealer   C. shellac   D. varnish

38. Adding titanium dioxide to a lead-zinc paint would probably yield a paint with all of the following characteristics EXCEPT

    A. greater durability
    B. hardened film
    C. increased hiding power
    D. reduced chalking

39. The BEST varnish for a wood floor is a ____ varnish.

    A. short-oil
    B. medium-oil
    C. fish oil
    D. latex

40. Of the following paints, the one which contains the GREATEST percentage of pigment is

    A. flat oil paint
    B. semi-gloss oil paint
    C. gloss oil paint
    D. enamel

KEY (CORRECT ANSWERS)

1.	C	11.	A	21.	C	31.	B
2.	B	12.	C	22.	C	32.	A
3.	C	13.	B	23.	D	33.	C
4.	A	14.	B	24.	C	34.	D
5.	B	15.	A	25.	A	35.	A
6.	C	16.	B	26.	D	36.	D
7.	C	17.	D	27.	D	37.	C
8.	D	18.	C	28.	D	38.	B
9.	D	19.	D	29.	B	39.	B
10.	B	20.	B	30.	D	40.	A

TEST 2

DIRECTIONS: Each question or incomplete statement is followed by several suggested answers or completions. Select the one that BEST answers the question or completes the statement. *PRINT THE LETTER OF THE CORRECT ANSWER IN THE SPACE AT THE RIGHT.*

1. The aluminum of a window frame has oxidized. Before painting the frames, the oxide 1.____

    A. should be removed with acid
    B. should be sealed with varnish
    C. should be removed by wire brushing
    D. may be left undisturbed

2. A dirty wall surface that is to be repainted should be washed starting at 2.____

    A. the bottom
    B. the top
    C. either the top or the bottom, whichever is easier
    D. the bottom with plaster walls and at the top with brick walls

3. The PROPER procedure to follow in connection with the priming of wood siding is that 3.____

    A. knots should be shellacked after priming
    B. knots should be shellacked before priming
    C. nail holes should be puttied before priming
    D. wood siding is never back primed

4. The one of the following statements concerning the repainting of interior wood that is CORRECT is: 4.____

    A. Worn spots should be spotprimed and sandpapered lightly after the primer has dried
    B. Greasy dirt should be wiped off with a dry cloth
    C. There is no objection to applying the paint over old varnish
    D. Yearly painting is better than less frequent painting

5. When an exterior paint that is chalking is rubbed lightly with a finger, the paint comes off right down to the bare wood. 5.____
   The one of the following statements that is CORRECT concerning this condition is:

    A. This is normal and no repainting is necessary
    B. The surface should be dusted and then repainted
    C. The surface should be scraped or wire-brushed and then repainted
    D. This indicates mildew. The surface should be washed with water and then repainted

6. A new concrete wall that was cast against smooth metal forms is to be painted with a water-cement paint. Preparation of the wall should include all of the following EXCEPT 6.____

    A. neutralization of alkalies
    B. removal of oil
    C. roughening of surface
    D. removal of efflorescence

7. A new concrete wall is to be painted with an oil-base paint.
   Before painting, it is BEST to treat the surface of the concrete with a solution of

   A. lime
   B. beatsal
   C. washing soda and trisodium phosphate
   D. phosphoric acid and zinc chloride

8. Two coats of masonry filler are applied to a cinder block wall before it is painted.
   The second coat should be allowed to dry for a MINIMUM of ____ hours.

   A. 6   B. 12   C. 18   D. 24

9. A strip about 1 inch wide and over a foot long has been gouged out of a plaster and metal lath wall. The depth of gouging varies but does not exceed 1/4 inch.
   Before filling this area with patching plaster, the area should be

   A. cut out down to the metal lath
   B. cut out to a uniform depth of 1/4 inch
   C. washed with turpentine
   D. painted with a sealer

10. When cracks in concrete are repaired by using portland cement grout, hydrated lime is often added to the grout in order to

    A. increase the strength of the grout
    B. slow up the curing of the grout
    C. change the color of the grout
    D. make the grout expand

11. Exterior woodwork that is to be repainted has some spots that are still glossy.
    The spots should

    A. not be repainted
    B. be coated very thinly
    C. be dulled by sanding or washing with a paint cleaning compound
    D. be treated exactly like the rest of the surface

12. There are traces of wax on interior woodwork that is to be repainted.
    After wiping the surface with turpentine, it is BEST practice to

    A. apply the new paint immediately
    B. wash the woodwork with a trisodium phosphate solution
    C. allow the wood to dry before dusting and repainting
    D. seal the woodwork and then stain it

13. Of the following colors, the one that is NOT a primary color is

    A. blue   B. green   C. red   D. yellow

14. The total number of primary and secondary colors is

    A. 4   B. 6   C. 9   D. 12

15. A small amount of orange paint is added to a bright blue paint.
    The color of the mixture is

    A. blue-green
    B. purple
    C. violet
    D. a less bright blue

16. A mixture of blue and yellow paints produces a ____ paint.

    A. cream   B. green   C. orange   D. violet

17. The complementary color of any warm color is a ____ color.

    A. secondary   B. tertiary   C. cool   D. warm

18. The pigments that could be mixed together to make a dark green paint are lampblack, prussian blue, and

    A. burnt sienna
    B. chromium hydroxide
    C. lemon chrome yellow
    D. Venetian red

19. The color of burnt umber is

    A. orange   B. purple   C. blue   D. red-yellow

20. A color is viewed in sunlight and then in incandescent light.
    The color will appear to

    A. acquire a greenish tinge in the incandescent light
    B. acquire a reddish tinge in the incandescent light
    C. acquire a whitish tinge in the fluorescent light
    D. be unchanged in the artificial light

21. Of the following requirements for the bristles of a paint brush, the one that is LEAST important is that the bristles

    A. be flagged
    B. be tapered
    C. vary in length
    D. be made of hog hair

22. A non-bleeder type gun for spray painting must be used with a(n)

    A. air tank
    B. compressor with two or more cylinders
    C. external-mix nozzle
    D. pressure feed

23. After selecting an air cap and a fluid tip for a spray gun, one of the BEST ways to balance air and paint flow is to

    A. use the fluid-adjusting screw
    B. thin or thicken the paint
    C. grease the pattern-adjustment screw
    D. jiggle the trigger as the gun is moved

24. A 45° nozzle should be used on a spray gun when painting

    A. a wall at an inside corner
    B. a wall at an outside corner
    C. the ceiling of a room
    D. the sides of cabinets

25. Parallel strokes, next to each other, from a spray gun should overlap

    A. not at all
    B. just enough to insure that there are no bare areas
    C. about 1/3 of the width of the stroke
    D. 2/3 to 3/4 of the width of the stroke

26. Paint has dried in the nozzle of a spray gun. The BEST way to clean the nozzle is to

    A. put clean thinner in the container and operate the gun
    B. loosen the paint with a wire and blow it out with air
    C. wipe the nozzle with a rag soaked in thinner
    D. disassemble the nozzle and soak the parts in thinner

27. The BEST solvent to use to clean a brush that has been used to apply shellac is

    A. denatured alcohol   B. lacquer thinner
    C. raw linseed oil   D. turpentine

28. Bleached shellac would MOST probably be used

    A. where a flexible coating is required
    B. where resistance to liquids is required
    C. on a light-colored wood
    D. on exterior woodwork

29. Of the following conditions, the one that is LEAST likely to indicate that a fiber rope is unsafe is

    A. broken fibers on the outside
    B. strands have begun to unlay
    C. dirt on the inside
    D. dirt on the outside

30. The CHIEF purpose of the stirrups sometimes attached to a boatswain's chair is to

    A. allow the occupant to reach a greater area from any one position of the chair
    B. keep the occupant from falling out
    C. keep the occupant's feet from *going to sleep*
    D. allow the occupant to control the swinging of the chair

31. The BEST knot to use to make a comfortable sling to set in is a

    A. running bowline   B. double bowline
    C. slip knot   D. cat's paw or rocking hitch

32. The BEST life line is made of

    A. manila rope
    B. nylon rope
    C. wire rope with a hemp center
    D. wire rope with a wire rope center

33. Of the following conditions, the one that is the MOST important requirement in the storage of manila rope is

    A. good air circulation
    B. exposure to sunlight
    C. exposure to a source of heat
    D. high humidity

34. A thimble would *most likely* be used when rope is

    A. made into a grommet
    B. unknotted
    C. reeved
    D. attached to a ring

35. The factor of safety (ratio of breaking strength to safe load) recommended for manila rope is *most nearly*

    A. 3   B. 5   C. 9   D. 11

36. A tackle has two triple pulley blocks. It is used to raise a load to the roof of a building with the lead line being pulled by men on the ground.
    To raise the load one foot, the lead line must move ____ feet.

    A. 3   B. 4   C. 6   D. 8

37. Vapor from a solvent in a closed space is

    A. explosive regardless of the concentration
    B. explosive for all concentrations exceeding a certain percentage
    C. not explosive if the concentration exceeds a certain percentage
    D. not explosive under any conditions

38. With respect to the erection and use of swinging scaffolds raised and lowered with block and tackle, it is CORRECT to say that

    A. life lines should be so arranged that if a man falls, the line will hang from a point no lower than the level he was working on
    B. the hook of the lower pulley block should be moused
    C. when two scaffolds are used end-to-end on a wall, they should be securely lashed together
    D. window cleaners' anchors may be used for tie-ins

39. With respect to the erection and use of movable scaffold mounted on wheels, it is CORRECT to say that

    A. men on the scaffold must stand still while it is being moved
    B. the working platform must have a guard rail on three sides
    C. casters or wheels should be securely chocked with hardwood blocks when the scaffold is in use
    D. a ladder used to reach the working platform must be fastened to the scaffold

40. For proper care, wood ladders should be

    A. painted at regular intervals
    B. coated with varnish, shellac, or linseed oil
    C. stored upright by leaning against a wall
    D. stored horizontally with supports at the ends only

KEY (CORRECT ANSWERS)

1. D	11. C	21. D	31. B
2. A	12. B	22. A	32. B
3. A	13. B	23. A	33. A
4. A	14. B	24. C	34. D
5. C	15. D	25. C	35. B
6. A	16. B	26. D	36. C
7. D	17. C	27. A	37. C
8. C	18. C	28. C	38. A
9. A	19. D	29. D	39. D
10. B	20. B	30. C	40. B

EXAMINATION SECTION
TEST 1

DIRECTIONS: Each question or incomplete statement is followed by several suggested answers or completions. Select the one that BEST answers the question or completes the statement. *PRINT THE LETTER OF THE CORRECT ANSWER IN THE SPACE AT THE RIGHT.*

1. Lacquer thinner would *most likely* be used to

    A. clean oil paint from a brush immediately after use
    B. clean a paint brush upon which paint has hardened
    C. rinse a new paint brush before using it
    D. remove paint from the hands

    1.____

2. Before repainting a glossy surface, the surface should be sanded to prevent

    A. crawling   B. blistering
    C. alligatoring   D. mildewing

    2.____

3. Raw linseed oil with a drier added could *best* be substituted for

    A. turpentine   B. varnish
    C. mineral spirits   D. boiled linseed oil

    3.____

4. A white lead paste consists *mainly* of white lead *and*

    A. turpentine   B. linseed oil
    C. water   D. varnish

    4.____

Questions 5 - 7.

Questions 5 through 7, inclusive, refer to the paint formulas which follow. These paints are to be used for a three-coat job on exterior new wood.

	Formula #1	Formula #2	Formula #3
White lead - lb.	100	100	100
Raw linseed oil - gal.	1 1/2	3 1/4	4
Turpentine - gal.	1 1/2	0	2
Liquid drier - pt.	1	1	1

5. The priming coat should be Formula # _____.

    A. 1   B. 1 or 2   C. 2   D. 3

    5.____

6. The body coat should be Formula # _____.

    A. 1   B. 2   C. 1 or 2   D. 3

    6.____

7. The finish coat should be Formula # _____.

    A. 1   B. 2   C. 2 or 3   D. 3

    7.____

8. The fire escapes of an apartment building are to be given a three-coat paint job. The difference between the priming coat and the body coat would, most probably be, in the

    A. vehicle   B. pigment
    C. thinner   D. drier

    8.____

9. A polishing wax consists of carnauba wax in an organic solvent. This wax polish should NOT be used on

   A. furniture
   B. hardwood floors
   C. softwood floors
   D. rubber-tile floors

10. The "length" of a varnish refers to the

    A. area covered per gallon
    B. period of time it will last without deterioration
    C. ratio of oil to resin
    D. type of resin used

11. Of the following coatings, the *one* which is *most likely* applied by spraying rather than brushing is

    A. oil paint
    B. lacquer
    C. shellac
    D. varnish

12. A solvent in a paint is classified as a

    A. pigment
    B. vehicle
    C. drying oil
    D. binder

13. A pigmented coating or paint is preferred to an unpigmented coating when the coating is exposed to

    A. wind
    B. sun
    C. rain
    D. wide temperature changes

14. Putty used for glazing wood sash should be applied _____ coat.

    A. *before* the prime
    B. *after* the finish
    C. *after* the prime
    D. *after* the body

15. Zinc oxide added to an exterior white oil paint reduces

    A. chalking
    B. checking and cracking
    C. hiding power
    D. film hardness

16. The length of the bristles of a paint brush, which has a width of 4 inches, should be *at least* _____ inches.

    A. 2   B. 3   C. 3 1/2   D. 4

17. In painting a wooden wall with a brush, the paint should be laid on with brush strokes in one direction and then smoothed with brush strokes at an angle to the lay-on strokes. The smoothing strokes should be

    A. parallel to the grain
    B. perpendicular to the grain
    C. vertical, regardless of grain
    D. horizontal, regardless of grain

18. Painting wood with a brush is better than using a spray gun *primarily* because brushing   18.____

    A. is cheaper
    B. is faster
    C. works the paint into the pores of the wood
    D. uses less paint

19. *Before* putty that has been used in glazing wood sash can be painted, it should be allowed to dry for *at least*   19.____

    A. 4 hours   B. 24 hours
    C. 48 hours   D. 4 days

20. Interior wood trim in a plasterboard room in which the plaster is not to be painted *should be* painted   20.____

    A. *as soon as* the plasterers have finished
    B. *as soon as* the plaster is hard
    C. *when* the plaster is relatively dry
    D. *only after* the plaster is equally moist and dry

21. Shellac, used as a sealer on knots and pitch streaks, should be allowed to dry for *at least*   21.____

    A. 4 hours   B. 24 hours
    C. 48 hours   D. one week

22. Of the following ready-mixed coatings, the *one* which is *least likely* to require re-mixing before use is   22.____

    A. exterior oil paint
    B. flat finish paint
    C. semi-gloss enamel
    D. varnish

23. Failure of exterior paint is *usually* most pronounced on the following side or sides of a building: 23.____

    A. North   B. South
    C. East and West   D. North and South

24. A painter would *most likely* use builder's acid (muriatic acid and water) before painting   24.____

    A. wood   B. steel
    C. plastic   D. brickwork

25. A painter pours a little turpentine into a half-full can of enamel in such a way that the turpentine forms a thin layer on top of the enamel.
    He does this, *most probably,* to   25.____

    A. thin the enamel
    B. prevent skinning
    C. make the enamel more glossy
    D. make the enamel less glossy

26. A brush which is used daily for the application of varnish has been suspended overnight in raw linseed oil. Before using, it is good practice to press the excess oil out of the brush *and*

    A. use the brush without further treatment
    B. rinse in clear water
    C. rinse in alcohol
    D. rinse in turpentine

27. Assume that a pigmented paint is stored in one-gallon cans and that it will not be used for at least one year. To insure that the paint will be usable when needed, the *usual* practice is to, occasionally,

    A. open the cans and mix throughly
    B. place the cans in a shaker
    C. turn the cans over end-for-end
    D. roll the cans and replace in the same position

28. Slimy matter that separates from some oils when they stand for a long time is *usually* known as

    A. foots
    B. efflorescence
    C. gum
    D. resin

29. "Spreading rate" is *usually* expressed in

    A. square feet per hour
    B. gallons per hour
    C. square feet per gallon
    D. gallons per square foot

30. The MOST viscous of the following fluids is

    A. boiled linseed oil
    B. raw linseed oil
    C. turpentine
    D. alcohol

31. Of the following ingredients, the *one* which would be classified as a drying oil is

    A. turpentine
    B. mineral spirits
    C. crude oil
    D. linseed oil

32. A concrete wall is to be painted using a cement-water paint. The paint is BEST applied by a

    A. spray gun
    B. white-wash brush
    C. stiff-fiber brush
    D. soft-fiber brush

33. The *principal* ingredient in white-wash is

    A. chalk
    B. lime paste
    C. whiting
    D. gypsum

34. Bichloride of mercury solution is NOT widely used to wash mildewed surfaces because

    A. trisodium phosphate solution is more efficient
    B. it is expensive
    C. it is a deadly poison
    D. it deteriorates rapidly

35. A can of paint is to be mixed before using.
    The use of a shaker to do the mixing is NOT recommended if the paint is

    A. enamel
    B. white lead outside wood paint
    C. red lead paint for steel
    D. deck paint

KEY (CORRECT ANSWERS)

1.	B	16.	D
2.	A	17.	A
3.	D	18.	C
4.	B	19.	C
5.	D	20.	C
6.	A	21.	A
7.	B	22.	D
8.	B	23.	B
9.	D	24.	D
10.	C	25.	B
11.	B	26.	D
12.	B	27.	C
13.	B	28.	A
14.	C	29.	C
15.	A	30.	A

31. D
32. C
33. B
34. C
35. A

TEST 2

DIRECTIONS: Each question or incomplete statement is followed by several suggested answers or completions. Select the one that BEST answers the question or completes the statement. *PRINT THE LETTER OF THE CORRECT ANSWER IN THE SPACE AT THE RIGHT.*

1. Weather conditions being the same, a paint is *most durable* when its color is   1.____

   A. white   B. red
   C. green   D. black

2. Of the following woods, the *one* which is POOREST in paint-holding quality is   2.____

   A. cedar   B. southern yellow pine
   C. northern white pine   D. spruce

3. A self-cleaning paint is one that   3.____

   A. checks   B. alligators
   C. chalks   D. scales

4. Blistering of paint on wood surfaces is *usually* caused by   4.____

   A. sunlight   B. cold
   C. heat   D. moisture

5. It is BEST to store paint in   5.____

   A. airtight rooms with windows
   B. airtight rooms without windows
   C. well-ventilated rooms with windows
   D. well-ventilated rooms without windows

6. Colors used in paints for painting concrete walls should be   6.____

   A. pigments in oil   B. mineral pigments
   C. water colors   D. tempera

7. Of the following, the BEST way to warm paint is to heat it   7.____

   A. in a hot water bath with the can lid loosened
   B. over an open flame with the can lid loosened
   C. in a hot water bath without loosening the can lid
   D. over an open flame without loosening the can lid

8. A rectangular wooden building occupies a ground space 27' 6" long by 18' 0" wide. The walls are 17' 6" high. Ignoring window and door spaces, the outside area requiring painting is, in square feet, most nearly,   8.____

   A. 1570   B. 1590   C. 1610   D. 1630

9. The type of paint which should *only* be applied to a damp surface is   9.____

   A. oil paint   B. lacquer
   C. cement paint   D. aluminum paint

10. If blue and yellow paint are mixed together in equal proportions, the color of the mixture will be

    A. red
    B. violet
    C. purple
    D. green

11. A gray-colored paint may be made by mixing together, in proper proportions, the following colored paints:

    A. red and yellow
    B. yellow and white
    C. white and blue
    D. black and white

12. An orange-colored paint may be made by mixing together, in proper proportions, the following colored paints:

    A. white and yellow
    B. yellow and red
    C. red and white
    D. white and ivory

Questions 13-15.

Questions 13 to 15, inclusive, are based on the following statement:
Tints are made by adding pigment-in-oil to white lead paste.

13. If the pigment used is burnt sienna, the color of the tint will, most likely, be

    A. brown
    B. green
    C. yellow
    D. orange

14. If the pigment used is Venetian red, the color of the tint will, most likely, be

    A. red
    B. yellow
    C. orange
    D. blue

15. If the pigment used is chromium oxide, the color of the tint will, most likely, be

    A. greenish blue
    B. pale orange
    C. yellowish green
    D. yellowish orange

Questions 16-17.

Questions 16 and 17 are based on the following statement:
An exterior oil paint which is ready-mixed is to be used for a three-coat job.

16. The addition of one pint of raw linseed oil to one gallon of the paint would *normally* be made for the

    A. priming coat
    B. body coat
    C. finish coat
    D. priming and body coats

17. The addition of up to one pint of turpentine to one gallon of the paint would *normally* be made for the

    A. priming coat
    B. body coat
    C. finish coat
    D. priming and body coats

18. Assume that a certain type of cabinet can be painted in twenty minutes by using a brush or 15 min. with spraygun. Assuming that three painters are put on the job but only one spray gun is available, the number of hours required by the three painters to paint 100 cabinets, one using the spray gun and the other two using brushes, is, most nearly,

    A. 9   B. 10   C. 11   D. 12

19. If it takes 5 painters 12 days to paint a building, the number of days it will take 9 painters to paint the same building, assuming all work is done at the same rate of speed, is, most nearly,

    A. 5 1/2   B. 6 1/2   C. 7 1/2   D. 8 1/2

20. Assume that one gallon of paint, costing $6.25, is able to cover 500 square feet. If a painter can spread 1.25 gallons per day and receives $60.00 per day, the cost per 100 square feet for labor and paint for a one-coat application is, most nearly,

    A. $12.00   B. $12.10   C. $12.20   D. $12.30

21. The strength of a swinging scaffold should be *at least* _____ the load it carries.

    A. twice
    B. 3 times
    C. 4 times
    D. 5 times

22. In order to maintain safety, *good* practice is that the maximum number of men that should be allowed on the ordinary swinging scaffold is

    A. 4   B. 3   C. 2   D. 1

23. Muriatic acid is being used by a painter.
    The acid is *most likely* to do serious damage to the following part of a swinging scaffold:

    A. metal stirrup or hangar
    B. wooden floor boards
    C. manila ropes
    D. all of the foregoing

24. The *proper* size of a toe board on a swinging scaffold is, approximately,

    A. 1" x 1"
    B. 2" x 2"
    C. 2" x 4"
    D. 1" x 6"

25. The BEST way to tell whether a ladder is safe for use is to

    A. place it horizontally on two supports and jump on it
    B. inspect it visually
    C. place it vertically and carefully place heavy weights on it
    D. place it vertically and have several men climb it at the same time

26. The one of the following which should NOT be used on a wooden ladder is:

    A. paint
    B. varnish
    C. shellac
    D. linseed oil

27. Wooden ladders stored horizontally should be supported 27.____

   A. throughout their length (that is, resting on the floor)
   B. by blocking at each end
   C. by two blocks near the middle
   D. by blocking at the ends and at intermediate points

28. A safety (life) line is *normally* used with a 28.____

   A. ladder   B. swinging scaffold
   C. single pole scaffold D. step ladder

29. The hook on the lower pulley block of a swinging scaffold *should* 29.____

   A. be moused with marlin
   B. be moused with wire
   C. NOT be moused
   D. be free so that it can be unhooked instantly

30. Nylon rope is better suited for life lines than manila rope *primarily* because of its 30.____

   A. elastic quality   B. strength
   C. smoothness   D. freedom from decay

31. Manila rope should be stored in a 31.____

   A. cool, dry, well-ventilated room   B. cool, dry room
   C. warm, dry, well-ventilated room   D. cool, damp room

32. Cracked and scaled paint on a wooden wall can BEST be removed by 32.____

   A. scraping   B. wire brushing and scraping
   C. burning and scraping D. burning

33. When sanding wood, the sandpaper should be moved 33.____

   A. at right angles to the grain   B. diagonally across the grain
   C. parallel to the grain   D. in a circular path

34. In comparing the lasting quality of a paint job on exterior wood doors done with three coats of a high grade oil paint as compared to three coats of spar varnish, the oil paint job will last _____ time. 34.____

   A. about the same length of   B. a much longer
   C. a much shorter   D. only a little longer

35. The total thickness of a three-coat paint job on exterior woodwork *should be* approximately _____ a two-coat paint job. 35.____

   A. twice the thickness of
   B. 50% thicker than the thickness of
   C. 25% thicker than the thickness of
   D. the same thickness as

KEY (CORRECT ANSWERS)

1.	D	16.	A
2.	B	17.	B
3.	C	18.	B
4.	D	19.	B
5.	D	20.	B
6.	B	21.	C
7.	A	22.	C
8.	B	23.	C
9.	C	24.	D
10.	D	25.	B
11.	D	26.	A
12.	B	27.	D
13.	A	28.	B
14.	A	29.	C
15.	C	30.	A
31.	A		
32.	C		
33.	C		
34.	B		
35.	D		

EXAMINATION SECTION
TEST 1

DIRECTIONS: Each question or incomplete statement is followed by several suggested answers or completions. Select the one that BEST answers the question or completes the statement. *PRINT THE LETTER OF THE CORRECT ANSWER IN THE SPACE AT THE RIGHT.*

Questions 1-28.

DIRECTIONS: Questions 1 through 28 are concerned with terms commonly used in the painting trade. Answer these questions by selecting the meaning as used in the trade.

1. BOXING is

    A. brushing B. mixing C. enclosing D. scaling

2. A HOLIDAY is a _____ spot.

    A. high B. faded C. depressed D. skipped

3. FLAG ends are found on

    A. ropes B. rollers C. ladders D. brushes

4. FOOTS refer to

    A. sediment B. skin C. crust D. bubbles

5. BOILED OIL is _____ oil.

    A. fish B. linseed C. rung D. cottonseed

6. WHIPPING is used with

    A. rollers B. brushes C. ropes D. ladders

7. JAPAN is a(n)

    A. pigment B. drier C. thinner D. extender

8. CALCIMINE is a(n) _____ paint.

    A. water B. latex C. oil D. alkyd

9. GRAPHITE is colored

    A. white B. black C. gold D. silver

10. CHINAWOOD oil is _____ oil

    A. tung
    C. cottonseed
    B. linseed
    D. soybean

11. LITHOPONE contains

    A. lead carbonate
    C. zinc sulfide
    B. lead sulfate
    D. zinc oxide

31

12. TURPENTINE is made from

    A. resin of pine trees
    B. benzine
    C. coal tar
    D. petroleum

13. PICKLING is

    A. drying
    B. preserving
    C. cleaning
    D. coloring

14. BLISTERING is caused by

    A. overthinning
    B. overheating
    C. moisture
    D. low temperature

15. EXTENDERS are

    A. driers
    B. inert fillers
    C. stainers
    D. vehicles

16. The VEHICLE in a paint is the

    A. liquid   B. base   C. body   D. pigment

17. RAW SIENNA is colored

    A. black   B. yellow   C. red   D. white

18. TITANIUM OXIDE is a

    A. solvent   B. drier   C. pigment   D. extender

19. LINSEED OIL is made from

    A. hempseed
    B. cottonseed
    C. poppy seed
    D. flaxseed

20. BURNT UMBER is colored

    A. yellow   B. white   C. red   D. brown

21. PIGMENT particles are bound together by

    A. driers   B. vehicles   C. solvents   D. extenders

22. CHECKING is

    A. bubbling
    B. blistering
    C. shrinking
    D. expansion

23. The COBALT used in tinting is

    A. yellow   B. blue   C. brown   D. red

24. CARNAUBA is a

    A. wax   B. pigment   C. putty   D. plaster

25. The MAIN disadvantage of WHITE LEAD was that it was

    A. difficult to tint
    B. poisonous
    C. expensive
    D. hard to thin

26. EFFLORESCENCE is normally found on walls made of 26.____

    A. cinder block B. gypsum block
    C. plaster D. brick

27. MILDEW is usually caused by 27.____

    A. high temperature B. low temperature
    C. insufficient mixing D. moisture

28. The main purpose of a SOLVENT is to 28.____

    A. make it easier to brush out the paint
    B. lower the cost of the paint
    C. strengthen the paint film
    D. increase the life of the paint

29. The purpose of adding zinc oxide to the formula for an exterior white house paint is to make the resulting paint film 29.____

    A. whiter B. harder C. smoother D. softer

30. A paint of good quality wears away by 30.____

    A. scaling B. chalking C. cracking D. flaking

31. Before a new hog-bristle paint brush is used for the first time with an oil paint, it would be good practice to soak the brush in 31.____

    A. benzine for eight hours
    B. water for two hours
    C. linseed oil overnight
    D. carbon tetrachloride overnight

32. The BEST type of brush to use for housepainting is one that is made of 32.____

    A. synthetic bristle B. nylon
    C. horsehair D. boar bristle

33. The area where manila scaffold ropes are stored should be 33.____

    A. cool and dry B. cool and humid
    C. hot and dry D. hot and humid

34. Application of an excessively heavy coat of paint which has too great an oil content will MOST likely cause 34.____

    A. washing B. wrinkling
    C. blistering D. alligatoring

35. Scaffold fibre ropes which have been exposed to muriatic acid should be 35.____

    A. discarded immediately
    B. treated with sodium hydroxide
    C. oiled with warm linseed oil
    D. washed with soap and warm water

KEY (CORRECT ANSWERS)

1.	B	16.	A
2.	D	17.	B
3.	D	18.	C
4.	A	19.	D
5.	B	20.	D
6.	C	21.	B
7.	B	22.	C
8.	A	23.	B
9.	B	24.	A
10.	A	25.	B
11.	C	26.	D
12.	A	27.	D
13.	C	28.	A
14.	C	29.	B
15.	B	30.	B

31. C
32. D
33. A
34. B
35. A

TEST 2

DIRECTIONS: Each question or incomplete statement is followed by several suggested answers or completions. Select the one that BEST answers the question or completes the statement. *PRINT THE LETTER OF THE CORRECT ANSWER IN THE SPACE AT THE RIGHT.*

1. Before a rusty iron surface is painted, it should be

    A. wire brushed
    B. treated with shellac
    C. washed with kerosene
    D. varnished

    1.____

2. If it is necessary to paint a new concrete floor that has not had time to dry thoroughly, it should be treated with a solution of

    A. zinc sulphate
    B. sodium chloride
    C. soap and water
    D. hydrochloric acid

    2.____

3. The main reason why it is NOT considered good practice to paint the portable ladders used by painters is that the paint

    A. will quickly wear off
    B. may mar the work area
    C. may hide serious defects
    D. may make the ladder slippery

    3.____

4. Painting specifications for a large job frequently require a different tint for each of the three coats.
   The MAIN reason for this requirement is that it

    A. helps spot missed areas
    B. reduces cost since only one paint need be purchased
    C. helps the painter to get the exact shade for the final coat
    D. is not feasible to get the right shade for all coats

    4.____

5. Paint mildew is BEST removed by

    A. applying paint with a high oil content
    B. covering it with a slow-drying paint
    C. washing it with linseed oil
    D. washing it with warm water and strong soap

    5.____

6. The color which should be added to a yellow paint in order to *gray* it is

    A. orange   B. red   C. violet   D. green

    6.____

7. A metal paint that is to be sprayed differs from one that is to be brush-applied in that it

    A. contains more oil
    B. contains more drier
    C. contains more pigment
    D. is of a thinner consistency

    7.____

8. Of the following, the BEST method of removing all foreign matter from structural steel prior to painting is

    A. sandblasting
    B. wire brushing
    C. scraping
    D. chipping

9. If the specifications call for the *stringer* to be enameled, the painter should check the paint on the

    A. roof beams
    B. door frames
    C. stairs
    D. windows

10. The PRIMARY objective in drawing up a set of specifications for painting materials is the

    A. control of quality
    B. outlining of intended use
    C. establishment of standard coverage
    D. establishment of inspection procedures

11. The varnish that is USUALLY specified because of its weather-resistant properties is _____ varnish.

    A. hard oil   B. rubbing   C. flat   D. spar

12. If a cement-block wall is to be painted with a cement-water paint, its surface should be

    A. varnished
    B. shellacked
    C. dry
    D. wetted

13. The BEST way to insure that a paint job on structural steel is long-lasting is to make sure the coats of paint are

    A. rigid and thin
    B. rigid and thick
    C. elastic and thin
    D. elastic and thick

14. The BEST method of removing loose and scaling paint from galvanized ducts that are to be repainted is to use

    A. a hammer and chisel
    B. coarse steel wool
    C. a putty knife
    D. a heavy scraper

15. The BEST material for cleaning brushes that have been used to apply shellac is

    A. soapy water
    B. benzine
    C. alcohol
    D. lacquer thinner

16. The ADVANTAGE of nylon bristle over hog bristle for brushes is that the nylon bristle

    A. will outwear the hog bristle
    B. is soluble in phenol
    C. does not soften in shellac
    D. has a greater pick-up capacity

17. The BEST practice for removing the excess paint on a brush is to

    A. tap the handle on the edge of the paint can
    B. tap the bristles lightly against the inside of the paint can

C. rub the bristles lightly across the inside edge of the paint can
D. hold the brush above the paint surface so the excess paint can drip back into the can

18. If paint is applied without being properly mixed, the USUAL result is

    A. cracking   B. scaling   C. running   D. spotting

19. To prevent paint from *crawling* when repainting a glossy surface, the surface should FIRST be

    A. shellacked
    B. sandpapered
    C. washed with naphtha
    D. wet down with water

20. The BEST thinner for varnishes is

    A. turpentine
    B. varnolene
    C. kerosene
    D. benzine

21. Before a water-based paint is applied to a recently plastered wall, the wall should be

    A. washed
    B. shellacked
    C. varnished
    D. sized

22. When painting a steel suspension bridge, a painter should use a *swab* to

    A. clean the steel
    B. remove rust
    C. spread the paint on rough surfaces
    D. get paint into narrow spaces

23. The MAIN purpose of a *drier* is to

    A. prevent the paint from scaling
    B. promote the oxidation of the linseed oil
    C. increase the penetration of the paint
    D. hasten the evaporation of the turpentine

24. A *fugitive* color is one that

    A. has little brightness value
    B. fuses easily with other colors
    C. has a tendency to run on metal
    D. fades in strong light

25. *Spotting* of paint on new wood occurs MAINLY when

    A. industrial gases are present
    B. the finish coat lacks elasticity
    C. an improper brushing procedure is used
    D. an inadequate amount of paint is used

26. *Benzol* should be added to the primary coat applied on

    A. white pine
    B. chestnut
    C. oak
    D. cypress

27. *Enamel* paint is a paint that contains

    A. lithopone as a pigment
    B. organic pigments only
    C. varnish as a vehicle
    D. whiting as a vehicle

28. The MAIN purpose of having a drying oil in paint is to

    A. permit air to reach the wood surface
    B. bind the pigment particles together
    C. dull the finish
    D. remove moisture from the wood

29. The BEST method of preparing a galvanized surface for painting is to FIRST

    A. prime it with graphite
    B. prime it with red lead
    C. wet it with a weak solution of muriatic acid
    D. wet it with a weak solution of tri-sodium phosphate

30. Before painting an old plastered wall that has been calcimined, it is advisable to FIRST

    A. apply paint remover to the plastered wall
    B. apply a solution of muriatic acid to the plastered wall
    C. wash off the calcimine with water
    D. wash off the calcimine with tri-sodium phosphate

31. A room will appear LARGER if it has been painted with a

    A. dark colored paint on all walls
    B. light colored paint on all walls
    C. design on at least one wall
    D. dark color on two walls, light color on the other walls

32. In sanding a wood surface with steel wool, the stroke should be

    A. with the grain
    B. crosswise to the grain
    C. circular
    D. oblique

33. Small cuts or injuries received on the job should be

    A. ignored since they are minor
    B. ignored unless they slow you down
    C. taken care of immediately to avoid infection
    D. taken care of if they continue to bleed

34. Artificial respiration should be started IMMEDIATELY on a painter who has suffered an electric shock if he is

    A. *unconscious* and badly burned
    B. *conscious* and in a daze
    C. *unconscious* and breathing heavily
    D. *unconscious* and not breathing

35. The MAIN purpose of giving first aid instruction to some selected painters is to 35._____
    A. avoid calling a doctor to the job
    B. save money
    C. enable them to give first aid in an emergency
    D. reduce the number of accidents

KEY (CORRECT ANSWERS)

1.	A	16.	A
2.	A	17.	B
3.	C	18.	C
4.	A	19.	B
5.	D	20.	A
6.	C	21.	D
7.	D	22.	D
8.	A	23.	B
9.	C	24.	D
10.	A	25.	D
11.	D	26.	D
12.	D	27.	C
13.	C	28.	B
14.	B	29.	C
15.	C	30.	C

31. B
32. A
33. C
34. D
35. C

EXAMINATION SECTION
TEST 1

DIRECTIONS: Each question or incomplete statement is followed by several suggested answers or completions. Select the one that BEST answers the question or completes the statement. *PRINT THE LETTER OF THE CORRECT ANSWER IN THE SPACE AT THE RIGHT.*

1. Of the following, the BEST method to use to remove smoke and soot discoloration from ceilings and walls in public halls before painting is by
   A. washing
   B. wire brushing
   C. scraping
   D. spackling

2. Of the following pigments, the one that contributes MOST to the mildew resistance of paints is
   A. zinc oxide
   B. yellow ochre
   C. prussian blue
   D. burnt sienna

3. Before priming unpainted galvanized iron, it should be washed with which of the following?
   A. Acetic acid
   B. Benzine
   C. Tri-sodium phosphate
   D. Gasoline

4. Areas missed by a painter during painting are called
   A. runs
   B. holidays
   C. clouds
   D. splashes

5. Of the following paint binders, the one that contains mineral spirits as a solvent is
   A. epoxy
   B. latex
   C. alkyd
   D. vinyl

6. A paint which stays where it is brushed without running down on to the surfaces below would have good resistance to
   A. sagging
   B. wrinkling
   C. flaking
   D. sweating

7. The ability of a coat of paint to conceal the underlying color is known as _____ power.
   A. reflective
   B. tinting
   C. hiding
   D. flatting

8. Paint on a wall develops a non-uniform surface appearance with a large number of tiny scales and cracks. This defect is called
   A. crawling
   B. caking
   C. cratering
   D. crazing

9. Of the following types of brushes, the one that is BEST for rough surfaces such as masonry is a _____ brush.
   A. nylon
   B. rayon
   C. horsehair
   D. badger hair

10. Efflorescence on unpainted brick can be BEST removed by cleaning with

    A. turpentine
    B. gasoline
    C. hydrochloric acid
    D. kerosene

11. Of the following types of interior paints, the one that contains lacquer thinner as a solvent is

    A. alkyd
    B. rubber base
    C. phenolic
    D. epoxy

12. Specifications for a painting contract state:
    The contractor at his own cost and expense shall be responsible for the following plastering work in all scheduled and move-out apartments to be painted under this contract:
    I. The patching of all holes and gouged plaster up to but not exceeding one square yard on any of the walls within apartments or public spaces to be painted
    II. The plastering of holes which exceed one square yard will be the responsibility of the authority.
    The one of the following sizes of holes that is the responsibility of the authority is a

    A. 2 3/4' x 3 1/4' rectangle
    B. 3 foot diameter circle
    C. 3'9" x 2'6" rectangle
    D. 2'10" x 2'10" square

13. Of the following, the MOST practical way to clean an enameled surface before painting is to wash it with

    A. turpentine
    B. wood alcohol
    C. acetone solvent
    D. tri-sodium phosphate solution

14. If an exterior surface is painted too many times over the years and the thickness of the coat is allowed to build up, the surface is MOST subject to

    A. cracking
    B. mildew
    C. crawling
    D. blistering

15. Of the following, the ingredient of a ready-mixed paint that MOST readily settles to the bottom of the can is the

    A. vehicle   B. solvent   C. pigment   D. drier

16. An exterior wood surface is newly painted. The FIRST effect of weathering, assuming good workmanship, is usually

    A. alligatoring of the surface
    B. reduction in gloss of the paint film
    C. bubbles of paint forming on the surface
    D. holidays

17. In comparison with putty, glazing compound is usually _____ expensive and _____ flexible.

    A. less; more
    B. more; more
    C. more; less
    D. less; less

18. The cementing material in sheets used for dry-wall construction is usually

    A. epoxy
    B. gypsum
    C. creosote
    D. asphaltum

19. Of the following materials, the one that is MOST frequently used to damp-proof the exposed surface of an exterior brick wall is

    A. vinyl
    B. silicone
    C. urethane
    D. phenol

20. Putty is usually whiting mixed with

    A. linseed oil
    B. alkyd
    C. phenol
    D. vinyl resin

KEY (CORRECT ANSWERS)

1.	A	11.	D
2.	A	12.	C
3.	A	13.	D
4.	B	14.	A
5.	C	15.	C
6.	A	16.	B
7.	C	17.	B
8.	D	18.	B
9.	A	19.	B
10.	C	20.	A

TEST 2

DIRECTIONS: Each question or incomplete statement is followed by several suggested answers or completions. Select the one that BEST answers the question or completes the statement. *PRINT THE LETTER OF THE CORRECT ANSWER IN THE SPACE AT THE RIGHT.*

1. To achieve best results when doing exterior painting on park playground fences, it is BEST to schedule the work when the weather is

    A. cool with high humidity
    B. warm with low humidity
    C. very hot and clear
    D. warm with high humidity

    1._____

2. Of the following types of work, the one for which MOST time should be allowed for contingencies is _____ painting of _____.

    A. interior; public areas
    B. exterior; buildings
    C. exterior; fences
    D. interior; fire exits

    2._____

3. Of the following solvents, the one that is MOST flammable is

    A. benzene
    B. refined kerosene
    C. turpentine
    D. carbon tetrachloride

    3._____

4. If the unsupported length of an extension ladder resting against a vertical wall is 14 feet, then the SAFEST horizontal distance, in feet, to set the foot of the ladder from the wall is MOST NEARLY

    A. 1.5
    B. 3.5
    C. 5.5
    D. 7.5

    4._____

5. When manila rope is used as a tie-back on a roof hook of a swinging scaffold, the diameter of the rope should be AT LEAST

    A. 5/8"
    B. 3/4"
    C. 1"
    D. 1 1/4"

    5._____

6. When using non-flammable paint removers, proper ventilation must be provided PRIMARILY to

    A. *decrease* the drying time of the paint removers
    B. *decrease* the toxicity of the air in the room
    C. *reduce* the temperature in the room
    D. *increase* the cutting power of the paint remover

    6._____

7. When using a swinging scaffold, the MAXIMUM number of men permitted on the scaffold is usually

    A. 2
    B. 3
    C. 4
    D. 5

    7._____

8. Scaffold planks are sometimes proof-tested with loads four times as great as they are expected to carry in service. This practice is

    A. *good,* because it insures that the planks are strong enough
    B. *good,* because the scaffold is occasionally overloaded
    C. *poor,* because the planks were inspected before they were shipped out
    D. *poor,* because it may cause concealed damage to the planks

    8._____

9. Of the following portable types of portable fire extinguishers, the one that should NOT be used on a flammable liquid fire such as paint, oil, or gasoline is

   A. foam
   B. dry chemical
   C. carbon dioxide
   D. soda acid

10. On a scaffold, the BEST type of knot to tie your safety-belt line (lanyard) to the safety line is a

    A. half hitch
    B. back hitch
    C. rolling hitch
    D. square knot

11. Paint-stained rags and oily rags should be kept in a metal container in which the

    A. cover has holes and the body none
    B. body has holes and the cover none
    C. both the cover and the body have no holes
    D. both the cover and the body have holes

12. Of the following federal agencies, the one that deals with safety and health on construction sites is the

    A. FTCA   B. CAB   C. OSHA   D. FEEA

13. Before painting sprinkler piping, the sprinkler heads should be

    A. removed after closing the sprinkler system
    B. closed by rotating the sprinkler clockwise
    C. turned upside down
    D. covered with a paper bag

14. A painter is found in a room unconscious from inhaling fumes. The FIRST thing to do is

    A. put a handkerchief over his face
    B. remove him from the room
    C. give him artificial respiration
    D. notify your immediate supervisor

15. A painter works MOST effectively when he

    A. does a full day's work and works carefully
    B. works carefully but overlooks doing minor areas because of job conditions
    C. varies the specifications to suit job conditions
    D. continually calls you up to talk about job conditions

16. A painter will respond MOST favorably to a foreman who has which of the following characteristics?

    A. Alertness
    B. Hostility
    C. Arrogance
    D. Domineering

Questions 17-20.

DIRECTIONS: Questions 17 through 20, inclusive, are based on the information given below.

A crew of 6 painters is going to paint only the walls of 75 rooms. The rooms have the following dimensions: 50 rooms are 35 feet long, 20 feet wide, with walls 10 feet high; and 25 rooms are 25 feet long, 15 feet wide, with walls 10 feet high. The walls are to be given two coats. The paint coverage is 400 square feet per gallon per coat. Assume a painter can cover 650 square feet of wall per 7-hour day. Assume that wall surfaces have windows and doors which constitute 10% of the wall surfaces and are not to be painted.

17. The total wall surface to be painted per coat of paint is MOST NEARLY _____ sq.ft.   17.___

    A. 65,300   B. 67,500   C. 69,500   D. 71,100

18. Assume that the total wall surface to be painted is 75,000 square feet. The total number   18.___
of gallons of paint needed for a complete job, neglecting any waste, is MOST NEARLY

    A. 358   B. 364   C. 370   D. 375

19. The total number of working days required for the crew to cover 75,000 square feet of   19.___
wall surface with 2 coats of paint is MOST NEARLY _____ days.

    A. 37   B. 39   C. 41   D. 43

20. If a painter earns $14.70 per hour for a 7-hour day, then the total cost in painter's wages   20.___
for a job that takes 27 working days for the 6-man crew is

    A. $16,312.80   B. $16,510.80
    C. $16,669.80   D. $16,913.40

KEY (CORRECT ANSWERS)

1.	B	11.	C
2.	B	12.	C
3.	A	13.	D
4.	B	14.	B
5.	B	15.	A
6.	B	16.	A
7.	A	17.	B
8.	D	18.	D
9.	D	19.	B
10.	C	20.	C

EXAMINATION SECTION
TEST 1

DIRECTIONS: Each question or incomplete statement is followed by several suggested answers or completions. Select the one that BEST answers the question or completes the Statement. *PRINT THE LETTER OF THE CORRECT ANSWER IN THE SPACE AT THE RIGHT.*

1. The *proper* planning of work assignments by a foreman should *generally* include *each* of the following factors EXCEPT: 1.____

   A. Location of the projects
   B. Painters' past productivity
   C. His ability to get along with painters
   D. Availability of equipment

2. Of the following, the BEST action you can take to insure that there are few delays on a paint job is to   2.____

   A. see that the men always have sufficient equipment and supplies
   B. concentrate your men in small areas
   C. spread your men widely
   D. allow your men to do the work of their own choice

3. If an in-house painting job in a public area is to take 135 man-days, the SMALLEST number of men needed to complete the job in 11 days is   3.____

   A. 11   B. 12   C. 13   D. 14

4. You have to get one of your painters to volunteer to cancel his approved vacation because another painter resigned. Of the following, the BEST way to do this is to   4.____

   A. use logic and reason on him
   B. use an emotional appeal only on him
   C. use logic and appeal to his good nature
   D. order him to relinquish his vacation

5. Of the following, the BEST way for a foreman painter to increase his efficiency is to   5.____

   A. devote less time to minor decisions
   B. keep a backlog of pending decisions
   C. always make a quick decision
   D. let a painter verify all decisions

6. Of the following, when assigning a painting job to a painter, the BEST way to insure that he knows what he is expected to do is to give him   6.____

   A. his orders orally
   B. a time schedule
   C. a list of tools and materials needed
   D. a list of things to be done

47

7. There is an item in a painting contract relating to insolvency. *Insolvency* means, most nearly,

    A. the improper mixing of paint
    B. the use of improper materials
    C. taking excessive time to complete the contract
    D. bankruptcy

8. Assume that you assign 3 painters to do a job in 12 days. After 4 days you add 3 more painters, all of whom work at the same pace.
   How many additional days will it take the 6 men to do the job?

    A. 2 Days   B. 3 Days   C. 4 Days   D. 5 Days

9. An inspector on a painting contract has to keep records on the progress of the work completed by a painting contractor. The following is the progress of the work completed by a contractor at the end of 8 months:

Apartment Size	Estimated Number of Apartments	Number of Apartments Painted
3 rooms	120	100
4 rooms	160	140
5 rooms	120	40

    The *percentage* of work completed on a room basis is, most nearly,

    A. 62%   B. 66%   C. 70%   D. 74%

10. On arriving at a public area being painted by three in-house painters, you learn another painter foreman has taken one of your most productive painters to work on his project.
    Of the following, the thing to do is to

    A. do nothing
    B. write a memo describing the problem
    C. bring the painter up on charges for disobeying your instructions
    D. contact your supervisor

11. The paint administrator tells you that you have to increase the productivity of the painters under your supervision. Of the following, the *BEST first* step would be to

    A. tell the painters there will be layoffs if they can not meet the increased work schedule
    B. discuss the matter with the painters
    C. say nothing to the painters about the matter
    D. increase the work load of the best painters

12. Of the following items, the *one* that would cut down on the productivity of painters the *MOST* is

    A. making the jobs as repetitive as possible
    B. varying the sequence of doing each job
    C. keeping a schedule of inspection
    D. letting painters set work schedules whenever possible

13. Of the following techniques for handling subordinates, the *one* that will *most likely* cause dissatisfaction among your subordinates is:

    A. Giving them routine jobs and making them feel proud of their work
    B. Encouraging them to make decisions and then criticizing them severely when they make mistakes
    C. Encouraging them to produce to the best of their abilities and setting high standards
    D. Listening to their legitimate gripes and attempting to solve them

14. Of the following, the *BEST* way for a foreman painter to check on in-house painters working at several locations is to visit *each* location

    A. *before* they start working
    B. *just before* they leave to go home
    C. *at* noon time
    D. *at* random hours

15. Of the following, the *BEST* way to gain the confidence of painters under your supervision is to

    A. be critical of their work
    B. make correct decisions
    C. be partial to some of the painters
    D. be humble

16. In preparing a work schedule for painters under your supervision, of the following, the *BEST* practice is to

    A. distribute work loads according to each painter's salary
    B. refer to previous schedules as a guide to distribute work loads to each painter
    C. increase each painter's work 10 percent above his current productivity
    D. schedule all painters' work load at 100 percent of each painter's capacity at all times

17. Of the following, the *BEST* action for a foreman painter to take when a painter under his supervision makes a mistake of consequence is to

    A. threaten to transfer him
    B. threaten to fire him
    C. reprimand him in private
    D. reprimand him in public

18. Of the following, the *BEST* way to resolve an argument between two painters under your supervision relating to the work is to

    A. discuss the matter with one of the men
    B. discuss the matter with both men together
    C. have your supervisor resolve the dispute
    D. have a group of painters discuss the dispute with the men

19. A foreman of painters will be MOST effective as a supervisor if he has a

    A. *mild* interest in the personnel under his jurisdiction and a *deep* interest in productivity
    B. *mild* interest in the personnel under his jurisdiction and a *mild* interest in productivity
    C. *deep* interest in the personnel under his jurisdiction and a *deep* interest in productivity
    D. *deep* interest in the personnel under his jurisdiction and a *mild* interest in productivity

20. Of the following, the characteristic *most likely* to be found in a successful supervisor is that he

    A. tends to be argumentative
    B. does little training
    C. is critical of change
    D. has an all-around knowledge of his trade

KEY (CORRECT ANSWERS)

1. C	11. B
2. A	12. B
3. C	13. B
4. C	14. D
5. A	15. B
6. D	16. B
7. D	17. C
8. C	18. B
9. B	19. C
10. D	20. D

TEST 2

DIRECTIONS: Each question or incomplete statement is followed by several suggested answers or completions. Select the one that *BEST* answers the question or completes the statement. *PRINT THE LETTER OF THE CORRECT ANSWER IN THE SPACE AT THE RIGHT.*

1. You are asked to select a painter under your supervision for a provisional appointment to foreman painter.
   Of the following sets of qualities, the *MOST* desirable set to be possessed by a candidate for the position would be:

   A. Long experience, good attendance, high seniority, good personality
   B. Long experience, good personality, good attendance, high productivity
   C. Long experience, high seniority, good personality, good attendance
   D. Low seniority, good attendance, good productivity, good personality

   1._____

2. One of your in-house painters comes in late several times in one week. As a foreman painter, the *FIRST* thing to do is to

   A. *write* a memo to your supervisor about it
   B. *write* a memo to the painter about it
   C. *talk* to your supervisor about it
   D. *talk* to the painter about it

   2._____

Questions 3.

DIRECTIONS: Question 3 is to be answered in accordance with the following paragraph:

Following is a description of a training method that could be used in the field to teach painters how to work with new equipment. In this method, you explain the operation of the equipment to the painter, show him how to do it, ask him to do it while you stand by to coach him, give encouragement, correct mistakes, and at last, when you decide he can do it alone, periodically check or follow up to make sure the work is satisfactory.

3. The training method described above is known as

   A. the lecture method
   B. job rotation
   C. vestibule training
   D. on-the-job training

   3._____

4. The *BEST* way to handle a false rumor is for you to

   A. try to find out who started it
   B. discuss the rumor with your painters
   C. do nothing about it as rumors are good for morale
   D. circulate another false rumor

   4._____

5. It is good policy to establish procedures for orienting new painters on the job.
   Of the following objectives to be achieved by these procedures, the one that would be *LEAST* desirable is that it should

   A. create positive impressions and generate favorable attitudes
   B. instill some anxiety
   C. facilitate learning and a cooperative spirit
   D. establish a feeling of belonging

   5._____

51

6. A competent supervisor should

   A. feel he can always satisfy his subordinates' requests
   B. feel it is not necessary to point out to his supervisors any risks involved in his supervisors' decisions
   C. apply the rules of discipline uniformly to his men
   D. demand the respect of his subordinates

7. Of the following personal characteristics of a foreman painter acting as an inspector on a painting contract, the MOST important is

   A. fluency   B. congeniality   C. integrity   D. individuality

8. One of the painters under your supervision turns out a great deal of work but the work is not up to your standards.
   Of the following, the BEST action to take in this matter is to

   A. have the man transferred since he cannot meet your standards
   B. tell the man to improve the quality of his work even if it means slowing down
   C. do nothing since the man is turning out a large quantity of work and that is the goal of the department
   D. tell the man that the quality of his work is unsatisfactory and that action will be taken against him if his work does not improve

9. You are sent to witness the demonstration of a new paint applicator and to present your recommendations in a report.
   Of the following elements of the report, the MOST important one is that it must

   A. be brief
   B. draw a conclusion
   C. be cleverly worded
   D. be ambiguous so as not to put anybody on the spot

10. Of the following words, the BEST one to use in a written report to describe a door twisted out of shape by heat is

    A. extruded   B. dangled   C. gutted   D. warped

11. You are asked to write a report on a painter recommending hin for a provisional appointment to foreman painter. One of his characteristics is that he never has to be told to start a job and he always works hard.
    Of the following words, the word that BEST describes this characteristic is

    A. indolent   B. flexible   C. industrious   D. infallible

12. When writing a formal accident report, the BEST rule of those listed below to follow is to use

    A. long sentences and short words
    B. long sentences and novel words
    C. short sentences and complex words
    D. short sentences and precise words

13. Of the following, the LAST action for you to take before submitting a written report is to be sure that

    A. there are no grammatical errors
    B. the date of the report is correct
    C. the report is signed
    D. the listing of names to receive a carbon copy is correct

14. The *part* of the written report that condenses the main points into a brief paragraph is the

    A. summary   B. salutation   C. body   D. heading

15. To have to prepare a written report on a new type of safety belt that is being introduced by a manufacturer. The MOST important item to cover in the report is whether or not the belt is

    A. expensive
    B. durable
    C. safe
    D. made by a reputable manufacturer

16. Of the following words, the BEST one to use in an accident report to describe the place at which an accident occurred is

    A. cite   B. site   C. sight   D. seen

17. As the foreman painter is discussing the selection of paint colors with a tenant, the tenant requests that the painting of the apartment be delayed.
    Of the following, the BEST action for the foreman painter to take is to

    A. deny the request   B. grant the request
    C. request a deposit of $10   D. request a reason

18. While you are inspecting an apartment that has been painted by one of your painters, a ten-year-old child asks you to explain how the primary colors are used to create colors.
    Of the following, the BEST action for you to take is to

    A. give the child a brief explanation of color matching
    B. ignore the child
    C. tell the child to ask her school teacher
    D. give the child an excuse to avoid answering the question

19. As far as possible, when dealing with the public, a foreman painter should be

    A. candid   B. argumentative
    C. ambiguous   D. vague

20. You receive a letter from a tenant criticizing the workmanship in the painting of her apartment. Your records show that you checked and accepted the painting.
    Of the following, the BEST approach for you to take is to

    A. file it and wait for a second letter of complaint
    B. reply, requesting permission to inspect the apartment
    C. reply, acknowledging receipt of the letter, and take no further action
    D. reply, stating nothing will be done in the matter since you accepted the workmanship

KEY (CORRECT ANSWERS)

1. B
2. D
3. D
4. B
5. B

6. C
7. C
8. B
9. B
10. D

11. C
12. D
13. C
14. A
15. C

16. B
17. B
18. A
19. A
20. B

WORK SCHEDULING
EXAMINATION SECTION
TEST 1

DIRECTIONS: Each question or incomplete statement is followed by several suggested answers or completions. Select the one that BEST answers the question or completes the statement. *PRINT THE LETTER OF THE CORRECT ANSWER IN THE SPACE AT THE RIGHT.*

Questions 1-8.

DIRECTIONS: Questions 1 through 8 are to be answered on the basis of the following information.

Assume that you are the supervisor of a unit that works seven days a week. You need to determine the work and vacation schedules of the employees you supervise for the month of July.

THE EMPLOYEES

Employee	Seniority	Position
Alan W.	9 years seniority	computer operator
Jane B.	4 1/2 years seniority	typist
Alex H.	5 years seniority	security staff
Tony E.	4 years seniority	security staff
Andre T.	4 2/3 years seniority	typist
Mary W.	11 years seniority	security staff
Andy R.	13 years seniority	computer operator
Rhonda L.	2 years seniority	computer operator
Ethel R.	15 years seniority	typist
Roger G.	3 years seniority	security staff

THE VACATION PREFERENCES OF THE EMPLOYEES:

	1st vacation day	last vacation day
Alan W.	7/1	7/19
Jane B.	7/15	7/29
Alex H.	7/8	7/22
Tony E.	7/22	7/30
Andre T.	7/1	7/14
Mary W.	7/1	7/22
Andy R.	7/15	7/30
Rhonda L.	7/20	7/31
Ethel R.	7/1	7/27
Roger G.	7/21	7/31

IMPORTANT REGULATIONS REGARDING VACATION LEAVE

Employees with seniority have first choice for their preferred vacation dates. Seniority should be calculated separately for each of the three occupational groups.

55

2 (#1)

There must be two security employees on duty each working day in July. This overrides any other considerations.

There must be one typist on duty each working day in July. This overrides any other considerations.

Employees with least seniority, when denied their first choice of vacation dates, should automatically be scheduled ahead for vacation on the very next date closest to the dates they had originally preferred and the length of the vacation extended the appropriate number of days. Example: A vacation originally requested for 7/13, but changed because of seniority, would be moved AHEAD to a date after 7/13 (to 7/16, for example).

You may want to use the calendar below to help you organize this information.

JULY

1	2	3	4	5	6	7
8	9	10	11	12	13	14
15	16	17	18	19	20	21
22	23	24	25	26	27	28
29	30	31				

1. The number of employees on vacation on July 16 should be   1.____
   A. four   B. five   C. six   D. seven

2. The number of employees on vacation on July 22 should be   2.____
   A. five   B. six   C. seven   D. eight

3. How many typists will be working on July 15?   3.____
   A. One   B. Two   C. Three   D. None

4. How many workers will be on vacation on July 31?   4.____
   A. Two   B. Three   C. Four   D. Five

5. Which of the following is TRUE of the employees in the unit?   5.____
   I. Andy R., Jane B., Tony E., and Mary W. will be on vacation on 7/22.
   II. Ethel R., Andre T., Mary W., and Alex H. will be on vacation on 7/8.

    III. Rhonda L., Tony E., and Roger G. will be on vacation on 7/31,
    IV. Andy R., Jane B., and Ethel R. will be on vacation on 7/28.
  THE CORRECT ANSWER IS:

  A. I, II, III
  C. II, III
  B. I, II
  D. II

6. How many typists will be working on July 28?

   A. One
   B. Two
   C. Three
   D. Four

7. How many computer operators will be working on July 23?

   A. One
   B. Two
   C. Three
   D. Four

8. Roger G. will begin his vacation on July

   A. 21
   B. 22
   C. 23
   D. 24

Questions 9-15.

DIRECTIONS: Questions 9 through 15 are to be answered on the basis of the following information.

Assume that you are the supervisor of a unit that works seven days a week. You need to determine the work and vacation schedules of the employees you supervise for the month of August.

THE EMPLOYEES

	Years Seniority	Position
Robert L.	7	Security staff
Ann N.	7 1/2	Computer operator
Thomas B.	9	Typist
Phyllis P.	11	Computer operator
Mike D.	3	Security staff
Jane R.	2	Security staff
Alan R.	8	Computer operator
Susan T.	10	Typist
George W.	6	Computer operator
Barbara L.	4	Typist
Jack B.	13	Security staff
Grace N.	12	Typist

THE VACATION PREFERENCES OF THE EMPLOYEES

	1st vacation day	last vacation day
Robert L.	8/3	8/18
Ann N.	8/17	8/28
Thomas B.	8/19	8/28
Phyllis P.	8/5	8/20
Mike D.	8/14	8/21
Jane R.	8/20	8/27
Alan R.	8/12	8/26
Susan T.	8/5	8/26
George W.	8/3	8/14
Barbara L.	8/7	8/21
Jack B.	8/10	8/18
Grace N.	8/4	8/25

4 (#1)

IMPORTANT REGULATIONS REGARDING VACATION LEAVE.

Employees with seniority have first choice for their preferred vacation dates. Seniority should be calculated separately for each of the three occupational groups.

There must be two security employees on duty each working day in August. This overrides any other considerations.

There must be two typists on duty from 8/11 to 8/18. This overrides any other considerations.

There must be two computer operators on duty each working day in August. This overrides any other considerations.

Employees with least seniority, when denied their first choice of vacation dates, should automatically be scheduled ahead for their vacation on the very next date closest to the date they originally preferred, and the length of the vacation extended the appropriate number of days. Example: A vacation originally requested for 8/18, but changed because of seniority, would be moved AHEAD to a date after 8/18 (to 8/21, for example).

You may wish to use the calendar on the next page to help you organize this information.

AUGUST

1	2	3	4	5	6	7
8	9	10	11	12	13	14
15	16	17	18	19	20	21
22	23	24	25	26	27	28
29	30	31				

9. How many workers will be on vacation on August 21? 9._____
   A. Five B. Six C. Seven D. Eight

10. How many workers will be working on August 28? 10._____
    A. Six B. Seven C. Eight D. Nine

11. Of the following, who will NOT work on August 27? 11.____

   A. Alan R.   B. George W.   C. Mike D.   D. Susan T.

12. Of the following, who will work on August 19? 12.____

   A. Thomas B.   B. Barbara L.
   C. Ann N.   D. Mike D.

13. How many typists will be on vacation on August 19? 13.____

   A. One   B. Two   C. Three   D. Four

14. How many workers will be on vacation on August 17? 14.____

   A. Five   B. Six   C. Eight   D. Nine

15. How many workers will work on August 11? 15.____

   A. Seven   B. Eight   C. Five   D. Six

KEY (CORRECT ANSWERS)

1. C	6. B	11. B
2. B	7. A	12. C
3. A	8. C	13. D
4. B	9. D	14. B
5. C	10. C	15. A

EXAMINATION SECTION
TEST 1

DIRECTIONS: Each question or incomplete statement is followed by several suggested answers or completions. Select the one that BEST answers the question or completes the statement. *PRINT THE LETTER OF THE CORRECT ANSWER IN THE SPACE AT THE RIGHT.*

1. A *basic* method of operation that a *good* supervisor should follow is to

    A. check the work of subordinates constantly to make sure they are not making exceptions to the rules
    B. train subordinates so they can handle problems that come up regularly themselves and come to him only with special cases
    C. delegate to subordinates only those duties which he cannot do himself
    D. issue directions to subordinates only on special matters

2. To do a *good* job of performance evaluation, it is BEST for a supervisor to

    A. compare the employee's performance to that of another employee doing similar work
    B. give greatest weight to instances of unusually good or unusually poor performance
    C. leave out any consideration of the employee's personal traits
    D. measure the employee's performance against standard performance requirements

3. Of the following, the MOST important reason for a supervisor to have private face to face discussions with subordinates about their performance is to

    A. help employees improve their work
    B. give special praise to employees who perform well
    C. encourage the employees to compete for higher performance ratings
    D. discipline employees who perform poorly

4. Of the following, the CHIEF purpose of a probationary period for a new employee is to allow time for

    A. finding out whether the selection processes are satisfactory
    B. the employee to make adjustments in his home circumstances made necessary by the job
    C. the employee to decide whether he wants a permanent appointment
    D. determining the fitness of the employee to continue in the job

5. When a subordinate resigns his job, it is MOST important to conduct an exit interview in order to

    A. try to get the employee to remain on the job
    B. learn the true reasons for the employee's resignation
    C. see that the employee leaves with a good opinion of the agency
    D. ask the employee if he would consider a transfer

6. Chronic lateness of employees is generally LEAST likely to be due to

    A. distance of job location from home   B. poor personnel administration
    C. unexpressed employee grievances   D. low morale

61

7. Of the following, the LEAST effective stimulus for motivating employees toward improved performance over a long-range period is

   A. their sense of achievement
   B. their feeling of recognition
   C. opportunity for their self-development
   D. an increase in salary

8. Suppose that NOT ONE of a group of employees has turned in an idea to the employees suggestion system during the past year.
   The *most probable* reason for this situation is that the

   A. money awards given for suggestions used are not high enough to make employees interested
   B. employees in this group are not able to develop any good ideas
   C. supervisor of these employees is not doing enough to encourage them to take part in the program
   D. methods and procedures of operation do not need improvement

9. A subordinate tells you that he is having trouble concentrating on his work due to a personal problem at home.
   Of the following, it would be BEST for you to

   A. refer him to a community service agency
   B. listen quietly to the story because he may just need a sympathetic ear
   C. tell him that you cannot help him because the problem is not job related
   D. ask him questions about the nature of the problem and tell him how you would handle it

10. For you as a supervisor to give each of your subordinates *exactly* the same type of supervision is

    A. *advisable,* because doing this insures fair and impartial treatment of each individual
    B. *not advisable,* because individuals like to think that they are receiving better treatment than others
    C. *advisable,* because once a supervisor learns how to deal with a subordinate who brings a problem to him, he can handle another subordinate with this problem in the same way
    D. *not advisable,* because each person is different and there is no one supervisory procedure for dealing with individuals that applies in every case

11. A senior employee under your supervision tells you that he is reluctant to speak to one of his subordinates about his poor work habits, because this worker is "strong-willed" and he does not want to antagonize him.
    For you to offer to speak to the subordinate about this matter yourself would be

    A. *advisable,* since you are in a position of greater authority
    B. *inadvisable,* since handling this problem is a basic supervisory responsibility of the senior employee
    C. *advisable,* since the senior employee must work more closely with the worker than you do
    D. *inadvisable,* since you should not risk antagonizing the employee yourself

12. Some of your subordinates have been coming to you with complaints you feel are unimportant. For you to hear their stories out is

    A. *poor practice,* you should spend your time on more important matters
    B. *good practice,* this will increase your popularity with your subordinates
    C. *poor practice,* subordinates should learn to come to you only with major grievances
    D. *good practice,* it may prevent minor complaints from developing into major grievances

13. Assume that an agency has an established procedure for handling employee grievances. An employee in this agency, comes to his immediate supervisor with a grievance. The supervisor investigates the matter and makes a decision.
    However, the employee is not satisfied with the decision made by the supervisor. The BEST action for the supervisor to take is to

    A. tell the employee he will review the matter further
    B. remind the employee that he is the supervisor and the employee must act in accordance with his decision
    C. explain to the employee how he can carry his complaint forward to the next step in the grievance procedure
    D. tell the employee he will consult with his own superiors on the matter

14. Subordinate employees and senior employees often must make quick decisions while in the field. The supervisor can BEST help subordinates meet such situations by

    A. training them in the appropriate action to take for every problem that may come up
    B. limiting the areas in which they are permitted to make decisions
    C. making certain they understand clearly the basic policies of the bureau and the department
    D. delegating authority to make such decisions to only a few subordinates on each level

15. Studies have shown that the CHIEF cause of failure to achieve success as a supervisor is

    A. an unwillingness to delegate authority to subordinates
    B. the establishment of high performance standards for subordinates
    C. the use of discipline that is too strict
    D. showing too much leniency to poor workers

16. When a supervisor delegates to a subordinate certain work that he normally does himself, it is MOST important that he give the subordinate

    A. responsibility for also setting the standards for the work to be done
    B. sufficient authority to be able to carry out the assignment
    C. written, step-by-step instructions for doing the work
    D. an explanation of one part of the task at a time

17. It is particularly important that disciplinary actions be equitable as between individuals. 17._____
    This statement *implies* that

    A. punishment applied in disciplinary actions should be lenient
    B. proposed disciplinary actions should be reviewed by higher authority
    C. subordinates should have an opportunity to present their stories before penalties are applied
    D. penalties for violations of the rules should be standardized and consistently applied

18. You discover that from time to time a number of false rumors circulate among your subordinates. 18._____
    Of the following, the BEST way for you to handle this situation is to

    A. ignore the rumors since rumors circulate in every office and can never be eliminated
    B. attempt to find those responsible for the rumors and reprimand them
    C. make sure that your employees are informed as soon as possible about all matters that affect them
    D. inform your superior about the rumors and let him deal with the matter

19. Supervisors who allow the "halo effect" to influence their evaluations of subordinates are *most likely* to 19._____

    A. give more lenient ratings to older employees who have longer service
    B. let one highly favorable or unfavorable trait unduly affect their judgment of an employee
    C. evaluate all employees on one trait before considering a second
    D. give high evaluations in order to avoid antagonizing their subordinates

20. For a supervisor to keep records of reprimands to subordinates about infractions of the rules is 20._____

    A. *good practice,* because these records are valuable to support disciplinary actions recommended or taken
    B. *poor practice,* because such records are evidence of the supervisor's inability to maintain discipline
    C. *good practice,* because such records indicate that the supervisor is doing a good job
    D. *poor practice,* because the best way to correct subordinates is to give them more training

21. When a new departmental policy has been established, it would be MOST advisable for you, as a supervisor, to 21._____

    A. distribute a memo which states the new policy and instruct your subordinates to read it
    B. explain specifically to your subordinates how the policy is going to affect them
    C. make sure your subordinates understand that you are not responsible for setting the policy
    D. tell your subordinates whether you agree or disagree with the policy

22. As a supervisor, you receive several complaints about the rude conduct of a subordinate. The FIRST action you should take is to

    A. request his transfer to another office
    B. prepare a charge sheet for disciplinary action
    C. assign a senior employee to work with him for a week
    D. interview the employee to determine possible reason, and warn that correction is necessary

23. A supervisor is *most likely* to get subordinates to work cooperatively toward accomplishing bureau goals if he

    A. creates an atmosphere that contributes to their feeling of security
    B. backs up subordinates even when they occasionally disobey regulations
    C. shows interest in subordinates by helping them solve their personal problems
    D. uses an authoritarian or "bossy" approach to supervision

24. A supervisor is holding a staff meeting with his senior employees to try to find an acceptable solution to a problem that has come up.
    Of the following, the CHIEF role of the supervisor at this meeting should be to

    A. see that every member of the group contributes at least one suggestions
    B. act as chairman of the meeting, but take no other active part to avoid influencing the senior employees
    C. keep the participants from wandering off into discussions of irrelevant matters
    D. make certain the participants hear his views on the matter at the beginning of the meeting

25. An employee shows you a certificate that he has just received for completing two years of study in conversational Spanish. As his supervisor, it would be BEST for you to

    A. put a note about this accomplishment in his personnel folder
    B. assign him to areas in which people of Spanish origin live
    C. congratulate him on this accomplishment, but tell him frankly that you doubt this is likely to have any direct bearing on his work
    D. encourage him to continue his studies and become thoroughly fluent in speaking the language

KEY (CORRECT ANSWERS)

1.	B	11.	B
2.	D	12.	D
3.	A	13.	C
4.	D	14.	C
5.	B	15.	A
6.	A	16.	B
7.	D	17.	D
8.	C	18.	C
9.	B	19.	B
10.	D	20.	A

21. B
22. D
23. A
24. C
25. A

TEST 2

DIRECTIONS: Each question or incomplete statement is followed by several suggested answers or completions. Select the one that BEST answers the question or completes the statement. *PRINT THE LETTER OF THE CORRECT ANSWER IN THE SPACE AT THE RIGHT.*

1. Of the following, the factor affecting employee morale which the immediate supervisor is LEAST able to control is

    A. handling of grievances
    B. fair and impartial treatment of subordinates
    C. general presonnel rules and regulations
    D. accident prevention

2. When one of your workers does outstanding work, you should

    A. explain to your other employees that you expect the same kind of work of them
    B. praise him for his work so that he will know it is appreciated
    C. say nothing, because other employees may think you are showing favoritism
    D. show him how his work can be improved still more so that he will not sit back

3. For you as a supervisor to consider a suggestion from a probationary worker for improving a procedure would be

    A. *poor practice,* because this employee is too new on the job to know much about it
    B. *good practice,* because you may be able to share credit for the suggestion
    C. *poor practice,* because it may hurt the morale of the older employees
    D. *good practice,* because the suggestion may be worthwhile

4. If you find you must criticize the work of one of your workers, it would be BEST for you to

    A. mention the good points in his work as well as the faults
    B. caution him that he will receive an unsatisfactory performance report unless his work improves
    C. compare his work to that of the other agents you supervise
    D. apologize for making the criticism

5. As a senior employee which one of the following matters would it be BEST for you to talk over with your supervisor before you take final action?

    A. One of the workers you supervise continues to disregard your instructions repeatedly in spite of repeated warnings
    B. One of your workers tells you he wants to discuss a personal problem
    C. A probationary employee tells you he does not understand a procedure
    D. One of your workers tells you he disagrees with the way you rate his work

6. If one of your subordinates asks you a question about a department rule and you do not know the answer, you should tell him that

    A. he should try to get the information himself
    B. you do not have the answer, but you will get it for him as soon as you can
    C. he should ask you the question again a week from now
    D. he should put the question in writing

7. If, as a supervisor, you realize that you have been unfair in criticizing one of your subordinates, the BEST action for you to take is to

    A. say nothing, but overlook some error made by this employee in the future
    B. be frank and tell the employee that you are sorry for the mistake you made
    C. let the employee know in some indirect way without admitting your mistake, that you realize he was not at fault
    D. say nothing, but be more careful about criticizing subordinates in the future

8. Of the following, the MOST important reason for a supervisor to write an accident report as soon as possible after an accident has happened is to

    A. make sure that important facts about the accident are not forgotten
    B. avoid delay in getting compensation for the injured person
    C. get adequate medical treatment for the injured person
    D. keep department accident statistics up to date

9. In any matter which may require disciplinary action, the FIRST responsibility of the supervisor is to

    A. decide what penalty should be applied for the offense
    B. refer the matter to a higher authority for complete investigation
    C. place the interests of the department above those of the employee
    D. investigate the matter fully to get all the facts

10. Suppose you find it necessary to criticize one of the subordinates you supervise. You should

    A. send an official letter to his home
    B. speak to him about the matter privately
    C. speak to him at a staff meeting
    D. ask another worker who is friendly with him to talk to him about the matter

11. Some of your subordinates have been coming to you with complaints you feel are unimportant. For you to hear their stories out is

    A. *poor practice,* you should spend your time on more important matters
    B. *good practice,* this will increase your popularity with your subordinates
    C. *poor practice,* subordinates should learn to come to you only with major grievances
    D. *good practice,* it may prevent minor complaints from developing into major grievances

12. Suppose that NOT ONE of a group of employees has turned in an idea to the employees' suggestion system during the past year. The *most probable* reason for this situation is that the

    A. supervisor of these employees is not doing enough to encourage them to take part in this program
    B. employees in this group are not able to develop any good ideas
    C. money awards given for suggestions used are not high enough to make employees interested
    D. methods and procedures of operation do not need improvement

13. For you as a supervisor to give each of your subordinates *exactly* the same type of supervision is

    A. *advisable,* because doing this insures fair and impartial treatment of each individual
    B. *not advisable,* because each person is different and there is no one supervisory procedure for dealing with individuals that applies in every case
    C. *advisable,* because once a supervisor learns how to deal with a subordinate who brings a problem to him, he can handle another subordinate with this problem in the same way
    D. *not advisable,* because individuals like to think that they are receiving better treatment than others

14. In evaluating personnel, a supervisor should keep in mind that the MOST important objective of performance evaluations is to

    A. encourage employees to compete for higher performance ratings
    B. give recognition to employees who perform well
    C. help employees improve their work
    D. discipline employees who perform poorly

15. A subordinate tells you that he is having trouble concentrating on his work due to a personal problem at home. Of the following, it would be BEST for you to

    A. refer him to a community service agency
    B. listen quietly to the story because he may just need a sympathetic ear
    C. tell him that you cannot help him because the problem is not job-related
    D. ask him some questions about the nature of the problem and tell him how you would handle it

16. To do a good job of performance evaluation, it is BEST for a supervisor to

    A. measure the employee's performance against standard performance requirements
    B. compare the employee's performance to that of another employee doing similar work
    C. leave out any consideration of the employee's personal traits
    D. give greatest weight to instances of unusually good or unusually poor performance

17. It is particularly important that disciplinary actions be equitable as between individuals. This statement *implies* that

    A. punishment applied in disciplinary actions should be lenient
    B. proposed disciplinary actions should be reviewed by higher authority
    C. subordinates should have an opportunity to present their stories before penalties are applied
    D. penalties for violations of the rules should be standardized and consistently applied

18. Assume that an agency has an established procedure for handling employee grievances. An employee in this agency comes to his immediate supervisor with a grievance. The supervisor investigates the matter and makes a decision. However, the employee is not satisfied with the decision made by the supervisor.
    The BEST action for the supervisor to take is to

A. tell the employee he will review the matter further
B. remind the employee that he is the supervisor and the employee must act in accordance with his decision
C. explain to the employee how he can carry his complaint forward to the next step in the grievance procedure
D. tell the employee he will consult with his own superiors on the matter

19. Of the following, the CHIEF purpose of a probationary period for a new employee is to allow time for   19._____

    A. finding out whether the selection processes are satisfactory
    B. determining the fitness of the employee to continue in the job
    C. the employee to decide whether he wants a permanent appointment
    D. the employee to make adjustments in his home circumstances made necessary by the job

20. Of the following, the subject that would be MOST important to include in a "break-in" program for new employees is   20._____

    A. explanation of rules, regulations and policies of the agency
    B. Instruction in the agency's history and programs
    C. explanation of the importance of the new employees' own particular job
    D. explanation of the duties and responsibilities of the employee

21. Suppose a new employee under your supervision seems slow to learn and is making mistakes in performing his duties. Your FIRST action should be to   21._____

    A. pass this information on to the bureau director
    B. reprimand the worker so he will not repeat these mistakes
    C. find out whether this worker understands your instructions
    D. note these facts for future reference when writing up the monthly performance evaluation

22. In training new employees to do a certain job it would be LEAST desirable for you to   22._____

    A. demonstrate how the job is done, step by step
    B. encourage the workers to ask questions if they aren't clear about any point
    C. tell them about the various mistakes other agents have made in doing this job
    D. have the workers do the job, explaining to you what they are doing and why

23. One of the workers under your supervision is resentful when you ask her to remove her jangling bracelets before she starts her tour of duty.   23._____
    Of the following, the BEST explanation you can give her for the rule against wearing such jewelry while on duty is that

    A. the jewelry may create a safety hazard
    B. employees must give up certain personal liberties if they want to keep their jobs
    C. workers cannot perform their duties as efficiently if they wear distracting jewelry
    D. citizens may receive an unfavorable impression of the department

24. Of the following, the LEAST important reason for having a department handbook and a bureau standard operating procedure is to

    A. help in training new employees
    B. provide a source of reference for department and bureau rules and procedures
    C. prevent errors in work by providing clear guidelines
    D. make the supervisor's job easy

25. On inspecting your squad prior to their tour of duty, you note an employee improperly and unacceptably dressed.
    The FIRST action you should take is to

    A. call the employee aside and insist on immediate correction if possible
    B. notify the district commander right away
    C. have the employee submit a memorandum explaining the reason for the improper uniform
    D. permit the employee to proceed on duty but warn him not to let this happen again

KEY (CORRECT ANSWERS)

1.	C		11.	D
2.	B		12.	A
3.	D		13.	B
4.	A		14.	C
5.	A		15.	B
6.	B		16.	A
7.	B		17.	D
8.	A		18.	C
9.	D		19.	B
10.	B		20.	D

21. C
22. C
23. D
24. D
25. A

EXAMINATION SECTION

TEST 1

DIRECTIONS: Each question or incomplete statement is followed by several suggested answers or completions. Select the one that BEST answers the question or completes the statement. *PRINT THE LETTER OF THE CORRECT ANSWER IN THE SPACE AT THE RIGHT.*

1. Of the following, the one MOST important quality required of a good supervisor is
   A. ambition   B. leadership   C. friendliness   D. popularity

   1.____

2. It is often said that a supervisor can delegate authority but never responsibility. This means MOST NEARLY that
   A. a supervisor must do his own work if he expects it to be done properly
   B. a supervisor can assign someone else to do his work, but in the last analysis, the supervisor himself must take the blame for any actions followed
   C. authority and responsibility are two separate things that cannot be borne by the same person
   D. it is better for a supervisor never to delegate his authority

   2.____

3. One of your men who is a habitual complainer asks you to grant him a minor privilege.
   Before granting or denying such a request, you should consider
   A. the merits of the case
   B. that it is good for group morale to grant a request of this nature
   C. the man's seniority
   D. that to deny such a request will lower your standing with the men

   3.____

4. A supervisory practice on the part of a foreman which is MOST likely to lead to confusion and inefficiency is for him to
   A. give orders verbally directly to the man assigned to the job
   B. issue orders only in writing
   C. follow up his orders after issuing them
   D. relay his orders to the men through co-workers

   4.____

5. It would be POOR supervision on a foreman's part if he
   A. asked an experienced maintainer for his opinion on the method of doing a special job
   B. make it a policy to avoid criticizing a man in front of his co-workers
   C. consulted his assistant supervisor on unusual problems
   D. allowed a cooling-off period of several days before giving one of his men a deserved reprimand

   5.____

6. Of the following behavior characteristics of a supervisor, the one that is MOST likely to lower the morale of the men he supervises is
   A. diligence
   B. favoritism
   C. punctuality
   D. thoroughness

7. Of the following, the BEST method of getting an employee who is not working up to his capacity to produce more work is to
   A. have another employee criticize his production
   B. privately criticize his production but encourage him to produce more
   C. criticize his production before his associates
   D. criticize his production and threaten to fire him

8. Of the following, the BEST thing for a supervisor to do when a subordinate has done a very good job is to
   A. tell him to take it easy
   B. praise his work
   C. reduce his workload
   D. say nothing because he may become conceited

9. Your orders to your crew are MOST likely to be followed if you
   A. explain the reasons for these orders
   B. warn that all violators will be punished
   C. promise easy assignments to those who follow these orders best
   D. say that they are for the good of the department

10. In order to be a good supervisor, you should
    A. impress upon your men that you demand perfection in their work at all times
    B. avoid being blamed for your crew's mistakes
    C. impress your superior with your ability
    D. see to it that your men get what they are entitled to

11. In giving instructions to a crew, you should
    A. speak in as loud a tone as possible
    B. speak in a coaxing, persuasive manner
    C. speak quietly, clearly, and courteously
    D. always use the word *please* when giving instructions

12. Of the following factors, the one which is LEAST important in evaluating an employee and his work is his
    A. dependability
    B. quantity of work done
    C. quality of work done
    D. education and training

13. When a District Superintendent first assumes his command, it is LEAST important for him at the beginning to observe
    A. how his equipment is designed and its adaptability
    B. how to reorganize the district for greater efficiency
    C. the capabilities of the men in the district
    D. the methods of operation being employed

14. When making an inspection of one of the buildings under your supervision, the BEST procedure to follow in making a record of the inspection is to
    A. return immediately to the office and write a report from memory
    B. write down all the important facts during or as soon as you complete the inspection
    C. fix in your mind all important facts so that you can repeat them from memory if necessary
    D. fix in your mind all important facts so that you can make out your report at the end of the day

14.____

15. Assume that your superior has directed you to make certain changes in your established procedure. After using this modified procedure on several occasions, you find that the original procedure was distinctly superior and you wish to return to it.
    You should
    A. let your superior find this out for himself
    B. simply change back to the original procedure
    C. compile definite data and information to prove your case to your superior
    D. persuade one of the more experienced workers to take this matter up with your superior

15.____

16. An inspector visited a large building under construction. He inspected the soil lines at 9 A.M., water lines at 10 A.M., fixtures at 11 A.M., and did his office work in the afternoon. He followed the same pattern daily for weeks.
    This procedure was
    A. *good*, because it was methodical and he did not miss anything
    B. *good*, because it gave equal time to all phases of the plumbing
    C. *bad*, because not enough time was devoted to fixtures
    D. *bad*, because the tradesmen knew when the inspection would occur

16.____

17. Assume that one of the foremen in a training course, which you are conducting, proposes a poor solution for a maintenance problem.
    Of the following, the BEST course of action for you to take is to
    A. accept the solution tentatively and correct it during the next class meeting
    B. point out all the defects of this proposed solution and wait until somebody thinks of a better solution
    C. try to get the class to reject this proposed solution and develop a better solution
    D. let the matter pass since somebody will present a better solution as the class work proceeds

17.____

18. As a supervisor, you should be seeking ways to improve the efficiency of shop operations by means such as changing established work procedures.
    The following are offered as possible actions that you should consider in changing established work procedures:
    I. Make changes only when your foremen agree to them
    II. Discuss changes with your supervisor before putting them into practice

18.____

4 (#1)

III. Standardize any operation which is performed on a continuing basis
IV. Make changes quickly and quietly in order to avoid dissent
V. Secure expert guidance before instituting unfamiliar procedures

Of the following suggested answers, the one that describes the actions to be taken to change established work procedures is

   A. I, IV, V   B. II, III, V   C. III, IV, V   D. All of the above

19. A supervisor determined that a foreman, without informing his superior, delegated responsibility for checking time cards to a member of his gang. The supervisor then called the foreman into his office where he reprimanded the foreman.
This action of the supervisor in reprimanding the foreman was
   A. *proper*, because the checking of time cards is the foreman's responsibility and should not be delegated
   B. *proper*, because the foreman did not ask the supervisor for permission to delegate responsibility
   C. *improper*, because the foreman may no longer take the initiative in solving future problems
   D. *improper*, because the supervisor is interfering in a function which is not his responsibility

20. A capable supervisor should check all operations under his control.
Of the following, the LEAST important reason for doing this is to make sure that
   A. operations are being performed as scheduled
   B. he personally observes all operations at all times
   C. all the operations are still needed
   D. his manpower is being utilized efficiently

21. A supervisor makes it a practice to apply fair and firm discipline in all cases of rule infractions, including those of a minor nature.
This practice should PRIMARILY be considered
   A. *bad*, since applying discipline for minor violations is a waste of time
   B. *good*, because not applying discipline for minor infractions can lead to a more serious erosion of discipline
   C. *bad*, because employees do not like to be disciplined for minor violations of the rules
   D. *good*, because violating any rule can cause a dangerous situation to occur

22. A maintainer would PROPERLY consider it poor supervisory practice for a foreman to consult with him on
   A. which of several repair jobs should be scheduled first
   B. how to cope with personal problems at home
   C. whether the neatness of his headquarters can be improved
   D. how to express a suggestion which the maintainer plans to submit formally

23. Assume that you have determined that the work of one of your foremen and the men he supervises is consistently behind schedule. When you discuss this situation with the foreman, he tells you that his men are poor workers and then complains that he must spend all of his time checking on their work.
The following actions are offered for your consideration as possible ways of solving the problem of poor performance of the foreman and his men:
   I.   Review the work standards with the foreman and determine whether they are realistic.
   II. Tell the foreman that you will recommend him for the foreman's training course for retraining.
   III. Ask the foreman for the names of the maintainers and then replace them as soon as possible.
   IV. Tell the foreman that you expect him to meet a satisfactory level of performance.
   V.   Tell the foreman to insist that his men work overtime to catch up to the schedule.
   VI. Tell the foreman to review the type and amount of training he has given the maintainers.
   VII. Tell the foreman that he will be out of a job if he does not produce on schedule.
   VIII. Avoid all criticism of the foreman and his methods.
   Which of the following suggested answers CORRECTLY lists the proper actions to be taken to solve the problem of poor performance of the foreman and his men?
   A. I, II, IV, VI   B. I, III, V, VII   C. II, III, VI, VIII   D. IV, V, VI, VIII

24. When a conference or a group discussion is tending to turn into a *bull session* without constructive purpose, the BEST action to take is to
   A. reprimand the leader of the bull session
   B. redirect the discussion to the business at hand
   C. dismiss the meeting and reschedule it for another day
   D. allow the bull session to continue

25. Assume that you have been assigned responsibility for a program in which a high production rate is mandatory. From past experience, you know that your foremen do not perform equally well in the various types of jobs given to them. Which of the following methods should you use in selecting foremen for the specific types of work involved in the program?
   A. Leave the method of selecting foremen to your supervisor
   B. Assign each foreman to the work he does best
   C. Allow each foreman to choose his own job
   D. Assign each foreman to a job which will permit him to improve his own abilities

KEY (CORRECT ANSWERS)

1. B
2. B
3. A
4. D
5. D

6. B
7. B
8. B
9. A
10. D

11. C
12. D
13. B
14. B
15. C

16. D
17. C
18. B
19. A
20. B

21. B
22. A
23. A
24. B
25. B

TEST 2

DIRECTIONS: Each question or incomplete statement is followed by several suggested answers or completions. Select the one that BEST answers the question or completes the statement. *PRINT THE LETTER OF THE CORRECT ANSWER IN THE SPACE AT THE RIGHT.*

1. A foreman who is familiar with modern management principles should know that the one of the following requirements of an administrator which is LEAST important is his ability to
    A. coordinate work
    B. plan, organize, and direct the work under his control
    C. cooperate with others
    D. perform the duties of the employees under his jurisdiction

    1.____

2. When subordinates request his advice in solving problems encountered in their work, a certain chief occasionally answers the request by first asking the subordinate what he thinks should be done.
    This action by the chief is, on the whole,
    A. *desirable*, because it stimulates subordinates to give more thought to the solution of problems encountered
    B. *undesirable*, because it discourages subordinates from asking questions
    C. *desirable*, because it discourages subordinates from asking questions
    D. *undesirable*, because it undermines the confidence of subordinates in the ability of their supervisor

    2.____

3. Of the following factors that may be considered by a unit head in dealing with the tardy subordinate, the one which should be given LEAST consideration is the
    A. frequency with which the employee is tardy
    B. effect of the employee's tardiness upon the work of other employees
    C. willingness of the employee to work overtime when necessary
    D. cause of the employee's tardiness

    3.____

4. The MOST important requirement of a good inspectional report is that it should be
    A. properly addressed   B. lengthy
    C. clear and brief   D. spelled correctly

    4.____

5. Building superintendents frequently inquire about departmental inspectional procedures.
    Of the following, it is BEST to
    A. advise them to write to the department for an official reply
    B. refuse as the inspectional procedure is a restricted matter
    C. briefly explain the procedure to them
    D. avoid the inquiry by changing the subject

    5.____

6. Reprimanding a crew member before other workers is a
   A. *good* practice; the reprimand serves as a warning to the other workers
   B. *bad* practice; people usually resent criticism made in public
   C. *good* practice; the other workers will realize that the supervisor is fair
   D. *bad* practice; the other workers will take sides in the dispute

7. Of the following actions, the one which is LEAST likely to promote good work is for the group leader to
   A. praise workers for doing a good job
   B. call attention to the opportunities for promotion for better workers
   C. threaten to recommend discharge of workers who are below standard
   D. put into practice any good suggestion made by crew members

8. A supervisor notices that a member of his crew has skipped a routine step in his job.
   Of the following, the BEST action for the supervisor to take is to
   A. promptly question the worker about the incident
   B. immediately assign another man to complete the job
   C. bring up the incident the next time the worker asks for a favor
   D. say nothing about the incident but watch the worker carefully in the future

9. Assume you have been told to show a new worker how to operate a piece of equipment.
   Your FIRST step should be to
   A. ask the worker if he has any questions about the equipment
   B. permit the worker to operate the equipment himself while you carefully watch to prevent damage
   C. demonstrate the operation of the equipment for the worker
   D. have the worker read an instruction booklet on the maintenance of the equipment

10. Whenever a new man was assigned to his crew, the supervisor would introduce him to all other crew members, take him on a tour of the plant, tell him about bus schedules and places to eat.
    This practice is
    A. *good*; the new man is made to feel welcome
    B. *bad*; supervisors should not interfere in personal matters
    C. *good*; the new man knows that he can bring his personal problems to the supervisor
    D. *bad*; work time should not be spent on personal matters

11. The MOST important factor in successful leadership is the ability to
    A. obtain instant obedience to all orders
    B. establish friendly personal relations with crew members
    C. avoid disciplining crew members
    D. make crew members want to do what should be done

12. Explaining the reasons for departmental procedure to workers tends to
    A. waste time which should be used for productive purposes
    B. increase their interest in their work
    C. make them more critical of departmental procedures
    D. confuse them

13. If you want a job done well do it yourself.
    For a supervisor to follow this advice would be
    A. *good*; a supervisor is responsible for the work of his crew
    B. *bad*; a supervisor should train his men, not do their work
    C. *good*; a supervisor should be skilled in all jobs assigned to his crew
    D. *bad*; a supervisor loses respect when he works with his hands

14. When a supervisor discovers a mistake in one of the jobs for which his crew is responsible, it is MOST important for him to find out
    A. whether anybody else knows about the mistake
    B. who was to blame for the mistake
    C. how to prevent similar mistakes in the future
    D. whether similar mistakes occurred in the past

15. A supervisor who has to explain a new procedure to his crew should realize that questions from the crew USUALLY show that they
    A. are opposed to the new practice
    B. are completely confused by the explanation
    C. need more training in the new procedure
    D. are interested in the explanation

16. A good way for a supervisor to retain the confidence of his or her employees is to
    A. say as little as possible
    B. check work frequently
    C. make no promises unless they will be fulfilled
    D. never hesitate in giving an answer to any question

17. Good supervision is ESSENTIALLY a matter of
    A. patience in supervising workers
    B. care in selecting workers
    C. skill in human relations
    D. fairness in disciplining workers

18. It is MOST important for an employee who has been assigned a monotonous task to
    A. perform this task before doing other work
    B. ask another employee to help
    C. perform this task only after all other work has been completed
    D. take measures to prevent mistakes in performing the task

19. One of your employees has violated a minor agency regulation. 19.____
    The FIRST thing you should do is
    A. warn the employee that you will have to take disciplinary action if it should happen again
    B. ask the employee to explain his or her actions
    C. inform your supervisor and wait for advice
    D. write a memo describing the incident and place it in the employee's personnel file

20. One of your employees tells you that he feels you give him much more work 20.____
    than the other employees, and he is having trouble meeting your deadlines.
    You should
    A. ask if he has been under a lot of non-work related stress lately
    B. review his recent assignments to determine if he is correct
    C. explain that this is a busy time, but you are dividing the work equally
    D. tell him that he is the most competent employee and that is why he receives more work

21. A supervisor assigns one of his crew to complete a portion of a job. A short 21.____
    time later, the supervisor notices that the portion has not been completed.
    Of the following, the BEST way for the supervisor to handle this is to
    A. ask the crew member why he has not completed the assignment
    B. reprimand the crew member for not obeying orders
    C. assign another crew member to complete the assignment
    D. complete the assignment himself

22. Supposes that a member of your crew complains that you are *playing favorites* 22.____
    in assigning work.
    Of the following, the BEST method of handling the complaint is to
    A. deny it and refuse to discuss the matter with the worker
    B. take the opportunity to tell the worker what is wrong with his work
    C. ask the worker for examples to prove his point and try to clear up any misunderstanding
    D. promise to be more careful in making assignments in the future

23. A member of your crew comes to you with a complaint. After discussing the 23.____
    matter with him, it is clear that you have convinced him that his complaint was not justified.
    At this point, you should
    A. permit him to drop the matter
    B. make him admit his error
    C. pretend to see some justification in his complaint
    D. warn him against making unjustified complaints

24. Suppose that a supervisor has in his crew an older man who works rather 24.____
    slowly. In other respects, this man is a good worker; he is seldom absent,
    works carefully, never loafs, and is cooperative.

The BEST way for the supervisor to handle this worker is to
- A. try to get him to work faster and less carefully
- B. give him the most disagreeable job
- C. request that he be given special training
- D. permit him to work at his own speed

25. Suppose that a member of your crew comes to you with a suggestion he thinks will save time in doing a job. You realize immediately that it won't work. Under these circumstances, your BEST action would be to
- A. thank the worker for the suggestion and forget about it
- B. explain to the worker why you think it won't work
- C. tell the worker to put the suggestion in writing
- D. ask the other members of your crew to criticize the suggestion

25._____

KEY (CORRECT ANSWERS)

1.	D		11.	D
2.	A		12.	B
3.	C		13.	B
4.	C		14.	C
5.	C		15.	D
6.	B		16.	C
7.	C		17.	C
8.	A		18.	D
9.	C		19.	B
10.	A		20.	B

21. A
22. C
23. A
24. D
25. B

ARITHMETICAL REASONING
EXAMINATION SECTION
TEST 1

DIRECTIONS: Each question or incomplete statement is followed by several suggested answers or completions. Select the one that BEST answers the question or completes the statement. *PRINT THE LETTER OF THE CORRECT ANSWER IN THE SPACE AT THE RIGHT.*

1. A room is 7'6" wide by 9'0" long with a ceiling height of 8'0". One gallon of flat paint will cover approximately 400 square feet of wall.
   The number of gallons of this paint required to paint the walls of this room, making no deductions for windows or doors, is MOST NEARLY _____ gallon.

   A. 1/4   B. 1/2   C. 2/3   D. 1

   1.____

2. The cost of a certain job is broken down as follows:
   Materials $3,750
   Rental of equipment 1,200
   Labor   3,150
   The percentage of the total cost of the job that can be charged to materials is MOST NEARLY

   A. 40%   B. 42%   C. 44%   D. 46%

   2.____

3. By trial it is found that by using two cubic feet of sand, a 5 cubic foot batch of concrete is produced.
   Using the same proportions, the amount of sand required to produce 2 cubic yards of concrete is MOST NEARLY _____ cubic feet.

   A. 20   B. 22   C. 24   D. 26

   3.____

4. It takes 4 men 6 days to do a certain job.
   Working at the same speed, the number of days it will take 3 men to do this job is

   A. 7   B. 8   C. 9   D. 10

   4.____

5. The cost of rawl plugs is $27.50 per gross.
   The cost of 2,448 rawl plugs is

   A. $467.50   B. $472.50   C. $477.50   D. $482.50

   5.____

6. A box contains an equal number of iron and brass castings. Each iron casting weighs 2 pounds, and each brass casting weighs 1 pound.
   If the box contents weigh 240 pounds, the number of brass pieces in the box is

   A. 40   B. 80   C. 120   D. 160

   6.____

7. The sum of 5 feet 2 3/4 inches, 8 feet 1/2 inch, and 12 1/2 inches is _____ feet _____ inches.

   A. 25; 3 3/4   B. 14; 3 3/4
   C. 13; 5 3/4   D. 13; 3 3/4

   7.____

8. A vertical cylindrical tank 4 feet in diameter and 5 feet high has a capacity of 470 gallons. The number of gallons in the tank when filled to a depth of 1'6" is NEAREST to

   A. 45   B. 95   C. 140   D. 180

9. A crate contains 3 pieces of equipment weighing 43, 59, and 66 pounds, respectively. If the crate is lifted by 4 men each lifting one corner of the crate, the average number of pounds lifted by each of the men is

   A. 56   B. 51   C. 42   D. 36

10. The sum of the following numbers, 1 3/4, 3 1/6, 5 1/2, 6 5/8, and 9 1/4, is closest to

    A. 26 1/8   B. 26 1/4   C. 26 1/2   D. 26 3/4

11. If a piece of plywood measures 5'1 1/4" x 3'2 1/2", the number of square feet in this board is MOST NEARLY

    A. 15.8   B. 16.1   C. 16.4   D. 16.7

12. Assume that in quantity purchases, the city receives a discount of 33 1/3%. If a one-gallon can of paint retails at $16.00 per gallon, the cost of 375 gallons of this paint is MOST NEARLY

    A. $3,997.50   B. $3,998.25   C. $3,999.00   D. $4,000.00

13. Assume that eight barrels of cement together weigh a total of 3,004 pounds and 12 ounces.
    If there are four bags of cement per barrel, then the weight of one bag of cement is MOST NEARLY _____ pounds.

    A. 93.1   B. 93.5   C. 93.9   D. 94.3

14. Assume that one man cuts 50 nameplates per hour, whereas his co-worker cuts 55 nameplates per hour.
    At the end of 7 hours, the first man will have cut fewer nameplates than the second man by

    A. 9.1%   B. 9.5%   C. 9.7%   D. 9.9%

15. The jaws of a vise close 3/16 of an inch for each turn of the screw.
    If the vise is open 6 inches, the number of turns required to close the jaw is

    A. 8   B. 16   C. 32   D. 64

16. If the inside diameter of a pipe is 3/8 of an inch and the wall thickness is .091 inches, the outside diameter of the pipe is _____ inches.

    A. .193   B. .284   C. .466   D. .557

17. If one dozen 1/8" welding rods cost $4.80, 37 rods would cost

    A. $14.40   B. $14.80   C. $15.20   D. $15.60

18. The sum of the following numbers, 6 5/8, 3 3/4, 4 1/2, 5 1/8, is

    A. 19 3/4   B. 19 7/8   C. 20   D. 20 1/8

19. The sum of 5 feet 4 1/4 inches, 8 feet 7 1/2 inches, and 13 feet 5 3/4 inches is _____ feet _____ inches. 19.____

   A. 26; 6 3/4
   B. 27; 5 1/2%
   C. 27; 7 1/2
   D. 28; 8 3/4

20. If the floor area of one shop is 17 feet by 19 feet 3 inches and the floor area of an adjacent shop is 22 feet by 28 feet 6 inches, then the total floor area of these two shops is MOST NEARLY _____ square feet. 20.____

   A. 856   B. 946   C. 948   D. 954

21. A carton contains 9 dozen drill bits.
   If a helper removes 73 drill bits, the number of bits remaining in the carton is 21.____

   A. 27   B. 35   C. 47   D. 62

22. One inch is MOST NEARLY equal to _____ feet. 22.____

   A. 0.8   B. 0.08   C. 0.008   D. 0.0008

23. The circumference of a circle is given by the formula C = 2 π R, where C is the circumference, R is the radius, and π is approximately 3 1/7.
   The circumference of an oil drum having a diameter of one foot and nine inches is, therefore, about _____ inches. 23.____

   A. 132   B. 66   C. 33   D. 17

24. Tubing with an outside diameter of 2" and a wall thickness of 1/16" has an inside diameter which is 24.____

   A. 1 1/2"   B. 1 3/4"   C. 1 7/8"   D. 1 15/16"

25. The decimal which is NEAREST 33/64 is 25.____

   A. 0.516   B. 0.500   C. 0.643   D. 1.939

KEY (CORRECT ANSWERS)

1. C
2. D
3. B
4. B
5. A

6. B
7. B
8. C
9. C
10. B

11. C
12. D
13. C
14. A
15. C

16. D
17. B
18. C
19. B
20. D

21. B
22. B
23. B
24. C
25. A

SOLUTIONS TO PROBLEMS

1. The area of the four walls = (2) (7 1/2') (8') + (2)(9')(8') = 264 sq.ft. Then, 264÷400=.66 or about 2/3 gallon of paint.

2. $3750÷($3750+$1200+$3150)=$3750÷$8100 ≈ 46%

3. 2 cu.yds. = 54 cu.ft. Then, 54 ÷ 5 = 10.8. Finally, (10.8)(2) ≈ 22 cu.ft. of sand.

4. (4)(6) = 24 man-days. Then, 24 ÷ 3 = 8 days

5. 2440 ÷ 144 = 17 gross of plugs. Then, (17)($27.50) = $467.50

6. Each 3 lbs. in the box means 1 iron casting and 1 brass casting.
   Then, 240 lbs. ÷ 3 lbs. = 80. Thus, there are 80 iron castings and 80 brass castings.

7. 5 ft. 2 3/4 in. + 8 ft. 1/2 in. + 0 ft. 12 1/2 in. = 13 ft. 15 3/4 in. = 14 ft. 3 3/4 in.

8. 1 1/2 ft. ÷ 5 ft. = .3 Then, (470 gallons)(.3) ≈ 140 gallons

9. 43 + 59 + 66 = 168 lbs. Then, 168 ÷ 4 = 42 lbs.

10. $1\frac{3}{4}+3\frac{1}{6}+5\frac{1}{2}+6\frac{5}{8}+9\frac{1}{4} = 24\frac{55}{24} = 26\frac{7}{24}$, closest to 26 1/4

11. (5'1 1/4")(3'2 1/2") = (61.25")(38.5") = 2358.125 sq. in.
    Since 1 sq.ft. = 144 sq. in., 2358.125 sq.in. ≈ 16.4 sq.ft.

12. (375)($16) = $6000. With a 33 1/3% discount, the cost becomes 67 2/3% of $6000 = $4000

13. (8)(4) = 32 bags of cement with a total weight of 3004.75 pounds. This means each bag weighs 3004.75 ÷ 32 ≈ 93.9 pounds.

14. In 7 hours, the first man cuts 350 nameplates, whereas the second man cuts 385 nameplates. The percentage pertaining to the amount done less by the first man is (35/385)(100) ≈ 9.1%

15. 6 in. ÷ $\frac{3}{16}$ in. = 32 turns required

16. Outside diameter = .375" + .091" + .091" = .557"

17. 37÷12=3.08$\overline{3}$ Then, (3.08$\overline{3}$)($4.80)=$14.80

18. $6\frac{5}{8}+3\frac{3}{4}+4\frac{1}{2}+5\frac{1}{8}=18\frac{16}{8}=20$

19. $5'4\frac{1}{4}" + 8'7\frac{1}{2}" + 13'5\frac{3}{4}" = 26'17\frac{1}{2}" = 27'5\frac{1}{2}"$

20. Total area = $(17)(19\frac{1}{4}) + (22)(28\frac{1}{2}) \approx 954$ sq.ft.

21. $(9)(12) - 73 = 35$ remaining drill bits

22. 1 inch = $\frac{1}{12}$ ft. = $.08\overline{3} \approx .08$ ft

23. $C = (2)(\pi)(10.5 \text{ in.}) = 21\pi$ inches ≈ 66 inches

24. Inside diameter = $2" - \frac{1}{16}" - \frac{1}{16}" = 1\frac{7}{8}"$

25. $\frac{33}{64} = .515625 \approx .516$

TEST 2

DIRECTIONS: Each question or incomplete statement is followed by several suggested answers or completions. Select the one that BEST answers the question or completes the statement. *PRINT THE LETTER OF THE CORRECT ANSWER IN THE SPACE AT THE RIGHT.*

1. A floor that is 9' wide by 12' long measures _____ square feet. 1._____

   A. 12   B. 21   C. 108   D. 150

2. The sum of 5 1/16, 4 1/4, 4 3/8, and 3 7/16 is 2._____

   A. 17 1/8   B. 17 7/16   C. 17 1/4   D. 17 3/8

3. From a length of pipe 6 feet 9 inches long, you are asked to cut a piece 4 feet 5 inches long. 3._____
   The length of the remainder, in inches, should be

   A. 24   B. 26   C. 28   D. 53

4. The jaws of a vise close 3/16 inch for each turn of the screw. 4._____
   If the vise is open 3 3/8 inches, then the number of turns needed to close the jaws is

   A. 16   B. 17   C. 18   D. 24

5. 627 cubic feet contains MOST NEARLY _____ cubic yards. 5._____

   A. 21   B. 22   C. 23   D. 24

6. The right angle shown at the right has been divided into three parts. 6._____
   The number of degrees in the unmarked part is
   A. 46
   B. 36
   C. 21
   D. 6

7. It ordinarily requires 5 days for 2 men to complete a certain job. 7._____
   If the management wants to have this work done in two days, the number of men required would be

   A. 10   B. 7   C. 6   D. 5

8. A room 20' x 25' in area with a ceiling height of 9'6" is to be painted. One gallon of paint will cover 400 square feet. 8._____
   The MINIMUM number of gallons necessary to give the four walls and the ceiling one coat of paint is

   A. 2   B. 3   C. 4   D. 5

9. An office has floor dimensions of 16 feet 6 inches wide by 22 feet 0 inches long. 9._____
   The floor area of this office, in square feet, is MOST NEARLY

   A. 143   B. 263   C. 363   D. 463

10. A supplier quotes a list price of $14.00 for a replacement part less discounts of 25, 10, and 5 percent.
    The cost of the item is MOST NEARLY

    A. $5.50   B. $6.00   C. $8.50   D. $9.00

11. An equipment rental allowance includes the rental charge plus 9%.
    If a piece of equipment is rented for 11 days at $36 per day, the total equipment allowance is MOST NEARLY

    A. $360   B. $390   C. $430   D. $450

12. A plumbing sketch is drawn to a scale of 1/8" = 1 foot.
    A horizontal water line measuring 6 3/4 inches on the sketch would be equivalent to _____ feet of water pipe.

    A. 27   B. 41   C. 54   D. 64

13. A rectangular yard is 50'0" long by 8'6" wide.
    The area of the yard, in square feet, is

    A. 420.0   B. 422.5   C. 425.0   D. 427.5

14. A rectangular court is 23'0" long by 9'6" wide.
    The length of the diagonal is MOST NEARLY

    A. 24'8"   B. 24'10"   C. 25'2"   D. 25'6"

15. Concrete weighs 150 pounds per cubic foot.
    A slab of concrete 6'0" long by 3'6" wide by 1'4" thick weighs MOST NEARLY _____ pounds.

    A. 4,150   B. 4,200   C. 4,250   D. 4,300

16. A building 32'0" by 65'0" occupies a lot 60'0" by 110'0".
    The ratio of building area to lot area is MOST NEARLY

    A. 0.32   B. 0.33   C. 0.34   D. 0.35

17. The decimal equivalent of 31/64 of an inch is MOST NEARLY

    A. 0.45   B. 0.46   C. 0.47   D. 0.48

18. The decimal equivalent of 27/32 is MOST NEARLY

    A. 0.813   B. 0.828   C. 0.844   D. 0.859

19. If a scaled measurement of 1'3" on the drawing of a sheet metal layout represents an actual length of 10'0", then the drawing has been made to a scale of _____ inch to the foot.

    A. 3/4   B. 1 1/4   C. 1 1/2   D. 1 3/4

20. If it takes 4 painters 5 1/2 days to do a certain paint job, then the time that it should take 5 painters working at the same speed to do the same job is MOST NEARLY _____ days.

    A. 3 1/2   B. 4   C. 4 1/2   D. 5

21. The number of square feet in a flat rectangular roof measuring 42'6" x 83'4" is MOST NEARLY 21._____

   A. 3,520   B. 3,530   C. 3,540   D. 3,550

22. The sum of the following dimensions, 3 5/8", 4 1/4", 6 5/16", 7 3/4", and 8 1/2", is 22._____

   A. 30 3/8"   B. 30 7/16"   C. 30 1/2"   D. 30 9/16"

23. Assume that 1 1/2 pounds of pitch are required for each square foot of roof. 23._____
    The number of pounds that would be required for a roof 55 feet by 96 feet is MOST NEARLY _____ pounds.

   A. 5,000   B. 6,000   C. 7,000   D. 8,000

24. A rectangular plot is 30 feet wide by 60 feet long. 24._____
    The length of the diagonal, in feet, is MOST NEARLY

   A. 68   B. 67   C. 66   D. 65

25. The volume, in cubic feet, of a room 8'6" wide by 10'6" long by 8'8" high is MOST NEARLY 25._____

   A. 770   B. 774   C. 778   D. 782

KEY (CORRECT ANSWERS)

1. C   11. C
2. A   12. C
3. C   13. C
4. C   14. B
5. C   15. B

6. B   16. A
7. D   17. D
8. C   18. C
9. C   19. C
10. D   20. C

21. C
22. B
23. D
24. B
25. B

SOLUTIONS TO PROBLEMS

1. (9')(12') = 108 sq.ft.

2. 5 1/16 + 4 1/4 + 4 3/8 + 3 7/16 = 16 18/16 = 17 1/8

3. 6 ft. 9 in. - 4 ft. 5 in. = 2 ft. 4 in. = 28 in.

4. $3\frac{3}{8} \div \frac{3}{16} = \frac{27}{8} \cdot \frac{16}{3} = 18$

5. Since 1 cu.yd. = 27 cu.ft., 627 cu. ft. ≈ 23 cu. yds.

6. The unmarked part = 90° - 33° - 21° = 36°

7. (5)(2) = 10 man-days. Then, 10 ÷ 2 = 5 men

8. The area of the four walls = (2)(20)(9 1/2) + (2)(25)(9 1/2) = 855 sq.ft.
   The area of the ceiling is (20)(25) = 500 sq.ft. Total area to be painted = 1355 sq.ft.
   Finally, 1355 ÷ 400 ≈ 3.3875 gallons, which means 4 gallons will need to be used.

9. (16 1/2')(22') = 363 sq.ft.

10. ($14.00)(.75)(.90)(.95) = $8.9775 ≈ $9.00

11. $36 + (.09)($36) = $39.24 Then, ($39.24)(11) ≈ $430

12. $6\frac{3}{4} \div \frac{1}{8} = (\frac{27}{4})(8) = 54$. Then, (54)(1 ft.) = 54 ft.

13. Area = (50')(8 1/2') = 425 sq. ft.

14. The diagonal = $\sqrt{(23)^2 + (9.5)^2} = \sqrt{619.25} \approx 24.885$ ft. ≈ 24 ft. 10 in.

15. (6')(3 1/2')(1 1/3') = 28 cu.ft. Then, (28)(150 pounds) = 4200 pounds

16. (32')(65') ÷ (60')(110') = 2080 ÷ 6600 = .3$\overline{15}$ ≈ .32

17. $\frac{31}{64} = .484375 \approx .48$

18. $\frac{27}{32} = .84375 \approx .844$

19. 1'3" ÷ 10 = 15" ÷ 10 = $1\frac{1}{2}$"

20. $(4)(5\frac{1}{2}) = 22$ painter-days. Then, $22 \div 5 \approx 4.5$ days

21. $(42\frac{1}{2}')(83\frac{1}{3}') = 3541\frac{2}{3}$ sq.ft. ≈ 3540 sq.ft.

22. $3\frac{5}{8}" + 4\frac{1}{4}" + 6\frac{5}{16}" + 7\frac{3}{4}" + 8\frac{1}{2}" = 28\frac{39}{16}" = 30\frac{7}{16}"$

23. $(55)(96) = 5280$ sq.ft. Then, $(5280)(1\frac{1}{2}) = 7920 \approx 8000$ pounds

24. Diagonal $= \sqrt{30^2 + 60^2} = \sqrt{4500} \approx 67$ ft.

25. $(8\frac{1}{2}')(10\frac{1}{2}')(8\frac{2}{3}') = 773.5 \approx 774$ cu.ft.

TEST 3

DIRECTIONS: Each question or incomplete statement is followed by several suggested answers or completions. Select the one that BEST answers the question or completes the statement. *PRINT THE LETTER OF THE CORRECT ANSWER IN THE SPACE AT THE RIGHT.*

Questions 1-5.

DIRECTIONS: Questions 1 through 5, inclusive, are to be answered on the basis of the information given below. In answering these questions, refer to this information.

A crew of 5 painters are going to paint 55 rooms. They will be painting only the walls, which are all 10 feet high. The rooms have the following dimensions: 30 rooms are 25 ft. long and 15 ft. wide, and the remaining rooms are 20 ft. long and 15 ft. wide. All walls will be painted the same color and will require 2 coats. Coverage is 500 square feet per gallon. Each painter can cover 700 square feet of wall per day and works 7 hours per day.

1. Assume that 20% of the total wall surface consists of windows which are not to be painted.
   The total wall surface, in square feet, to be painted is MOST NEARLY

   A. 15,600   B. 21,800   C. 33,200   D. 41,500

2. Assume the total wall surface to be painted is 49,500 square feet per coat of paint.
   The total number of gallons of paint needed for a complete job is MOST NEARLY

   A. 250   B. 200   C. 150   D. 100

3. The total number of working days required for this crew to cover 49,500 square feet of wall surface with two coats of paint is MOST NEARLY

   A. 17   B. 23   C. 28   D. 35

4. Assuming each painter earns $11.20 per hour, the total cost in painter's wages for a job which takes 21 working days to complete is MOST NEARLY

   A. $10,460   B. $8,240   C. $6,020   D. $4,720

5. If two painters are sick for two days each and they are not replaced, the total time to complete this job would be extended APPROXIMATELY _____ day(s).

   A. 1   B. 2   C. 3   D. 4

6. A rectangular wooden building occupies a ground space 27'6" long by 18'0" wide. The walls are 17'6" high. Ignoring window and door spaces, the outside area requiring painting is, in square feet, MOST NEARLY

   A. 1,570   B. 1,590   C. 1,610   D. 1,630

7. Assume that a certain type of cabinet can be painted in twenty minutes by using a brush and 15 min. by spraygun.
   Assuming that three painters are put on the job but only one spray gun is available, the number of hours required by the three painters to paint 100 cabinets, one using the spray gun and the other two using brushes, is MOST NEARLY

   A. 9   B. 10   C. 11   D. 12

8. If it takes 5 painters 12 days to paint a building, the number of days it will take 9 painters to paint the same building, assuming all work is done at the same rate of speed, is MOST NEARLY

   A. 5 1/2   B. 6 1/2   C. 7 1/2   D. 8 1/2

9. Assume that one gallon of paint, costing $12.50, is able to cover 500 square feet.
   If a painter can spread 1.25 gallons per day and receives $120 per day, the cost per 100 square feet for labor and paint for a one-coat application is MOST NEARLY

   A. $21.70   B. $24.20   C. $24.40   D. $24.60

Questions 10-13.

DIRECTIONS: Questions 10 through 13 are to be answered on the basis of the information given below.

A crew of 6 painters is going to paint only the walls of 75 rooms. The rooms have the following dimensions: 50 rooms are 35 feet long, 20 feet wide, with walls 10 feet high; and 25 rooms are 25 feet long, 15 feet wide, with walls 10 feet high. The walls are to be given two coats. The paint coverage is 400 square feet per gallon per coat. Assume a painter can cover 650 square feet of wall per 7-hour day. Assume that wall surfaces have windows and doors which constitute 10% of the wall surfaces and are not to be painted.

10. The total wall surface to be painted per coat of paint is MOST NEARLY _____ square feet.

    A. 65,300   B. 67,500   C. 69,500   D. 71,100

11. Assume that the total wall surface to be painted is 75,000 square feet.
    The total number of gallons of paint needed for a complete job, neglecting any waste, is MOST NEARLY

    A. 358   B. 364   C. 370   D. 375

12. The total number of working days required for the crew to cover 75,000 square feet of wall surface with 2 coats of paint is MOST NEARLY _____ days.

    A. 37   B. 38   C. 41   D. 43

13. If a painter earns $7.35 per hour for a 7-hour day, then the TOTAL cost in painter's wages for a job that takes 27 working days for the 6-man crew is

    A. $8,156.40   B. $8,255.40
    C. $8,334.90   D. $8,456.70

14. Assume that you assign 3 painters to do a job in 12 days. After 4 days, you add 3 more painters, all of whom work at the same pace.
How many additional days will it take the 6 men to do the job?

    A. 2   B. 3   C. 4   D. 5

15. Assume that a given paint has a covering capacity of 375 square feet per gallon. In order to paint 10,125 square feet, you would need _____ gallons.

    A. 21   B. 23   C. 25   D. 27

16. The sum of the following dimensions, 3'2 1/4", 0'8 7/8", 2'6 3/8", 2'9 3/4", and 1'0", is

    A. 9'2 7/8"   B. 10'3 1/4"   C. 10'7 3/8"   D. 11'4 1/4"

17. If the scale of a drawing is 1/8" to the foot, then a 1/2" measurement on the drawing would represent an actual length of _____ feet.

    A. 2   B. 4   C. 8   D. 16

18. The average 40-hour weekly pay of 3 painters who earn $8.50, $9.00, and $9.50 an hour is

    A. $340   B. $360   C. $380   D. $400

19. If it takes 10 gallons of paint to cover a 1,500 square foot room, how many gallons of paint will be needed to paint a 3,750 square foot room?

    A. 20   B. 22   C. 25   D. 27

20. A maintenance man is getting a 5% raise on his $8.00 an hour wage.
What will be his weekly earnings if he works a 44-hour week and is paid 1 1/2 times for hours over 40 hours?

    A. $320   B. $336   C. $369.60   D. $386.40

KEY (CORRECT ANSWERS)

1.	C	11.	D
2.	B	12.	B
3.	C	13.	C
4.	B	14.	C
5.	A	15.	D
6.	B	16.	B
7.	B	17.	B
8.	B	18.	B
9.	A	19.	C
10.	B	20.	D

4 (#3)

SOLUTIONS TO PROBLEMS

1. Total area of the walls in all 55 rooms = [(2)(25)(10)+(2)(10)(15)] [30] + [(2)(10)(20)+(2)(10)(15)][25] = 24,000 + 17,500 = 41,500 sq.ft. Since 20% of the wall surface consists of windows, the wall surface to be painted = (.80)(41,500) = 33,200 sq.ft.

2. $49,500 \div 500 = 99$ gallons required for 1 coat of paint. Then, $(2)(99) \approx 200$ gallons will be needed for 2 coats of paint.

3. (700)(5) = 3500 sq.ft. can be covered each day with 1 coat of paint. To cover 49,500 sq.ft. with 2 coats of paint will require $(49,500 \div 3500)(2) \approx 28$ days.

4. Total cost = (5)($11.20)(7)(21) = $8232, which is nearest to answer B ($8240).

5. (5)(21) = 105 man-days. If 2 painters are sick for 2 days, a total of (3)(21) + (2)(19) = 101 man-days. The remaining 4 man-days will be done by 3 painters, and this will take $4 \div 3 = 1\frac{1}{3} \approx 1$ more day.

6. (2)(27 1/2')(17 1/2') + (2)(18')(17 1/2') = $1592 \approx 1590$ sq.ft.

7. The spray painter paints 4 cabinets/hr. [60÷15=4] ; the brush painters each paint 3 cabinets/hr. [60÷20=3] ; ten cabinets/hr. for 10 hrs. = 100 cabinets.

8. (5) (12) = 60 man-days. Then, $60 \div 9 = 6\frac{2}{3} \approx 6\frac{1}{2}$ 64 days

9. In one day, a painter can cover (500)(1.25) = 625 sq.ft.
   Labor cost per 100 sq.ft. = $120 ÷ 6.25 = $19.20
   Paint cost per 100 sq.ft. = 12.50 ÷ 5 = $2.50
   Total cost (per 100 sq.ft.) of labor and paint = $21.70

10. Total area of the walls in 75 rooms = [50][(2)(10)(35)+(2)(10)(20)] + [25][(2)(10)(25)+(2)(15)(10)] = 55,000 + 20,000 = 75,000 sq.ft. Since 10% of this area will not be painted, the amount of area to be painted = (.90)(75,000) = 67,500 sq.ft.

11. 75,000 ÷ 400 = 187.5 gallons required for 1 coat of paint. Then, (187.5)(2) = 375 gallons will be needed for 2 coats of paint.

12. (6)(650) = 3900 sq.ft. can be covered each day with 1 coat of paint. To cover 75,000 sq.ft. with 2 coats of paint will require $(75,000 \div 3900)(2) \approx 38$ days.

13. Total cost = (6)($7.35)(7)(27) = $8334.90

14. (3)(12) = 36 man-days. After 4 days, (3)(4) = 12 man-days have been used, which means 24 man-days are left to complete the job. If 6 men are used for the remainder of this job, 24 ÷ 6 = 4 more days will be needed.

5 (#3)

15. 10,125 ÷ 375 = 27 gallons

16. 3'2 1/4" + 0'8 7/8" + 2'6 3/8" + 2'9 3/4" + 1'0" = 8'25 18/8" = 10'3 1/4"

17. $\frac{1}{2}" \div \frac{1}{8}" = 4$. So, the actual length is 4 ft.

18. [(40)($8.50)+(40)($9.00)+(40)($9.50)] ÷ 3 = $360

19. 3750 ÷ 1500 = 2.5 Then, (2.5)(10) = 25 gallons

20. ($8.00)(1.05) = $8.40/hr. for regular pay and ($8.40)(1.5) = $12.60/hr. overtime. Total pay = ($8.40)(40) + ($12.60)(4) = $386.40

SUPERVISION STUDY GUIDE

Social science has developed information about groups and leadership in general and supervisor-employee relationships in particular. Since organizational effectiveness is closely linked to the ability of supervisors to direct the activities of employees, these findings are important to executives everywhere.

IS A SUPERVISOR A LEADER?

First-line supervisors are found in all large business and government organizations. They are the men at the base of an organizational hierarchy. Decisions made by the head of the organization reach them through a network of intermediate positions. They are frequently referred to as part of the management team, but their duties seldom seem to support this description.

A supervisor of clerks, tax collectors, meat inspectors, or securities analysts is not charged with budget preparation. He cannot hire or fire the employees in his own unit on his say-so. He does not administer programs which require great planning, coordinating, or decision making.

Then what is he? He is the man who is directly in charge of a group of employees doing productive work for a business or government agency. If the work requires the use of machines, the men he supervises operate them. If the work requires the writing of reports, the men he supervises write them. He is expected to maintain a productive flow of work without creating problems which higher levels of management must solve. But is he a leader?

To carry out a specific part of an agency's mission, management creates a unit, staffs it with a group of employees and designates a supervisor to take charge of them. Management directs what this unit shall do, from time to time changes directions, and often indicates what the group should not do. Management presumably creates status for the supervisor by giving him more pay, a title, and special privileges.

Management asks a supervisor to get his workers to attain organizational goals, including the desired quantity and quality of production. Supposedly, he has authority to enable him to achieve this objective. Management at least assumes that by establishing the status of the supervisor's position, it has created sufficient authority to enable him to achieve these goals—not his goals, nor necessarily the group's, but management's goals.

In addition, supervision includes writing reports, keeping records of membership in a higher-level administrative group, industrial engineering, safety engineering, editorial duties, housekeeping duties, etc. The supervisor as a member of an organizational network, must be responsible to the changing demands of the management above him. At the same time, he must be responsive to the demands of the work group of which he is a member. He is placed in the difficult position of communicating and implementing new decisions, changed programs and revised production quotas for his work group, although he may have had little part in developing them.

It follows, then, that supervision has a special characteristic: achievement of goals, previously set by management, through the efforts of others. It is in this feature of the supervisor's job that we find the role of a leader in the sense of the following definition: *A leader is that person who <u>most</u> effectively influences group activities toward goal setting and goal achievements.*

This definition is broad. It covers both leaders in groups that come together voluntarily and in those brought together through a work assignment in a factory, store, or government agency. In the natural group, the authority necessary to attain goals is determined by the group membership and is granted by them. In the working group, it is apparent that the establishment of a supervisory position creates a predisposition on the part of employees to accept the authority of the occupant of that position. We cannot, however, assume that mere occupation confers authority sufficient to assure the accomplishment of an organization's goals.

Supervision is different, then, from leadership. The supervisor is expected to fulfill the role of leader but without obtaining a grant of authority from the group he supervises. The supervisor is expected to influence the group in the achieving of goals but is often handicapped by having little influence on the organizational process by which goals are set. The supervisor, because he works in an organizational setting, has the burdens of additional organizational duties and restrictions and requirements arising out of the fact that his position is subordinate to a hierarchy of higher-level supervisors. These differences between leadership and supervision are reflected in our definition: *Supervision is basically a leadership role, in a formal organization, which has as its objective the effective influencing of other employees.*

Even though these differences between supervision and leadership exist, a significant finding of experimenters in this field is that supervisors <u>must</u> be leaders to be successful.

The problem is: How can a supervisor exercise leadership in an organizational setting? We might say that the supervisor is expected to be a natural leader in a situation which does not come about naturally. His situation becomes really difficult in an organization which is more eager to make its supervisors into followers rather than leaders.

LEADERSHIP: NATURAL AND ORGANIZATIONAL

Leadership, in its usual sense of *natural* leadership, and supervision are not the same. In some cases, leadership embraces broader powers and functions than supervision; in other cases, supervision embraces more than leadership. This is true both because of the organization and technical aspects of the supervisor's job and because of the relatively freer setting and inherent authority of the natural leader.

The natural leader usually has much more authority and influence than the supervisor. Group members not only follow his command but prefer it that way. The employee, however, can appeal the supervisor's commands to his union or to the supervisor's superior or to the personnel office. These intercessors represent restrictions on the supervisor's power to lead.

The natural leader can gain greater membership involvement in the group's objectives, and he can change the objectives of the group. The supervisor can attempt to gain employee support only for management's objectives; he cannot set other objectives. In these instances leadership is broader than supervision.

The natural leader must depend upon whatever skills are available when seeking to attain objectives. The supervisor is trained in the administrative skills necessary to achieve management's goals. If he does not possess the requisite skills, however, he can call upon management's technicians.

A natural leader can maintain his leadership, in certain groups, merely by satisfying members' need for group affiliation. The supervisor must maintain his leadership by directing and organizing his group to achieve specific organizational goals set for him and his group by management. He must have a technical competence and a kind of coordinating ability which is not needed by many natural leaders.

A natural leader is responsible only to his group which grants him authority. The supervisor is responsible to management, which employs him, and also to the work group of which he is a member. The supervisor has the exceedingly difficult job of reconciling the demands of two groups frequently in conflict. He is often placed in the untenable position of trying to play two antagonistic roles. In the above instance, supervision is broader than leadership.

ORGANIZATIONAL INFLUENCES ON LEADERSHIP

The supervisor is both a product and a prisoner of the organization wherein we find him. The organization which creates the supervisor's position also obstructs, restricts, and channelizes the exercise of his duties. These influences extend beyond prescribed functional relationships to specific supervisory behavior. For example, even in a face-to-face situation involving one of his subordinates, the supervisor's actions are controlled to a great extent by his organization. His behavior must conform to the organization policy on human relations, rules which dictate personnel procedures, specific prohibitions governing conduct, the attitudes of his own superior, etc. He is not a free agent operating within the limits of his work group. His freedom of action is much more circumscribed than is generally admitted. The organizational influences which limit his leadership actions can be classified as structure, prescriptions, and proscriptions.

The organizational structure places each supervisor's position in context with other designated positions. It determines the relationships between his position and specific positions which impinge on his. The structure of the organization designates a certain position to which he looks for orders and information about his work. It gives a particular status to his position within a pattern of statuses from which he perceives that (1) certain positions are on a par, organizationally, with his, (2) other positions are subordinate, and (3) still others are superior.

The organizational structure determines those positions to which he should look for advice and assistance, and those positions to which he should give advice and assistance.

For instance, the organizational structure has predetermined that the supervisor of a clerical processing unit shall report to a supervisory position in a higher echelon. He shall have certain relationships with the supervisors of the work units which transmit work to and receive work from his unit. He shall discuss changes and clarification of procedures with certain staff units, such as organization and methods, cost accounting, and personnel. He shall consult supervisors of units which provide or receive special work assignments.

The organizational structure, however, establishes patterns other than those of the relationships of positions. These are the patterns of responsibility, authority, and expectations.

The supervisor is responsible for certain activities or results; he is presumably invested with the authority to achieve these. His set of authority and responsibility is interwoven with other sets to the end that all goals and functions of the organization are parceled out in small, manageable lots. This, of course, establishes a series of expectations: a single supervisor can perform his particular set of duties only upon the assumption that preceding or contiguous sets of duties have been, or are being carried out. At the same time, he is aware of the expectations of others that he will fulfill his functional role.

The structure of an organization establishes relationships between specified positions and specific expectations for these positions. The fact that these relationships and expectations are established is one thing; whether or not they are met is another.

PRESCRIPTIONS AND PROSCRIPTIONS

But let us return to the organizational influences which act to restrict the supervisor's exercise of leadership. These are the prescriptions and proscriptions generally in effect in all organizations, and those peculiar to a single organization. In brief these are the *thou shalt's* and the *thou shalt not's*.

Organizations not only prescribe certain duties for individual supervisory positions, they also prescribe specific methods and means of carrying out these duties and maintaining management-employee relations. These include rules, regulations, policy, and tradition. It does no good for the supervisor to say, *This seems to be the best way to handle such-and-such,* if the organization has established a routine for dealing with problems. For good or bad, there are rules that state that firings shall be executed in such a manner, accompanied by a certain notification; that training shall be conducted, and in this manner. Proscriptions are merely negative prescriptions; you may not discriminate against any employee because of politics or race; you shall not suspend any employee without following certain procedures and obtaining certain approvals.

Most of these prohibitions and rules apply to the area of interpersonal relations, precisely the area which is now arousing most interest on the part of administrators and managers. We have become concerned about the contrast between formally prescribed relationships and interpersonal relationships, and this brings us to the often discussed informal organization.

FORMAL AND INFORMAL ORGANIZATIONS

As we well know, the functions and activities of any organization are broken down into individual units of work called positions. Administrators must establish a pattern which will link these positions to each other and relate them to a system of authority and responsibility. Man-to-man are spelled out as plainly as possible for all to understand. Managers, then, build an official structure which we call the formal organization.

In these same organizations, employees react individually and in groups to institutionally determined roles. John, a worker, rides in the same carpool as Joe, a foreman. An unplanned communication develops. Harry, a machinist knows more about high-speed machining than his foreman or anyone else in his shop. An unofficial tool boss comes into being. Mary, who fought with Jane, is promoted over her. Jane now gives Mary's directions. A planned relationship fails to develop. The employees have built a structure which we call the informal organization.

Formal organization is a system of management-prescribed relations between positions in an organization.

Informal organization is a network of unofficial relations between people in an organization.

These definitions might lead us to the absurd conclusion that positions carry out formal activities and that employe4es spend their time in unofficial activities. We must recognize that organizational activities are in all cases carried out by people. The formal structure provides a needed framework within which interpersonal relations occur. What we call informal organization is the complex of normal, natural relations among employees. These personal relationships may be negative or positive. That is, they may impede or aid the achievement of organizational goals. For example, friendship between two supervisors greatly increases the probability of good cooperation and coordination between their sections. On the other hand, *buck passing* nullifies the formal structure by failure to meet a prescribed and expected responsibility.

It is improbable that an ideal organization exists where all activities are carried out in strict conformity to a formally prescribed pattern of functional roles. Informal organization arises because of the incompleteness and ambiguities in the network of formally prescribed relationships, or in response to the needs or inadequacies of supervisors or managers who hold prescribed functional roles in an organization. Many of these relationships are not prescribed by the organizational pattern; many cannot be prescribed; many should not be prescribed.

Management faces the problem of keeping the informal organization in harmony with the mission of the agency. One way to do this is to make sure that all employees have a clear understanding of and are sympathetic with that mission. The issuance of organizational charts, procedural manuals, and functional descriptions of the work to be done by divisions and sections helps communicate management's plans and goals. Issuances alone, of course, cannot do the whole job. They should be accompanied by oral discussion and explanation. Management must ensure that there is mutual understanding and acceptance of charts and procedures. More important is that management acquaint itself with the attitudes, activities, and peculiar brands of logic which govern the informal organization. Only through this type of knowledge can they and supervisors keep informal goals consistent with the agency mission.

SUPERVISION STATUS AND FUNCTIONAL ROLE

A well-established supervisor is respected by the employees who work with him. They defer to his wishes. It is clear that a superior-subordinate relationship has been established. That is, status of the supervisor has been established in relation to other employees of the same work group. This same supervisor gains the respect of employees when he behaves in as certain manner. He will be expected, generally, to follow the customs of the group in such matters as dress, recreation, and manner of speaking. The group has a set of expectations as to his behavior. His position is a functional role which carries with it a collection of rights and obligations.

The position of supervisor usually has a status distinct from the individual who occupies it: it is much like a position description which exists whether or not there is an incumbent. The status of a supervisory position is valued higher than that of an employee position both because of the functional role of leadership which is assigned to it and because of the status symbols of titles, rights, and privileges which go with it.

Social ranking, or status, is not simple because it involves both the position and the man. An individual may be ranked higher than others because of his education, social background, perceived leadership ability, or conformity to group customs and ideals. If such a man is ranked higher by the members of a work group than their supervisor, the supervisor's effectiveness may be seriously undermined.

If the organization does not build and reinforce a supervisor's status, his position can be undermined in a different way. This will happen when managers go around rather than through the supervisor or designate him as a straw boss, acting boss, or otherwise not a real boss.

Let us clarify this last point. A role, and corresponding status, establishes a set of expectations. Employees expect their supervisor to do certain things and to act in certain ways. They are prepared to respond to that expected behavior. When the supervisor's behavior does not conform to their expectations, they are surprised, confused, and ill-at-ease. It becomes necessary for them to resolve their confusion, if they can. They might do this by turning to one of their own members for leadership. If the confusion continues, or their attempted solutions are not satisfactory, they will probably become a poorly motivated, non-cohesive group which cannot function very well.

COMMUNICATION AND THE SUPERVISOR

In a recent survey, railroad workers reported that they rarely look to their supervisor for information about the company. This is startling, at least to us, because we ordinarily think of the supervisor as the link between management and worker. We expect the supervisor to be the prime source of information about the company. Actually, the railroad workers listed the supervisor next to last in the o5rder of their sources of information. Most surprising of all, the supervisors, themselves, stated that rumor and unofficial contacts were their principal sources of information. Here we see one of the reasons why supervisors may not be as effective as management desires.

The supervisor is not only being bypassed by his work group, he is being ignored, and his position weakened, by the very organization which is holding him responsible for the activities of his workers. If he is management's representative to the employee, then management has an obligation to keep him informed of its activities. This is necessary if he is to carry out his functions efficiently and maintain his leadership in the work group. The supervisor is expected to be a source of information; when he is not, his status is not clear, and employees are dissatisfied because he has not lived up to expectations.

By providing information to the supervisor to pass along to employees, we can strengthen his position as leader of the group, and increase satisfaction and cohesion within the group. Because he has more information than the other members, receives information sooner, and passes it along at the proper times, members turn to him as a source and also provide him with information in the hope of receiving some in return. From this, we can see an increase in group cohesiveness because:

- Employees are bound closer to their supervisor because he is *in the know*.
- There is less need to go outside the group for answers
- Employees will more quickly turn to the supervisor for enlightenment

The fact that he has the answers will also enhance the supervisor's standing in the eyes of his men. This increased status will serve to bolster his authority and control of the group and will probably result in improved morale and productivity.

The foregoing, of course, does not mean that all management information should be given out. There are obviously certain policy determinations and discussions which need not or cannot be transmitted to all supervisors. However, the supervisor must be kept as fully informed as possible so that he can answer questions when asked and can allay needless fears and anxieties. Further, the supervisor has the responsibility of encouraging employee questions and submissions of information. He must be able to present information to employees so that it is clearly understood and accepted. His attitude and manner should make it clear that he believes in what he is saying, that the information is necessary or desirable to the group, and that he is prepared to act on the basis of the information.

SUPERVISION AND JOB PERFORMANCE

The productivity of work groups is a product; employees' efforts are multiplied by the supervision they receive. Many investigators have analyzed this relationship and have discovered elements of supervision which differentiate high and low production groups. These researchers have identified certain types of supervisory practices which they classify as *employee-centered* and other types which they classify as *production centered*.

The difference between these two kinds of supervision lies not in specific practices but in the approach or orientation to supervision. The employee-centered supervisor directs most of his efforts toward increasing employee motivation. He is concerned more with realizing the potential energy of persons than with administrative and technological methods of increasing efficiency and productivity. He is the man who finds ways of causing employees to want to work harder with the same tools. These supervisors emphasize the personal relations between their employees and themselves.

Now, obviously, these pictures are overdrawn. No one supervisor has all the virtues of the ideal type of employee-centered supervisor. And, fortunately, no one supervisor has all the bad traits found in many production-centered supervisors. We should remember that the various practices that researchers have fond which distinguish these two kinds of supervision represent the many practices and methods of supervisors of all gradations between these extremes. We should be careful, too, of the implications of the labels attached to the two types. For instance, being production-centered is not necessarily bad, since the principal responsibility of any supervisor is maintaining the production level that is expected of his work group. Being employee-centered may not necessarily be good, if the only result is a happy, chuckling crew of loafers. To return to the researchers' findings, employee-centered supervisors:

- Recommend promotions, transfers, pay increases
- Inform men about what is happening in the company
- Keep men posted on how well they are doing
- Hear complaints and grievances sympathetically
- Speak up for subordinates

Production-centered supervisors, on the other hand, don't do those things. They check on employees more frequently, give more detailed and frequent instructions, don't give reasons for changes, and are more punitive when mistakes are made. Employee-centered supervisors were reported to contribute to high morale and high production, whereas production-centered supervision was associated with lower morale and less production.

More recent findings, however, show that the relationship between supervision and productivity is not this simple. Investigators now report that high production is more frequently associated with supervisory practices which combine employee-centered behavior with concern for production. (This concern is not the same, however, as anxiety about production, which is the hallmark of our production-centered supervisor.) Let us examine these apparently contradictory findings and the premises from which they are derived.

SUPERVISION AND MORALE

Why do supervisory activities cause high or low production? As the name implies, the activities of the employee-centered supervisor tend to relate him more closely and satisfactorily to his workers. The production-centered supervisor's practices tend to separate him from his group and to foster antagonism. An analysis of this difference may answer our question.

Earlier, we pointed out that the supervisor is a type of leader and that leadership is intimately related to the group in which it occurs We discover, now, that an employee-centered supervisor's primary activities are concerned with both his leadership and his group membership. Such a supervisor is a member of a group and occupies a leadership role in that group.

These facts are sometimes obscured when we speak of the supervisor as management's representative, or as the organizational link between management and the employee, or as the end of the chain of command. If we really want to understand what it is we expect of the supervisor, we must remember that he is the designated leader of a group of employees to whom he is bound by interaction and interdependence.

Most of his actions are aimed, consciously or unconsciously, at strengthening membership ties in the group. This includes both making members more conscious that he is a member of their group) and causing members to identify themselves more closely with the group. These ends are accomplished by:

- making the group more attractive to the worker: they find satisfaction of their needs for recognition, friendship, enjoyable work, etc.;
- maintaining open communication: employees can express their views and obtain information about the organization
- giving assistance: members can seek advice on personal problems as well as their work; and
- acting as a buffer between the group and management: he speaks up for his men and explains the reasons for management's decisions.

Such actions both strengthen group cohesiveness and solidarity and affirm the supervisor's leadership position in the group.

DEFINING MORALE

This brings us back to a point mentioned earlier. We had said that employee-centered supervisors contribute to high morale as well as to high production. But how can we explain units which have low morale and high productivity, or vice versa? Usually production and morale are considered separately, partly because they are measured against different criteria and partly because, in some instances, they seem to be independent of each other.

Some of this difficulty may stem from confusion over definitions of morale. Morale has been defined as, or measured by, absences from work, satisfaction with job or company, dissension among members of work groups, productivity, apathy or lack of interest, readiness to help others, and a general aura of happiness as rated by observers. Some of these criteria of morale are not subject to the influence of the supervisor, and some of them are not clearly related to productivity. Definitions like these invite findings of low morale coupled with high production.

Both productivity and morale can be influenced by environmental factors not under the control of group members or supervisors. Such things as plant layout, organizational structure and goals, lighting, ventilation, communications, and management planning may have an adverse or desirable effect.

We might resolve the dilemma by defining morale on the basis of our understanding of the supervisor as leader of a group; morale is the degree of satisfaction of group members with their leadership. In this light, the supervisor's employee-centered activities bear a clear relation to morale. His efforts to increase employee identification with the group and to strengthen his leadership lead to greater satisfaction with that leadership. By increasing group cohesiveness and by demonstrating that his influence and power can aid the group, he is able to enhance his leadership status and afford satisfaction to the group.

SUPERVISION, PRODUCTION, AND MORALE

There are factors within the organization itself which determine whether increased production is possible:

- Are production goals expressed in terms understandable to employees and are they realistic?
- Do supervisors responsible for production respect the agency mission and production goals?
- If employees do not know how to do the job well, does management provide a trainer—often the supervisor—who can teach efficient work methods?

There are other factors within the work group which determine whether increased production will be attained:

- Is leadership present which can bring about the desired level of production?
- Are production goals accepted by employees as reasonable and attainable?
- If group effort is involved, are members able to coordinate their efforts?

Research findings confirm the view that an employee-centered supervisor can achieve higher morale than a production-centered supervisor. Managers may well ask what is the relationship between this and production.

Supervision is production-oriented to the extent that it focuses attention on achieving organizational goals, and plans and devises methods for attaining them; it is employee-centered to the extent that it focuses attention on employee attitudes toward those goals, and plans and works toward maintenance of employee satisfaction.

High productivity and low morale result when a supervisor plans and organizes work efficiently but cannot achieve high membership satisfaction. Low production and high morale result when a supervisor, though keeping members satisfied with his leadership, either has not gained acceptance of organizational goals or does not have the technical competence to achieve them.

The relationship between supervision, morale, and productivity is an interdependent one, with the supervisor playing an integral role due to his ability to influence productivity and morale independently of each other.

A supervisor who can plan his work well has good technical knowledge, and who can install better production methods can raise production without necessarily increasing group satisfaction. On the other hand, a supervisor who can motivate his employees and keep them satisfied with his leadership can gain high production in spite of technical difficulties and environmental obstacles.

CLIMATE AND SUPERVISION

Climate, the intangible environment of an organization made up of attitudes, beliefs, and traditions, plays a large part in morale, productivity, and supervision. Usually when we speak of climate and its relationship to morale and productivity, we talk about the merits of *democratic* versus *authoritarian* climate. Employees seem to produce more and have higher morale in a democratic climate, whereas in an authoritarian climate, the reverse seems to be true or so the researchers tell us. We would do well to determine what these terms mean to supervision.

Perhaps most of our difficulty in understanding and applying these concepts comes from our emotional reactions to the words themselves. For example, authoritarian climate is usually painted as the very blackest kind of dictatorship. This is not surprising, because we are usually expected to believe that it is invariably bad. Conversely, democratic climate is drawn to make the driven snow look impure by comparison.

Now these descriptions are most probably true when we talk about our political processes, or town meetings, or freedom of speech. However, the same labels have been used by social scientists in other contexts and have also been applied to government and business organizations, without it, it seems, any recognition that the meanings and their social values may have changed somewhat

For example, these labels were used in experiments conducted in an informal classroom setting using 11-year-old boys as subjects. The descriptive labels applied to the climate of the setting as well as the type of leadership practiced. When these labels were transferred to a management setting, it seems that many presumed that they principally meant the king of leadership rather than climate. We can see that there is a great difference between the experimental and management settings and that leadership practices for one might be inappropriate for the other.

It is doubtful that formal work organizations can be anything but authoritarian, in that goals are set by management and a hierarchy exists through which decisions and orders from the top are transmitted downward. Organizations are authoritarian by structure and need; direction and control are placed in the hands of a few in order to gain fast and efficient decision making. Now this does not mean to describe a dictatorship. It is merely the recognition of the fact that direction of organizational affairs comes from above. It should be noted that leadership in some natural groups is, in this sense, authoritarian.

Granting that formal organizations have this kind of authoritarian leadership, can there be a democratic climate? Certainly there can be, but we would want to define and delimit this term. A more realistic meaning of democratic climate in organizations is the use of permissive and participatory methods in management-employee relations. That is, a mutual exchange of information and explanation with the granting of individual freedom within certain restricted and defined limits. However, it is not our purpose to debate the merits of authoritarianism versus democracy. We recognize that within the small work group there is a need for freedom from constraint and an increase in participation in order to achieve organizational goals within the framework of the organizational movement.

Another aspect of climate is best expressed by this familiar, and true, saying: actions speak louder than words. Of particular concern to us is this effect of management climate on the behavior of supervisors, particularly in employee-centered activities.

There have been reports of disappointment with efforts to make supervisors ore employee-centered. Managers state that, since research has shown ways of improving human relations, supervisors should begin to practice these methods. Usually a training course in human relations is established; and supervisors are given this training. Managers then sit back and wait for the expected improvements, only to find that there are none.

If we wish to produce changes in the supervisor's behavior, the climate must be made appropriate and rewarding to the changed behavior. This means that top-level attitudes and behavior cannot deny or contradict the change we are attempting to effect. Basic changes in organizational behavior cannot be made with any permanence, unless we provide an environment that is receptive to the changes and rewards those persons who do change.

IMPROVING SUPERVISION

Anyone who has read this far might expect to find *A Dozen Rules for Dealing With Employees* or *29 Steps to Supervisory Success*. We will not provide such a list.

Simple rules suffer from their simplicity. They ignore the complexities of human behavior. Reliance upon rules may cause supervisors to concentrate on superficial aspects of their relations with employees. It may preclude genuine understanding.

The supervisor who relies on a list of rules tends to think of people in mechanistic terms. In a certain situation, he uses *Rule No. 3*. Employees are not treated as thinking and feeling persons, but rather as figures in a formula: Rule 3 applied to employee X = Production.

Employees usually recognize mechanical manipulation and become dissatisfied and resentful. They lose faith in, and respect for, their supervisor, and this may be reflected in lower morale and productivity.

We do not mean that supervisors must become social science experts if they wish to improve. Reports of current research indicate that there are two major parts of their job which can be strengthened through self-improvement: (1) Work planning, including technical skills, and (2) motivation of employees.

The most effective supervisors combine excellence in the administrative and technical aspects of their work with friendly and considerate personal relations with their employees.

CRITICAL PERSONAL RELATIONS

Later in this chapter we shall talk about administrative aspects of supervision, but first let us comment on *friendly and considerate personal relations*. We have discussed this subject throughout the preceding chapters, but we want to review some of the critical supervisory influences on personal relations.

Closeness of Supervision: The closeness of supervision has an important effect on productivity and morale. Mann and Dent found that supervisors of low-producing units supervise very closely, while high-producing supervisors exercise only general supervision. It was found that the low-producing supervisors:

- check on employees more frequently
- give more detailed and frequent instructions
- limit employee's freedom to do job in own way

Workers who felt less closely supervised reported that they were better satisfied with their jobs and the company. We should note that the manner or attitude of the supervisor has an important bearing on whether employees perceive supervision as being close or general.

These findings are another way of saying that supervision does not mean standing over the employee and telling him what to do and when and how to do it. The more effective supervisor tells his employees what is required, giving general instructions.

COMMUNICATION

Supervisors of high-production units consider communication as one of the most important aspects of their job. Effective communication is used by these supervisors to achieve better interpersonal relations and improved employee motivation. Low-production supervisors do not rate communications as highly important.

High-producing supervisors find that an important aid to more effective communication is listening. They are ready to listen to both personal problems or interests and questions about the work. This does not mean that they are *nosey* or meddle in their employees' personal lives, but rather that they show a willingness to listen, and do listen, if their employees wish to discuss problems.

These supervisors inform employees about forthcoming changes in work; they discuss agency policy with employees; and they make sure that each employee knows how well he is doing. What these supervisors do is use two-way communication effectively. Unless the supervisor freely imparts information, he will not receive information in return.

Attitudes and perception are frequently affected by communication or the lack of it. Research surveys reveal that many supervisors are not aware of their employees' attitudes, nor do they know what personal reactions their supervision arouses. Through frank discussion with employees, they have been surprised to discover employee beliefs about which they were ignorant. Discussion sometimes reveals that the supervisor and his employees have totally different impressions about the same event. The supervisor should be constantly on the alert for misconceptions about his words and deeds. He must remember that, although his actions are perfectly clear to himself, they may be, and frequently are, viewed differently by employees.

Failure to communicate information results in misconceptions and false assumptions. What you say and how you say it will strongly affect your employees' attitudes and perceptions. By giving them available information, you can prevent misconceptions; by discussion, you may be able to change attitudes; by questioning, you can discover what the perceptions and assumptions really are. And it need hardly be added that actions should conform very closely to words.

If we were to attempt to reduce the above discussion on communication to rules, we would have a long list which would be based on one cardinal principle: Don't make assumptions!

- Don't assume that your employees know; tell them.
- Don't assume that you know how they feel; find out.
- Don't assume that they understand; clarify.

20 SUPERVISORY HINTS

1. Avoid inconsistency.
2. Always give employees a chance to explain their action before taking disciplinary action. Don't allow too much time for a "cooling off" period before disciplining an employee.
3. Be specific in your criticisms.
4. Delegate responsibility wisely.
5. Do not argue or lose your temper, and avoid being impatient.
6. Promote mutual respect and be fair, impartial, and open-minded.
7. Keep in mind that asking for employees' advice and input can be helpful in decision making.
8. If you make promises, keep them.
9. Always keep the feelings, abilities, dignity and motives of your staff in mind.
10. Remain loyal to your employees' interests.
11. Never criticize employees in front of others, or treat employees like children.
12. Admit mistakes. Don't place blame on your employees, or make excuses.
13. Be reasonable in your expectations, give complete instructions, and establish well-planned goals.
14. Be knowledgeable about office details and procedures, but avoid becoming bogged down in details.
15. Avoid supervising too closely or too loosely. Employees should also view you as an approachable supervisor.
16. Remember that employees' personal problems may affect job performance, but become involved only when appropriate.
17. Work to develop workers, and to instill a feeling of cooperation while working toward mutual goals.
18. Do not overpraise or underpraise, be properly appreciative.
19. Never ask an employee to discipline someone for you.
20. A complaint, even if unjustified, should be taken seriously.

NOTES

BASIC PAINTING OPERATIONS

TABLE OF CONTENTS

Section		Page
1.	Paint Shop	1
2.	Paint Materials	1
3.	Paint Conditioning and Mixing	3
4.	Preparation of Surfaces	6
5.	Repair of Surfaces	20
6.	Paint Application	24

BASIC
PAINTING OPERATIONS

SECTION 1 – PAINT SHOP

1.1 Functions. The paint shop is used for storage, paint preparation and painting of small items. It provides storage space for painting equipment and limited stocks of paints and paint materials. It is used for preparing paints for field use, i.e., conditioning, mixing, limited testing, thinning and straining. Special ventilated booths are located in the paint shop for spraying and drying small items. Lettering and sign painting are also done in this area.

1.2 Planning and Layout. Locate the paint shop in a firesafe area with all paint storage cabinets of non-combustible construction (see 2.3). Provide adequate space, facilities, heating, lighting and mechanical ventilation for storage, paint preparation and sign painting. Facilities include spray booths large enough to allow spraying of the largest anticipated signs or other items which will be painted. These booths should be of the water-wash type, capable of removing all fumes without leaving any solvent vapor in the working area. Provide all necessary safety equipment and post appropriate warning signs designating danger areas within the shop. For example, paint storage cabinets should be marked, "Danger, Flammable. Keep Flame and Excessive Heat Away". "No Smoking" signs should be posted at several locations within the shop. Equip the paint shop with all equipment, tools and supplies required for paint mixing, limited testing, thinning and straining, surface preparation and application by brush, roller or spray. Also provide all doors, windows and equipment storage spaces with adequate locking devices.

1.3 Equipment Operation and Maintenance. Cleaning of spray booths, either by scraping or high pressure washdown, should be performed at frequent intervals. Apply a thin coating of a water soluble material such as a liquid soap to the walls of spray booths to collect excess spray.

See Standard No. 33 of the National Fire Protection Association for details concerning the operation and maintenance of paint spray booths and associated equipment.

SECTION 2 – PAINT MATERIALS

2.1 Procurement. Purchase all paint materials in accordance with applicable procurement regulations. Procurement is to be by requisition, competitive bids, or by open market purchases.

2.2 Sampling and Testing. Specification paint materials furnished by a contractor or procured on the open market will be tested to determine acceptability before use. Tests will be made by a qualified government or qualified independent testing laboratory to insure compliance with applicable specifications. Limited testing will also be done just prior to use (see 2.2.2).

2.2.1 Sampling Procedure. Select samples from each lot of paint purchased by the government or supplied by the painting contractor. A representative of the contractor should be present to certify, in writing, that the sample was properly taken. Samples will be a full gallon if the paint is delivered in gallon containers, or two quarts if the paint is delivered in other sizes. Before taking a sample from a larger container, mix the paint thoroughly until it is of the same consistency from top to bottom. Inspect containers to determine that full measure has been received. Record the following on each sample container:

a. Number and exact title of specification including amendment or revisions, also class or type of paint.

b. Manufacturer's name and address.

c. Contractor's name and contract number when applicable.

d. Batch or lot number.

e. Date of manufacture.

f. Number of gallons represented by the sample.

Forward the samples to the laboratory with a written request for the tests required, whether for full compliance or the specific test desired. Include the above information in the request form.

2.2.2 Inspection and Paint Shop Testing. It should not be necessary to sample paint materials when it is known, by actual test, that the paint complies with specification requirements. Limited testing should be done when preparing the paint for use and during painting operations by contractors, to determine if paints have been adulterated. Limited field testing should not be considered as a substitute for standard professional laboratory techniques. Field testing does serve to discover major flaws or adulteration in a coating material. Sampling on the job is done by the paint inspector or his qualified representative (see 2.2.1).

Check for the following properties:

a. Weight per Gallon: Weigh an empty gallon can; then weigh a full gallon of the paint. The difference between these two weights gives a close enough approximation to the number of pounds of material which are included in each gallon of paint. The result should be within the requirements outlined in the product specification. Any greater variation may indicate improper mixing or unauthorized addition of thinners.

b. Application Properties, Dry Time, And Appearance:

Brush the paint on to a substrate which is similar to the substrate which will be coated and hang it vertically to dry. If the paint is intended for brush application, note its brushing qualities. Check to see if it dries within the specification limits. After it has dried, note its appearance and compare it with specification standards for such properties as gloss, color, leveling and resistance to sagging.

2.3 Materials Storage.

2.3.1 Storage Areas. Store paint materials in warm, dry and well ventilated areas. The best temperature range is 65°F to 85°F. Low temperatures cause paints to increase in viscosity and require conditioning for 24 hours before use. Freezing temperatures may ruin water-thinned paints and may also cause containers to bulge or burst. Conversely, high temperatures will cause paints to thin down and settle more rapidly. If the coating material is sensitive to heat, temperatures over 100°F may bring about reactivity within the container resulting in a viscosity increase to the point of gelation. Such paints are then not usable. Also, pressure build-up may cause covers to blow off, creating a serious fire hazard. Application is seriously affected when paint materials are drawn from stocks in overly cold or warm storage. Additional conditioning time and efforts are required to assure proper application and maximum surface protection. Other factors to be considered are high humidity which causes containers to corrode and labels to deteriorate, and poor ventilation which allows the collection of excessive concentrations of solvent vapors that are both toxic and combustible. Pumps for drawing liquids from steel drums must be types approved by fire underwriters. Do not use gravity spigots other than self-closing types for this purpose. Stock should be stored so that all labels can easily be read and so that containers can be rotated to use up older material first.

Provide an orderly method of maintaining records of paints entered into storage as well as an appropriate system of arranging paint materials in storage to be certain that all like types and colors are kept in their designated sections.

2.3.2 Issue. Issue paint materials so that oldest stocks are used first. Make all paints ready for use before issuance, e.g., conditioned at the proper temperature and mixed thoroughly. Avoid using left-over paint but, if necessary to do so, condition and strain before issuance.

2.3.3 Containers. Store paint material in full, tightly sealed containers. Avoid partially filled containers. Try to use paint on the job so as to have little or none left over (accuracy in advance estimating will accomplish this). It is safer to discard small quantities than to use paint that has skinned. Otherwise, place leftover paint in smaller containers, filling them full, and seal. Be certain to copy all information from the original container and mark this directly on the new container as follows:

a. Name or title of paint
b. Specification number
c. Stock number
d. Manufacturer
e. Date of manufacture
f. Contents by volume
g. Color
h. Batch number
i. Instructions for use.

2.3.4 Storage. Store smaller containers, e.g., ¼, 1, 2 and 5 gallon cans, on shelves or in cabinets constructed of noncombustible materials. Store full drums either vertically on concrete floors or horizontally on steel racks. Refill partially used drums into 5-gallon cans to prevent skinning. Storage spaces must be firesafe (See NFPA Standard No. 30 for guidance). Forebid smoking or open flames in the area. Post all necessary precautionary signs throughout the area. Take adequate safeguards as to temperature, humidity and ventilation (see 2.3.1).

2.4 Defective Paint Materials. When faulty paints are encountered, information should be furnished to the appropriate office.

The information should include:

a. Complete data from the label, Federal stock item number (if applicable), specification number, color, container size, batch number, date of manufacture, and name of the manufacturer.

b. Condition in container, such as mold growth, livering, skinning, putrefaction, lumps or particles, corrosion in container, permanent settling of pigment, color not as specified, putrid or irritating odor, or other.

c. Working properties, such as difficulty in application by brush, roller, or spray streaking, lifting, running, sagging, pinholes, incompatibility with thinner, or other.

d. Appearance of applied paint, whether sagging, pinholes, streaking, conspicuous laps, objectionable brush marks, or other.

e. Type of work, whether new construction or maintenance, exterior or interior. Also job number, installation, site, organization, and date.

SECTION 3—PAINT CONDITIONING AND MIXING

3.1 General. Essentially, paints consist of two principal components—the solid pigment and the liquid vehicle. The purpose of conditioning and mixing is to redisperse or reblend settled pigment with the vehicle, to eliminate lumps, skins or other detriments to proper application, and to bring the paint materials to their proper application temperature. All paint materials should be placed in the paint shop at least twenty-four hours before use in order to bring their temperatures between 65°F and 85°F. After this time paints are mixed, thinned or tinted if specified, and finally are strained, if necessary.

3.2 Mixing. Mix paint materials in the paint shop just prior to issuance. Mixing procedures will vary among different types of paints. Regardless of the procedure used, take care to avoid the incorporation of an excess of air through overmixing. Table 3 outlines the type of equipment and procedure to be followed for various types of coatings. Mixing is done by either manual or mechanical methods, but the latter is definitely preferred to insure maximum uniformity. The two most commonly used types of mechanical mixers are those which vibrate the full, sealed container, and those which utilize propellers that are inserted into the paint. Vibrating shakers are used for full containers, up to 5 gallons. Propeller mixers are used for containers ranging from 1 quart or larger. (See Figures 30 through 32.) Manual mixing is less efficient than mechanical methods in terms of time, effort and results. It is to be done only when absolutely necessary and should be limited to containers no larger than one gallon. Five gallon containers may be stirred manually, if done with care. To accomplish this, half of the paint is poured off into an empty container and the remainder is then stirred thoroughly, being certain to scrape off and break up any settled matter on the bottom or lower sides of the container. Stirring is continued as the other half of the paint is

Figure 30. Paint Mixer-Drill Attachment.

Figure 31. Paint Mixer-Vibrating Shaker.

Table 3. MIXING PROCEDURES

Coating	Equipment	Remarks
Enamel, semigloss or flat paints (oil type).	Manual, propeller or shaker	Mix until homogeneous.
Water based paints (latex type).	Manual or propeller	Use extreme care to avoid air entrapment.
Clear finishes	Manual, propeller or shaker	Generally require little or no mixing.
Extremely viscous finishes, e.g., coal tar paints.	Drum-type mixer	Use extreme care to avoid air entrapment.
Two package metallic paints, e.g., aluminum paints.	Propeller	Add small amount of liquid to paste; mix well. Slowly add remainder of vehicle, while stirring, until coating is homogeneous. With metallic powder, first make into a paste with solvent, and then proceed as above.
Two Component Systems	Propeller, shaker or drum-type mixer.	Mix until homogeneous. Check label for special instructions.

returned slowly to the original container. The stirred paint must have a completely blended appearance with no evidence of varicolored swirls at the top, indicating unmixed pigment or vehicle. Neither should there be evidence of lumps indicating the presence of unredispersed solids or foreign matter. (See Figure 33.)

3.2.1 Sequence of Operations. Complete conditioning and mixing of ready mixed paints (as received) is mandatory *prior* to introducing thinners or other additives, and these must be thoroughly blended into the paint *after* being introduced. In addition, use the same conditioning procedures for all components of multi-component paint materials before mixing. Manufacturers' label directions regarding proper mixing are to be strictly followed.

3.2.2 Boxing. Paints tend to settle during storage. To assure that they are uniform, box all paints before use. (See Figure 33). If different production batches are used (check batch nos.), compare them for color and gloss after boxing. If any differences are observed, either use them in different areas or box enough for the job using larger containers.

3.3 Tinting. Avoid tinting as a general practice. Purchase paints in the desired color to minimize waste and errors in on-the-job tinting. This procedure also eliminates

Notes

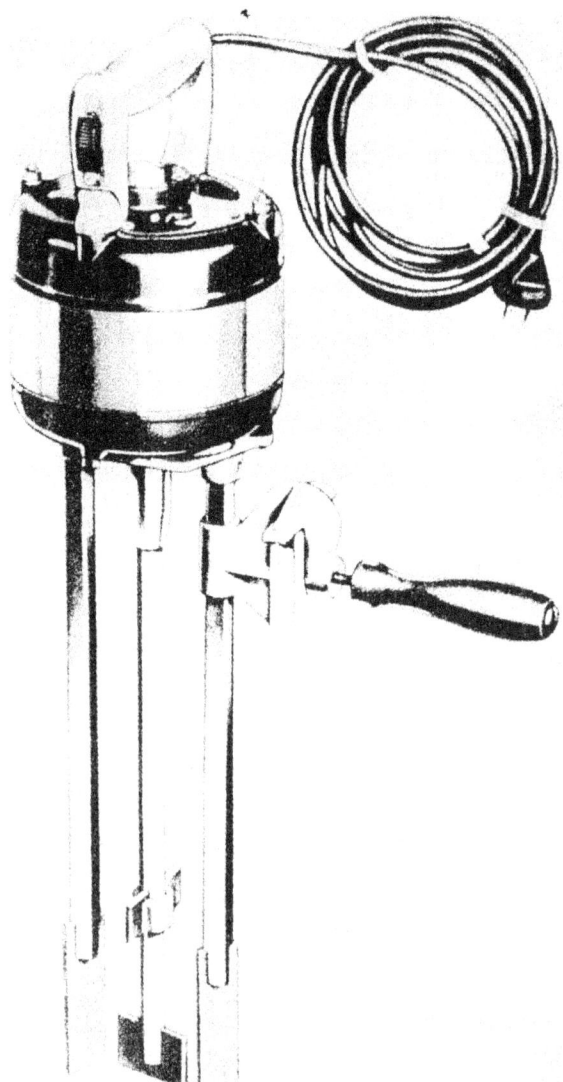

Figure 32. Paint Mixer-Propeller Type.

the problem of matching special colors at a later date. One exception is the tinting of intermediate coats which is done to differentiate between that coat and the topcoat so as to assure that there are no missed areas. Tinting colors affect the properties of the paint to which they are added, often reducing performance to some extent. Tinting should be done with care. Use only colors which are known to be compatible, and, add no more than 4 ozs. per gallon of paint, if at all possible. Never use more than 8 ozs. per gallon, otherwise, the paint may not dry well and will surely be degraded in performance. Do not tint chalking type exterior paint except for identification of intermediate coats.

3.3.1 Tinting Colors. There are two types of colors used for tinting: colors-in-oil and universal tinting colors.

a. Colors-in-Oil are limited to use with standard paints based on oil, alkyd resin, chlorinated rubber and butadiene styrene resin. They cannot be used with the other synthetics or with water thinned paints.

b. Universal Tinting Colors are used in the same manner as colors-in-oil. They are much more compatible with a wide variety of paint materials. Many can be used with both solvent-thinned and water-thinned paints. Follow the manufacturer's directions carefully when using these products.

3.3.2 Tinting Procedure. When tinting is necessary, it should be done in the paint shop, and only by experienced personnel. The paint must be at application viscosity before tinting. Colorants must be compatible, fresh and fluid, so as to mix in readily. Mechanical agitation is of utmost importance to insure uniform color distribution throughout the applied paint. Avoid overmixing (see 3.2). Test the resultant color by applying the paint and allowing it to dry for comparison with the manufacturer's reference chip, if one is used. Maintain a written record of the tinting formula and mark the container appropriately. Also apply a spot of the final paint to the can cover as a further reference.

3.4 Straining. Paint in freshly opened containers should not normally require straining. In all instances, however, strain paints after mixing, if there is any evidence of skins, lumps, color flecks or foreign materials. First remove skins from the paint surface, thoroughly mix the paint, thin to application viscosity, if necessary, e.g., for spraying, then strain through a fine sieve or commercial paint strainer. Use straining as a standard procedure in all instances where the paint is to be applied by spray to avoid clogging of the spray gun.

3.5 Thinning. Paints should be ready for application by brush or roller when received. While thinning is frequently re-

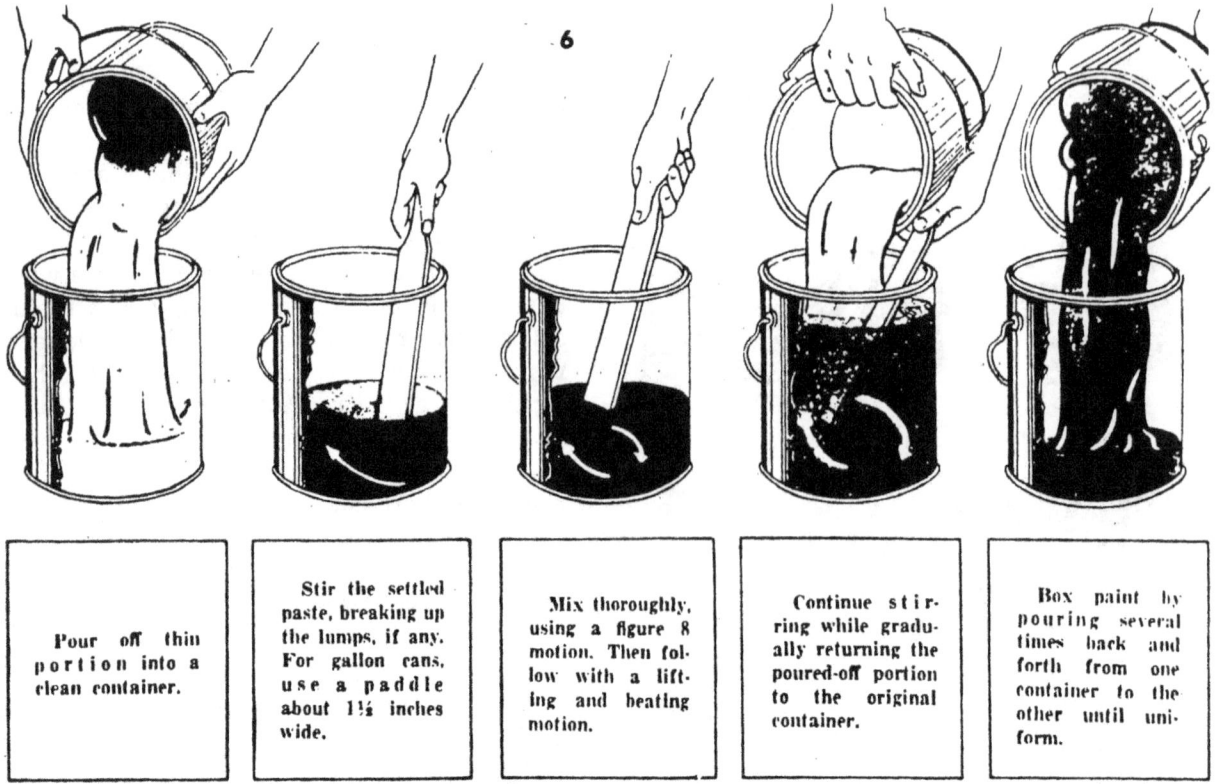

Figure 33. Manual Mixing and Boxing.

quired for spray application, avoid the arbitrary addition of thinners to any coating. Unnecessary or excessive thinning results in an inadequate film thickness, and drastically reduces the longevity and protective qualities of the applied coating. In all instances, measure the viscosity of the material to determine that it is correct for the method of application as established by the manufacturer. When thinning is necessary, it is to be done by competent personnel using only compatible thinning agents recommended in label or specification instructions. Thinner can be added for brush or roller application with only prior approval of the supervisor or inspector. Do not thin to improve brushing or rolling of paint materials which are overly cold. These should be pre-conditioned to bring them up to 65°F to 85°F.

SECTION 4 — PREPARATION OF SURFACES

4.1 General. Proper preparation of the surface prior to painting is essential to achieve maximum life of the coating. The best quality paint will not perform effectively if applied on a poorly prepared surface. The initial cost of adequate surface preparation is more than compensated for by increased durability, minimum repairs and repainting. The selection of surface preparation systems is dependent upon:

    a. nature of substrate
    b. condition of surface to be painted
    c. type of exposure
    d. practical limitations, i.e., time, location, space, and the availability of equipment
    e. economic considerations
    f. type of paint to be applied
    g. safety factors.

Many surface contaminants reduce adhesion and cause blistering, peeling, flaking, and underfilm rusting. Among these contaminants are: dirt, grease, rust, rust scale, mill scale, chemicals, moisture and efflorescence. In addition, the following surface defects will affect adhesion adversely: irregular weld areas, metal burrs, crevices, sharp edges, irregular areas, weld splatter, weld flux, knots, splinters, nail holes, loose aggregates and old paints in various stages of failure. Because of its importance, methods of preparing iron and steel for painting are given particular emphasis in the folowing paragraphs.

4.2 Mechanical Treatment.

4.2.1 Hand Cleaning. Hand cleaning will remove only loose or loosely adhering surface contaminants. These include rust scale, loose rust, mill scale and loosely adhering paint. Hand cleaning is not to be considered an appropriate procedure for removing tight mill scale and all traces of rust. In general terms, hand cleaning cannot be expected to do more than remove major surface contamination. As such, it is primarily recommended for spot-cleaning in areas where corrosion is not a serious factor. In extreme situations, as when areas are not accessible to power tools, hand cleaning may have to be used by necessity. Inasmuch as hand cleaning will remove only the loosest contamination, primers are required which will thoroughly wet the surface. All applied coats must be capable of overcoming the interference of contaminants left behind after hand cleaning to achieve satisfactory adhesion, assuring maximum anticipated coating life under normal conditions. Before hand cleaning, the surface must be free of oil, grease, dirt and chemicals. This can best be accomplished with solvent cleaners (see 4.3). Then remove rust scale and heavy build-up of old coatings with impact tools such as chipping hammers, chisels and scalers. Remove loose mill scale and nonadhering paint with wire brushes and scrapers. Finish up by sanding, especially on woodwork. All work must be done to avoid deep marking or scratches on the surface by the tools used. (See Figure 34.) Start painting as soon as possible after cleaning.

4.2.2 Power Tool Cleaning. Power tool cleaning methods provide faster and more adequate surface preparation than hand tool methods. Power tools are used for removing

Figure 34. Hand Cleaning Tools.

small amounts of tightly adhering contaminants which hand tools cannot remove, but they remain uneconomical and time consuming as compared with blasting for large area removal of tight mill scale, rust or old coatings. Power tools are driven either electrically or pneumatically and include a variety of attachments for the basic units. Chipping hammers are used for removing tight rust, mill scale and heavy paint coats. Rotary and needle scalers are used for removing rust, mill scale and old paint from large metallic and masonry areas. Wire brushes (cup or radial) are used for removing loose mill scale, old paint, weld flux, slag and dirt deposits. Grinders and sanders are used for complete removal of old paint, rust or mill scale on small surfaces and for smoothing rough surfaces. As with hand tools, care must be exercised with power impact and grinding tools not to cut too deeply into the surface, since this may result in burrs that are difficult to protect satisfactorily. Care must also be taken when using wire brushes to avoid polishing metal surfaces and thus prevent adequate adhesion of the subsequent coatings. Power tool cleaning is to be preceded by solvent or chemical treatment (see 4.3) and painting must be started and completed as soon after power cleaning as possible. (See Figures 35 thru 40.)

4.2.3 Flame Cleaning. (For Metal Only) Flame cleaning is a method of passing high-velocity, oxy-acetylene flames over a metal surface. This method is satisfactory

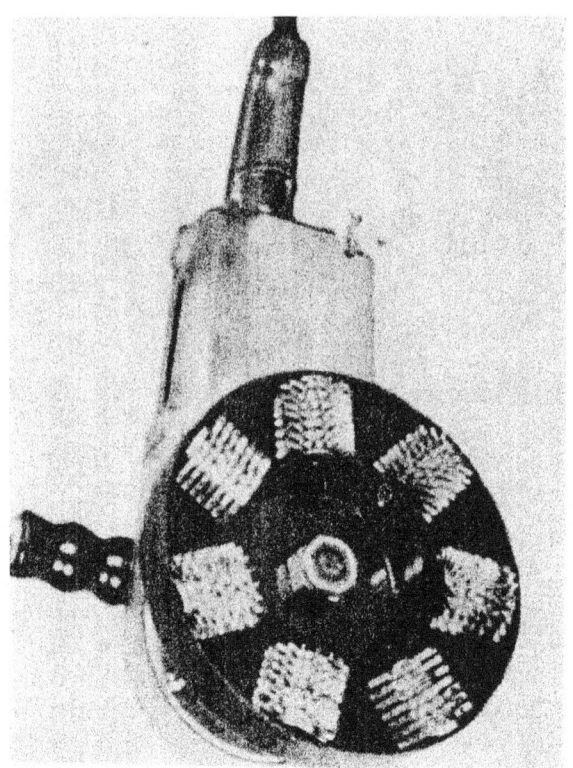

Figure 35. Typical Power Grinding Tool.

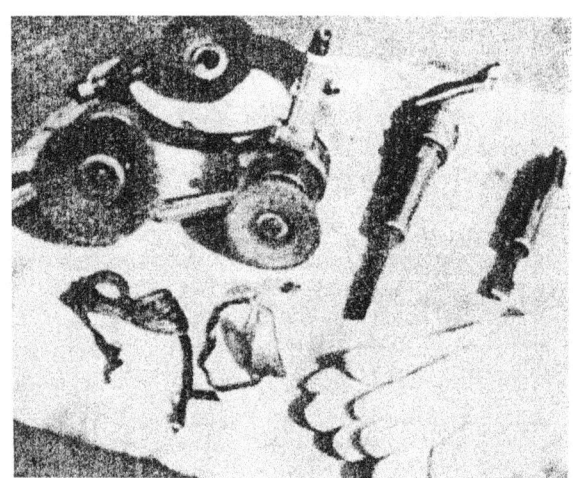

Figure 36. Air Powered Cleaning Tools.

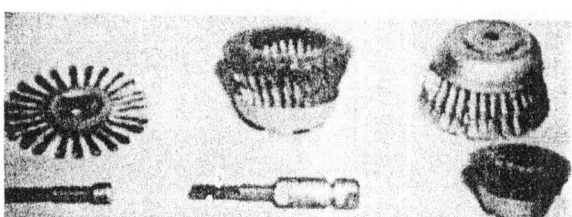

Figure 37. Power Tool Wire Brushes.

dents from the flame, and adequate ventilation must be provided during the process. The coating is applied while the substrate is still warm, thereby speeding up drying time and also permitting painting when ambient temperatures are somewhat below 50°F. However, avoid painting until completion of the cleaning operation because the flame presents a definite fire hazard with solvent thinned paints. (See Figures 41 and 42.)

4.2.4 *Blast Cleaning.* Blast cleaning abrades and cleans through the high velocity

for both new and maintenance work. Oil and grease must be removed prior to flame cleaning both for safety and adequacy of preparation. Wire brushing normally follows flame cleaning to remove loose matter. Extreme caution is necessary to prevent acci-

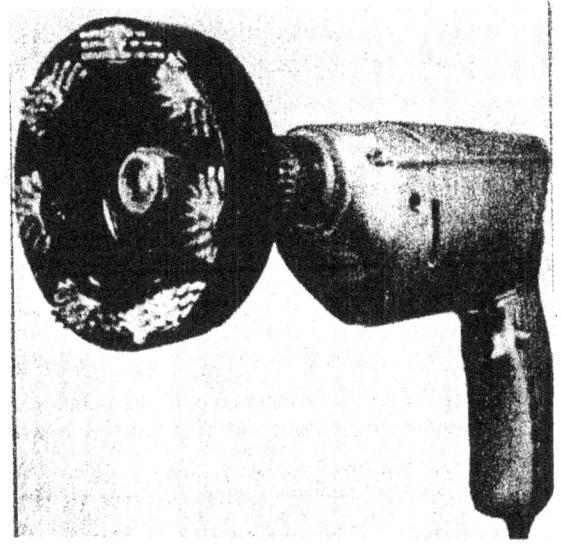

Figure 38. Typical Drill Attachment Tool.

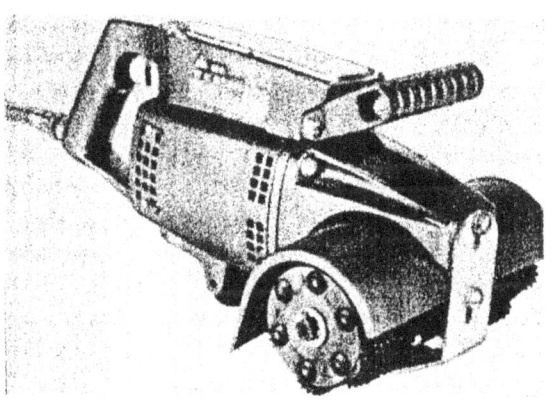

Figure 39. Rotary Impact Cleaning Tool.

Figure 40. Needle Scaler.

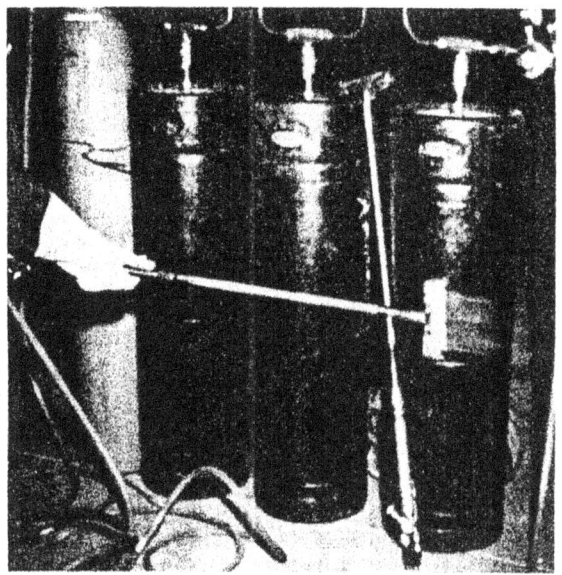

Figure 41. Flame Cleaning Equipment.

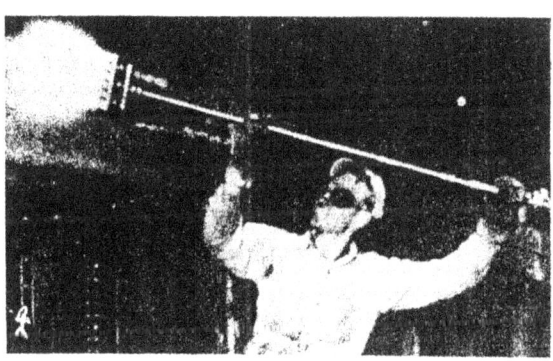

Figure 42. Flame Cleaning.

impact of sand, metal shot, metal or synthetic grit or other abrasive particles on the surface. Blast cleaning is most often used on metal structures in the field but may also be used, with caution, on masonry substrates. It is, by far, the most thorough of all mechanical treatments. There are four degrees of blast cleaning. Steel Structures Painting Council (SSPC) Manual No. 2 should be referred to for greater detail.

a. White Metal Blast: (SSPC-SP 5) Blast cleaning to white metal is the ultimate in blast cleaning. It is used for coatings which must withstand exposure to very corrosive atmospheres, where a high cost of surface preparation is considered to be warranted. Blast cleaning to white metal provides for the complete removal of all rust, mill scale and other contaminants from the surface. This will assist in maximum paint system performance.

    b. Near-White Metal Blast: (SSPC-SP 10) In this procedure the blasted surface will show shadows, streaks and/or discolorations but they will appear across the general surface area and not be concentrated in spots. Thus, the evaluation of the completed cleaning job must be of a visual judgment. This preparation effects a 10% to 35% savings over white metal blasting and has proven to be sufficiently adequate for many of the special coatings developed for long-term protection in moderately severe environments.

    c. Commercial Blast: (SSPC-SP 6) Commercial blast describes the removal of all loose scale, rust and other surface contaminants. This method of surface preparation will result in a high degree of cleaning, and is generally considered adequate to the long life of the majority of paint systems under normal exposure conditions.

    d. Brush-Off Blasting: (SSPC-SP 7) This is a relatively low cost method of cleaning to remove old finishes in poor condition, loose rust and loose mill scale. Brush-off blasting is not intended for use where severe corrosion is prevalent, but is, instead, intended to supplant hand tool and power tool cleaning where blast cleaning equipment is available. The brush-off method is also used for the removal of loose or degraded paint from masonry. (See Table 4.)

Table 4. RATE OF CLEANING

(Approximate cleaning rates using 100 PSI with a 5/16 inch nozzle.)

	sq. ft. per hour
White-Metal	100
Near-White	175
Commercial	370
Brush-Off	870

4.2.5 Procedures. Blast cleaning involves the high velocity impact of abrasive particles on the surface. The abrasive is discharged, either wet or dry, under pressure. The wet system differs from the dry in that water, or a solution of water and a rust inhibitor, is incorporated with the blast abrasive. The water is either mixed with the abrasive in the pressure tank or is introduced into the blast stream just behind or just in front of the blast nozzle. All blasted metal surfaces require that prime painting be started and completed the same day to prevent new rust from forming, since such blast cleaned surfaces are subject to rapid rusting if not coated. Metal or synthetic shot, grit or similar abrasives are used where recovery of the abrasive is possible. Sand is used when the agent is expendable, but this is a costly procedure. The grit, in any case, must be of a size sufficient to remove surface contamination without working the surface to excess. Overworking creates extreme peaks and valleys (anchor pattern) on the surface which require an additional buildup of the applied paint film for adequate protection. The peaks, even then, if too high,

*Table 5. EFFECT OF ABRASIVE**

	Average Mesh	Rate Sq. ft./hr.	Max. Height of Profile (mils)
Steel grit (dry honing)	100	120	1.5
Ottawa Sand—Very fine	80	175	1.5
Ottawa Sand—Fine	40	150	1.5
Ottawa Sand—Medium	18	115	2.0
Ottawa Sand—Coarse	12	90	2.8
Iron grit—Fine	50	100	2.0
Iron grit—Medium	25	65	3.2
Iron grit—Coarse	16	60	4.5
Iron shot	30	110	2.0
Iron shot	18	75	2.5

* 80 PSI using 5/16 in. Venturi nozzle at 18–24 ins. from mill scale covered mild steel plate.

represent possible areas of premature paint failure. (See Table 5.)

a. Dry Blasting: There are two general methods of dry blasting; conventional and vacuum.

(1) *Conventional blasting.* Conventional blast cleaning is a term used to designate the usual method of field blasting, in which no effort is made to alleviate the dust hazard or reclaim the blast abrasive. (See Figures 43 and 44.) This procedure precludes the need for special rinsing, as required for wet blasting, but requires that health precautions be taken to protect the operator and other personnel in the area from the fine, abrasive dust. Machinery in the vicinity must also be shielded. After blasting, the surface must be brushed, vacuumed, or air-cleaned to remove residues or trapped grit.

(2) *Vacuum blasting.* Vacuum blasting is a relatively new method, which minimizes the dust hazard and in which the blast abrasive is reclaimed. (See Figure 45.) This procedure, also known as dry honing, provides for practically no dust to escape and

Figure 43. Dry Blast Cleaning Setup.

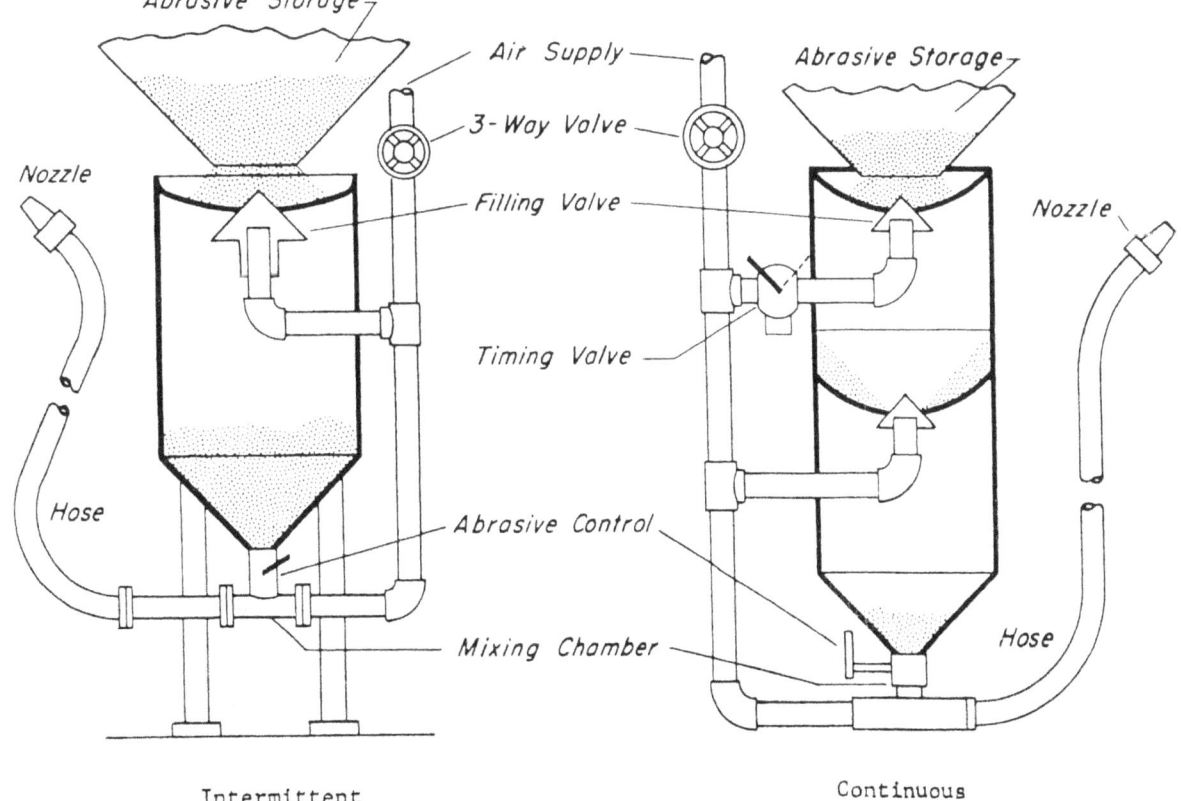

Figure 44. Direct Pressure Blast Cleaning Tanks.

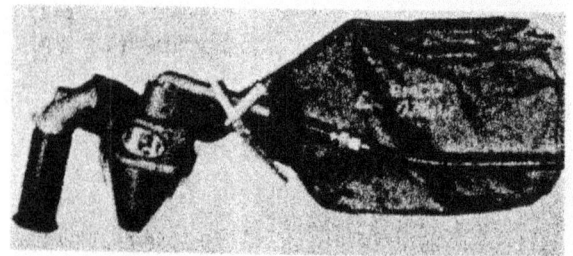

Figure 45. Vacuum Blast Cleaner.

contaminate the atmosphere. The vacuum method of blasting is less efficient than conventional blasting methods on highly irregular surfaces because of the poor vacuum on such surfaces. When the blasting cone is held firmly against the surface to prevent abrasive loss, and the surface is heavily contaminated with rust, algae, or other foreign matter, the machine may not be able to function more than a short time without becoming clogged. In such instances the vacuum blaster is used as a semi-open blasting device, i.e., the cone containing the nozzle is held at a slight distance away from the surface. The dust created is appreciable (workmen must wear respirators) but not nearly as great as with conventional blasting equipment. However, vacuum blasting is very efficient and economical for cleaning repetitive, small-scale surfaces in a shop. The process results in considerable savings in abrasive costs, and also reduces the dust and health hazard.

b. Wet Blasting: (See Figure 46.) This method reduces to a minimum the dust associated with blasting, but is not suitable for all types of work. Steel structures, containing a large number of ledges formed by upturned angles and horizontal girders, present a large amount of troublesome cleanup work if the wet method of blasting is used. Wet sand and other blast residues trapped on these ledges are more difficult to remove than dry materials. Also, a sufficient amount of sludge adheres to wet blasted surfaces to necessitate removal by rinsing, brushing, or compressed air. Moreover, there is a tendency for the wet-blasted surface to rust even though inhibitor is present in the mixing and rinsing water. The blasted surface must be thoroughly dry before coatings are applied.

★c. Centrifugal Blaster: (See Figures 47 and 48.) Large steel plates can be blast cleaned automatically and uniformly before erection. The abrasive grit is dropped into a spinning

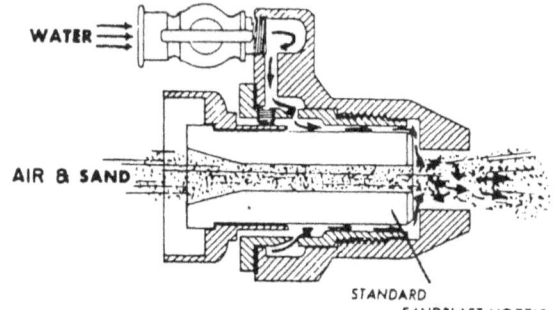

Cross section view of wet blast attachment which sucks water from any water supply for wet blast cleaning.

Figure 46. Wet Blast Attachment.

Figure 47. Centrifugal Blaster—Cutaway View.

For Descaling STRUCTURALS

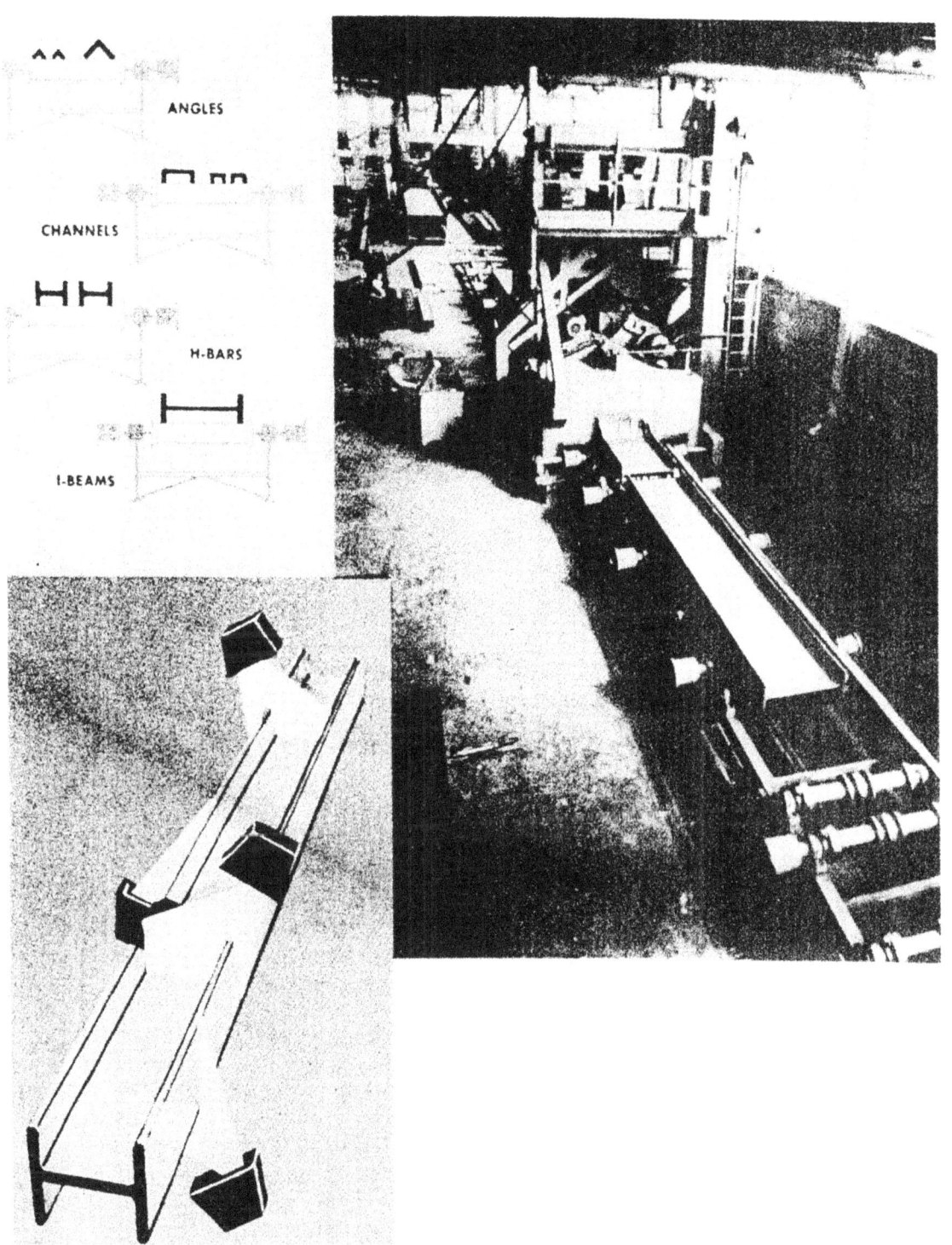

Figure 48. Centrifugal Blasting.

vaned wheel at a controlled rate. The grit is thus impinged against the steel plate moving beneath it at a predetermined rate. The result is a controlled, uniformly cleaned surface.

4.2.6 Precautions. Use goggles, gloves and dust respirators for all mechanical cleaning operations which create a threat to the health and safety of personnel. (See Chapter 3 and Figure 43.) Large amounts of surface grease or oil must be removed by solvent cleaning, prior to blasting (See 4.4.3.1). Avoid dry blasting if temperature of the steel is less than 5°F above the dew point to prevent condensation and subsequent rusting.

4.4.2.7 Summary. The principal mechanical surface preparation methods can be classified into four categories according to their increasing order of effectiveness:

Class 1: Nominal cleaning with hand or power tools where the corrosive environment is mild to normal, and coatings used will satisfactorily adhere to tight residues normally remaining on surfaces after cleaning.

Class 2: A better grade of surface preparation through flame cleaning or brush-off blasting. It extends the life of the applied coating when the severity of the environment increases.

Class 3: Commercial blast cleaning for preparation required in moderately corrosive atmospheres including immersion in water and exposure to industrial or marine environments.

Class 4: The optimum cleaning procedure including white metal or near-white blasting of ferrous metal surfaces exposed to, or in direct contact with strong chemicals, where any degree of rust formation on the surface would be intolerable or when maximum coating life demands warrant the ultimate in preparation procedures.

Refer to "Pictorial Surface Preparation Standards for Painting Steel Surfaces"—Steel Structures Painting Council SSPC-VIS 1 and ASTM Standard D2200. See also Table 6, "Treatment of Various Substrates".

4.4.3 Chemical and Solvent Treatment.

4.4.3.1 Solvent Wiping and Degreasing. Solvent cleaning is a procedure for removing oil, grease, dirt, chemical paint stripper residues and other foreign matter from the surfaces prior to painting or mechanical treatment. Solvents clean by dissolving and diluting to permit contaminants to be wiped or washed off the surface. The simplest procedure is to first remove soil, cement spatter and other dry materials with a wire brush. The surface is then scrubbed with brushes or rags saturated with solvent. Clean rags are used for rinsing and wiping dry. More effective methods include immersing the work in the solvent or spraying solvent over the surface. In either case, the solvent quickly becomes contaminated, so it is essential that several clean solvent rinses be applied to the surface. Mineral spirits is an effective solvent for cleaning under normal conditions. Toxic solvents and solvents with low flash points represent hazards to health and safety.

Do not use a solvent for cleaning if its flash point is below 100°F, or its maximum allowable concentration (M.A.C.) is less than 100 parts per million. Rags must be placed in fireproof containers after use.

4.4.3.2 Alkali Cleaning. Alkali cleaning is more efficient, less costly and less hazardous than solvent cleaning, but is more difficult to carry out. Alkaline cleaners are dissolved in water and used at relatively high temperatures (150°F–200°F) since cleaning efficiency increases with temperature. Alkalis attack oil and grease, converting them into soapy residues that wash away with water. Other active ingredients contained in the alkali cleaners aid in removing surface dirt and other contaminants such as mildew. These cleaners are also effective in removing old paint by saponifying the

Table 6. TREATMENT OF VARIOUS SUBSTRATES

	Wood	Metal Steel	Metal Other	Concrete Masonry	Plaster Wallboard
Mechanical					
Hand Cleaning	S	S	S	S	S
Power Tool Cleaning	S*	S		S	
Flame Cleaning		S			
Blast Cleaning:					
Brush-Off		S	S	S	
All Other		S			
Chemical and Solvent					
Solvent Cleaning	S	S	S		
Alkali Cleaning		S		S	
Steam Cleaning		S		S	
Acid Cleaning		S		S	
Pickling		S			
Pretreatments					
Hot Phosphate		S			
Cold Phosphate		S			
Wash Primers		S	S		
Conditioners, Sealers and Fillers					
Conditioners				S	
Sealers	S				
Fillers	S			S	

S—Satisfactory for use as indicated
*—Sanding only

dried vehicle. The most commonly used alkaline cleaners are trisodium phosphate, caustic soda and silicated alkalis. They can be applied by brushing, scrubbing, spraying or by immersion of the surface into soak tanks. Thorough water rinses are absolutely necessary to remove the soapy residue as well as all traces of alkali, to avoid reactivity with the applied paint. Otherwise, cleaning may do more harm than good. The water should be hot and, preferably, applied under pressure. If used on steel, these cleaners should contain 0.1% chromic acid or potassium dichromate to prevent corrosion. Universal pH test paper, placed against the wet steel, should be used to check for the presence of free alkali after rinsing. Do not use alkali cleaners on aluminum or stainless steel.

4.3.3 Steam Cleaning. Steam or hot water under pressure is used in this method of cleaning. A detergent should be included for added effectiveness. The steam or hot water removes oil and grease by liquefying them because of the high temperature, then emulsifying them and diluting them with water. When used on old paint, the vehicle is swelled so that it loses its adhesiveness and is easily removed. Steam or hot water alone is commonly used to remove heavy dirt deposits, soot and grime. Wire brushing and/or brush-off blast cleaning may be necessary to augment the steam cleaning process by removing remaining residues.

4.3.4 Acid Cleaning. This method is used for cleaning iron, steel, concrete and masonry by treating them with an acid solution.

a. Iron and Steel: These surfaces are treated with solutions of phosphoric acid containing small amounts of solvent, detergent and wetting agent. (Do not use on aluminum or stainless steel.)

Such cleaning effectively removes oil, grease, dirt and other foreign contaminants. In addition (and unlike alkali cleaners), it also removes light rust and faintly etches the surface to assure better adhesion of applied coatings. There are many types of phosphoric acid metal cleaners and rust removers, each formulated to perform a specific cleaning job. There also are four basic methods of using acid cleaners and each requires a variation in the phosphoric acid concentration as well as a different detergent system. The methods are:

Wash-off—This involves the application of the cleaner, a time allowance for it to act, a thorough rinsing and a drying period before painting.

Wipe-off—This is used when rinsing is impractical and involves the application of the cleaner, a time allowance for it to act, wiping of the surface with clean, damp cloths, final wiping with clean dry cloths and a drying period prior to painting.

Hot-dip—This involves immersion of the work in hot cleaner, a rinse in hot or cold water after the surface is sufficiently cleaned, a second rinse in weak cleaner solution (5 percent) and a drying time before painting.

Spray—This involves the same steps as with the wash-off method but requires pressurized spray equipment.

b. Concrete and Masonry: These surfaces are washed with 5 to 10% muriatic (hydrochloric) acid to remove efflorescence and laitance, to clean the surface, to remove any glaze, and to etch the surface. Efflorescence is a white, powdery, crystalline deposit often found on concrete and masonry surfaces. Laitance is fine cement powder which floats to the surface after concrete is poured. Coatings applied over loose deposits of efflorescence or laitance will loosen prematurely and result in early coating failure. Remove as much of the loose efflorescence or laitance as possible using a clean dry, wire or stiff fiber brush. Putty knives or scrapers may also be used. All oil and grease must also be removed prior to acid cleaning, either by solvent wiping or by steam or alkali cleaning. To acid clean these surfaces, thoroughly wet the surface with clean water, then scrub it with a 5 percent solution (by weight) of muriatic acid, using a stiff fiber brush. In extreme cases, up to a 10 percent muriatic acid solution may be used, and may be allowed to remain on the surface up to five minutes before scrubbing. Work should be done on small areas, not greater than four square feet in size. Immediately after the surface is scrubbed, wash the acid solution completely from the surface by thoroughly sponging or rinsing with clean water. Rinsing must be done immediately to avoid formation of salts on the surface which are difficult to remove. The above procedure is also used when it is desired to etch the surface, e.g., to remove the glaze. Often, when concrete surfaces are steel troweled they may become so dense, smooth and even glazed that paint will not adhere to the surface. A simple method to determine whether etching is required is to pour a few drops of water on the surface. If water is quickly absorbed, etching is unnecessary. In addition to this acid washing, glaze may be removed by rubbing with an abrasive stone, lightly sandblasting, or allowing the surface to weather for six to twelve months. It may also be removed by treatment with a solution of 3% zinc chloride plus 2% phosphoric acid to etch the surface. This is not flushed off but is allowed to dry to produce a paintable surface. It may be necessary, in certain instances, to use acid cleaning methods to neutralize concrete and masonry surfaces before applying a coating which is sensitive to alkali. To detect the presence of free alkali, dampen the surface in several spots and applied dampened pH testing paper.

4.3.5 Pickling. This method is used in the shop to completely remove all mill scale, rust and rust scale. Sulfuric, hydrochloric, nitric, hydrofluoric and phosphoric acid are used individually or in combination. Sulfuric acid is most frequently employed because of its low cost, high boiling point and general suitability. Pickling is usually accomplished by immersing work in tanks, but the same principles apply if the solution is sprayed or washed over the contaminated surface. Because mill scale itself is not chemically consistent throughout its composition, the outer layer tends to resist the acid solution, but the lower layers (and base metal) are soluble in the acid. Thus, the diluted acid penetrates cracks in the outer scale layer, dissolves some of the scale beneath, penetrates to the lowest layer and base metal to dissolve them rapidly and cause all of the scale to eventually flake off the surface. During this process, any rust or rust scale is dissolved completely in the acid solution, being considerably less resistant to the acid action. Inhibitors are added to the solution to minimize acid action on base metal exposed in those portions of the surface that have cleaned faster than others. Work must be solvent-or alkali-cleaned to remove oil and grease before pickling (pickling will not suitably accomplish this). Following pickling several rinses are necessary to remove acids and salts with a final rinse in a weak alkali solution to retard rusting. It should be noted that pickling is a low-cost shop procedure, provided there is sufficient work to keep the equipment in regular use. Do not use this method on aluminum or stainless steel. See also SSPC–SP 8.

4.3.6 Paint Removers. Paint and varnish removers generally are used for small areas. Solvent type removers or solvent mixtures are selected according to the type and condition of the old finish as well as the nature of the substrate. Removers are available as flammable or non-flammable types, also liquid or semi-paste in consistency. While most paint removers require scraping or steel wool to physically remove the softened paint, types are available that allow the loosened finish to be flushed off with steam or hot water. Many of the flammable and non-flammable removers contain paraffin wax to retard evaporation. It is absolutely essential that this residue be removed from the surface prior to painting to prevent loss of adhesion of the applied coating. In such instances, follow the manufacturer's label directions or use mineral spirits to remove any wax residue. As a safety precaution, it should be noted that, while non-flammable removers eliminate fire hazards, they are toxic to a degree (as are all removers). Proper ventilation must be provided whenever they are used.

4.3.7 Summary. Chemical methods of surface cleaning are usually more suited to paint shop application while mechanical methods are generally more practical in field work. On the basis of overall effectiveness and efficiency, chemical cleaning is superior to mechanical methods, with the exception of blast cleaning. The paint or paint system selected for any given surface and environment is of primary importance. The coating and environment then, determine the degree of surface cleaning required. The existing surface conditions, job location, equipment availability and economic factors will serve as a guide to the cleaning method required. Project specifications also will provide a guide to the recommended cleaning method. In the case of paint systems, manufacturer's directions will probably be even more specific, including the cleaning methods recommended. See Table 6 for a list of substrates and satisfactory cleaning procedures.

4.3.8 Precautions. Use goggles and rubber gloves when handling chemical cleaners, and protective clothing where acid or alkaline solutions are used. Adequate ventilation is essential. Use respirators when cleaners must be applied in confined areas. Flammable cleaners necessitate that all proper fire precautions be taken. Only experienced personnel will be permitted to perform cleaning by steam, acid, pickling or other methods that constitute a hazard if mishandled or improperly supervised. Under no circumstances will procedures be followed without full and complete knowledge of the operation.

4.4. Pretreatments. Pretreatments are applied on metal surfaces after cleaning to improve the adhesion and to improve the effectiveness of the applied paint. Refer also to Steel Structures Painting Council Manual No. 2.

4.4.1 Hot Phosphate Treatments. Hot phosphate treatments utilize zinc or iron phosphate solutions to form crystalline deposits on the surface of the metal. They greatly increase the bond and adhesion of applied paints while reducing underfilm corrosion. Zinc phosphate generally produces the best results and is most widely used. The hot phosphate solutions are somewhat critical in their application and require carefully controlled conditions and cleaned surfaces. As these deposits thicken, the system becomes more brittle. However, adhesion increases and rust prevention is more effective. When painting, it usually is necessary to apply thicker paint coats over the heavier phosphate coatings if a gloss finish is desired, because the heavier phosphate coatings absorb considerably more paint. If a higher gloss finish is desired, iron phosphate is preferred to the zinc phosphate pretreatment, because it produces a finer crystalline structure and hence a thinner film. The hot phosphate treatments are excellent procedures leading to tight bonds between the surface and applied paint. The mechanics of hot phosphate treatment limit its use to the paint shop. See also SSPC-PT 4.

4.4.2 Cold Phosphate Treatments. These treatments are produced with a mixture of phosphoric acid, wetting agent, water miscible solvent and water. An acid concentration of about 5 to 7% (by weight) will produce the desired reaction with steel when the area to be treated is not exposed to high summer temperatures, direct sunlight, or high wind velocities. Such environmental conditions cause rapid evaporation and consequent high acid concentration. When a dry, powdery surface, grayish-white in color, develops within a few minutes after application, the acid has reacted properly and has the proper dilution. If a dark color develops and the surface is somewhat sticky, the acid is too concentrated. In such cases, if the area is small, wiping with damp rags may bring about the desired appearance. Otherwise, rinse the surface with water and re-treat with a more dilute solution. Although cold phosphate treatments produce a crystalline deposit on the metal surface, the density of the deposit is not as great as the hot phosphate treatment; therefore, paint adhesion is not quite as good. The procedures used for cold phosphating are adaptable to field use on large or small structures. See also SSPC–PT 2.

4.4.3 Wash Primers. Wash primers are actually a form of cold phosphatizing. They perform more efficiently than the standard cold phosphating treatments and are generally replacing them for field use. Wash primers are so called, because they are applied in very thin or "wash" coats. They contain polyvinyl butyral resin, phosphoric acid, and a rust inhibitive pigment such as basic zinc chromate or lead chromate. Wash primers develop extremely good adhesion to blast cleaned or pickled steel, and provide a sound base for topcoating. They are also used to promote adhesion of coatings to surfaces generally considered difficult to paint, such as galvanized or stainless steel and aluminum.

4.4.4 Chemical Conversion Coatings. The chemical conversion coatings are chromate conversion coatings. These coatings are specifically formulated for aluminum, magnesium, zinc, cadmium, copper and silver to prevent or retard corrosion and when required to provide a good base on which to apply primer and finish coats. The coatings impart a light iridescent gold to light green color to the white metals, when properly applied. When this treatment is to be applied to aluminum, the surface should be alkaline etched and the coating applied by brush or dip until the appropriate color is obtained as described in MIL-C-5541. The reaction may be stopped by water rinsing the excess chemical from the surface. Care should be exercised to prevent splashing this toxic chemical on one's skin! Materials suitable for producing chromate conversion coatings conform to MIL-C-81706.

4.5 Conditioners, Sealers, and Fillers. Conditioners are often applied on masonry to seal a chalky surface in order to improve adhesion of water-based topcoats. Sealers are used on wood to prevent resin exudation or bleeding. Fillers are used to produce a smooth finish on open grain wood and rough masonry. (See Table 6.)

4.5.1 Conditioners. Latex (water-thinned) paints do not adhere well to chalky masonry surfaces. To overcome this problem, an oil-based conditioner is applied to the chalky substrate before the latex paint is applied. The entire surface should be vigorously wire brushed by hand or power tools, then dusted to remove all loose particles and chalk residue. The conditioner is then brushed on freely to assure effective penetration and allowed to dry. This surface conditioner is not intended for use as a finish coat.

4.5.2 Knot Sealers. Sealers are used on bare wood to prevent resin exudation (bleeding) through applied paint coatings. Freshly exuded resin, while still soft, may be scraped off with a putty knife and the affected area solvent cleaned with alcohol. Hardened resin may be removed by scraping or sanding. Since the sealer is not intended for use as a priming coat, it should be used only when necessary, and applied only over the affected area. When previous paint on pine lumber has become discolored over knots, the sealer should be applied over the old paint before the new paint is applied.

4.5.3 Fillers. Fillers are used on porous wood, concrete, and masonry to fill the pores to provide a smoother finish coat.

   a. Wood Fillers: Wood filters are used on open-grained hardwoods. In general, those hardwoods with pores larger than in birch should be filled. (See Table 7.) When filling is necessary, it is done after any staining operations. Stain should be allowed to dry for 24 hours before filler is applied. If staining is not warranted, natural (uncolored) filler is applied directly to the bare wood. The filler may be colored with some of the stain in order to accentuate the grain pattern of the wood. To apply, first thin the filler with mineral spirits to a creamy consistency, then liberally brush it across the grain, followed by light brushing along the grain. Allow to stand five to ten minutes until most of the thinner has evaporated, at which time the finish will have lost its glossy appearance. Before it has a chance to set and harden, wipe the filler off *across* the grain using burlap or other coarse cloth, rubbing the filler into the pores of the wood while removing the excess. Finish by stroking along the grain with clean rags. It is essential that all excess filler be removed.

Table 7. Characteristics of Wood

Name of Wood	Soft Closed	Hard Open	Hard Closed	Notes on Finishing
Ash		X		Requires filler.
Alder	X			Stains well.
Aspen			X	Paints well.
Basswood			X	Paints well.
Beech			X	Paints poorly; varnishes well.
Birch			X	Paints and varnishes well.
Cedar	X			Paints and varnishes well.
Cherry			X	Varnishes well.
Chestnut		X		Requires filler; paints poorly.
Cottonwood			X	Paints well.
Cypress			X	Paints and varnishes well.
Elm		X		Requires filler; paints poorly.
Fir	X			Paints poorly.
Gum			X	Varnishes well.
Hemlock	X			Paints fairly well.
Hickory		X		Requires filler.
Mahogany		X		Requires filler.
Maple			X	Varnishes well.
Oak		X		Requires filler.
Pine	X			Variable depending on grain.
Teak		X		Requires filler.
Walnut		X		Requires filler.
Redwood	X			Paints well.

Note: Any type finish may be applied unless otherwise specified.

Knowing when to start wiping is important; wiping too soon will pull the filler out of the pores, while allowing the filler to set too long will make it very difficult to wipe off. A simple test for dryness consists of rubbing a finger across the surface. If a ball is formed, it is time to wipe. If the filler slips under the pressure of the finger, it is still too wet for wiping. Allow the filler to dry for 24 hours before applying finish coats.

b. Masonry Fillers: Masonry fillers, are intended for use on porous surfaces as rough concrete, concrete block, stucco and other masonry surfaces. The purpose of the filler is to fill the open pores and voids by brushing the filler into the surface to produce a fairly smooth finish suitable for painting. There are two types of filler coatings, one a solvent-thinned material, i.e., TT-F-1098, which cannot be applied to damp masonry, and the other a water-thinned cementitious or latex emulsion coating which can be applied to damp masonry. Prior to the use of fillers, the surfaces must be clean, whether they are new, old or have been previously painted. On previously painted surfaces, only the solvent-type filler should be used. Uncoated surfaces should be prepared as described in 4.3.4.b. Residual form oil or other organic material on the surface should be removed by sandblasting, or strong detergent treatment, including proper rinsing, or if time permits, allowing natural weathering to remove the oils. On previously painted surfaces, all loose, powdery or flaking material, dirt and old paint may be removed effectively by sandblasting. Application of either type coatings should be at ambient temperatures of 50° F or higher. Allow the filler to dry for 24 hours before painting. When applying a cement-water or emulsion-type filler, a brush with relatively short bristles, for example, Tampico fiber, is needed to work the filler into the voids. Solvent-thinned filler may be applied by brush, roller or spray, however, a brush is preferred to most effectively work the material into the pores. Before this filler becomes tacky, usually 3 to 5 minutes, excess material is removed with a rubber squeegee. The moderate pressure exerted using the squeegee helps to fill the voids and smooth the surface besides removing excess filler.

4.6 Applicable Specifications. The specified products which are recommended for surface preparation before painting are listed.

SECTION 5—REPAIR OF SURFACES

5.1 General. All surfaces must be in good condition before painting. Repair or replace degraded wood, concrete, masonry, stucco, metal, plaster and wallboard. Remove and replace all loose mortar in brickwork. Replace broken windows and loose putty or glazing compound. Securely fasten or replace loose gutter hangers and downspout bands. Fill all cracks, crevices and joints with calking compound, or sealants. Drive all exposed nail heads below the surface. Patch all cracks or holes in wood, masonry and plaster. The final surface should be smooth, with no openings or defects of any kind. These preparatory procedures eliminate the major areas for the entrance of moisture which can lead to blistering and peeling of the paint film.

5.2 Calking Compounds and Sealants. Calking compounds are oil and/or resin based. They are used in fixed joints of wood, metal, or masonry, also in joints with very limited movement. Sealants, on the other hand, are elastomeric, rubber-like compounds. They are intended for use in expansion or other movable joints. Sealants are available as one or two component compounds.

5.2.1 Calking Compounds. Calking compounds are used to fill joints and crevices around doors and windows in wood, brick, concrete and other masonry surfaces. They are supplied in two grades, a gun grade and a knife grade. The gun grade is most popular since it is easier to use and faster in application because it employs the use of a calking gun, whereas the knife grade must be applied by hand using a putty knife. The gun grade is supplied in two forms, i.e., in bulk and in factory prefilled cartridges. The cartridge type fits directly into a calking gun and is preferred for convenience of use. Triggering the gun extrudes the calking compound directly into the crevice. A variety of different shaped tips aid in speeding up the work. Calking compounds tend to dry on the surface but remain soft and tacky within the crevice. The applied calking should be painted each time the surrounding area is painted to help extend its life.

5.2.2 Sealants. Sealants are an advanced and much more durable type of calking compound. Compared with calking compounds, they have better adhesion to the walls of the crevices, have better extensibility so that they do not pull away when the walls contract in cold weather, and they remain flexible for much longer periods of time. Although they are considerably more expensive than calking compounds, their longer life is often well worth the difference in cost. There are many types of sealants, and they may be divided into three groups:

a. One Component: These are similar to calking compounds in general handling. All are available in bulk and some are also available in cartridges. They are applied in a manner similar to calking compounds.

b. Two Component: These are supplied only in bulk since they must be pre-mixed before use. Their useful, or pot-life when mixed, is normally, not less than three hours. High temperatures may drastically shorten this time. The two components react to form a tough rubbery seal with excellent adhesion, extensibility and durability.

c. Preformed Tapes: These sealants are supplied in an extruded bead so that they can be applied simply by pressing the tape into crevices by hand without the use of tools.

5.3 Putty. Putty is used to fill nail holes, cracks and imperfections in wood surfaces. It is supplied in bulk form and is applied with a putty knife. Putty is not flexible and should not be used for joints or crevices. It dries to a harder surface than calking compound.

5.4 Glazing Compounds. Glazing compounds are used on both interior and exterior wood and metal window sash either as bedding or face glazing. They are used to cushion glass in metal or wood frames and are not intended to keep or hold the glass in position. Glazing compounds set firmly, but not hard, and have some limited flexibility. They are more flexible than putty. They tend to harden upon exposure with life expectancy estimated to be approximately ten years, if they are properly applied. Painting over glazing compounds will extend their useful life. Glazing compounds are relatively inexpensive though more costly than putty.

5.5 Application of Calking and Glazing Compounds, Putty and Sealants. All surfaces must be clean and dry to obtain good adhesion. Remove all oil, grease, soot, dirt or loose paint, or old materials. Be sure the crevice openings are large enough to allow an adequate amount of material to be inserted. Prime substrate, when recommended by the manufacturer, in accordance with directions given. If the opening is deep, first insert back-up materials such as oakum, foamed plastic or rubber, fiberglass, or fiberboard.

5.5.1 Gun Grade Calking Compounds and Sealants. When applying gun grade material, move the gun along the crevice while triggering so that the compound is extruded directly into the crevice. Move the gun slowly and steadily, so as to push the bead into the crevice rather than pull it away. Allow the compound to overlap the opening slightly for a better seal, and to allow sufficient surface area for adhesion. The best position to hold the gun is at a slight angle with the bevel parallel to the work. (See Figure 49.) Compound should finally be tooled to insure close contact with the joint surfaces.

5.5.2 Knife Grade Calking Compounds, Sealants and Putty. When applying knife grade material or putty, use a putty knife and press firmly into cracks or holes until full. Then smooth with the flat side of the knife by sliding it across the surface. The exposed area should be slightly convex to allow for shrinkage. (See Figure 50.)

5.5.3 Face Glazing. For face glazing, apply a generous quantity of glazing compound into the glazing rabbet, and gently press the glass into the rabbet leaving a bed of back glazing material of approximately 1/16". Apply glazing points to hold the glass in place. Strip surplus glazing compound at an angle to allow for run-off of condensation. Apply additional glazing compound to the face and tool into place with the aid of a

Figure 49. Calking.

Covering nail heads with putty, after priming coat has dried. The putty should be squeezed into the nail hole and cut off with a putty knife while under pressure. The surface of the putty should be slightly convex to allow for shrinkage, as shown in the detail.

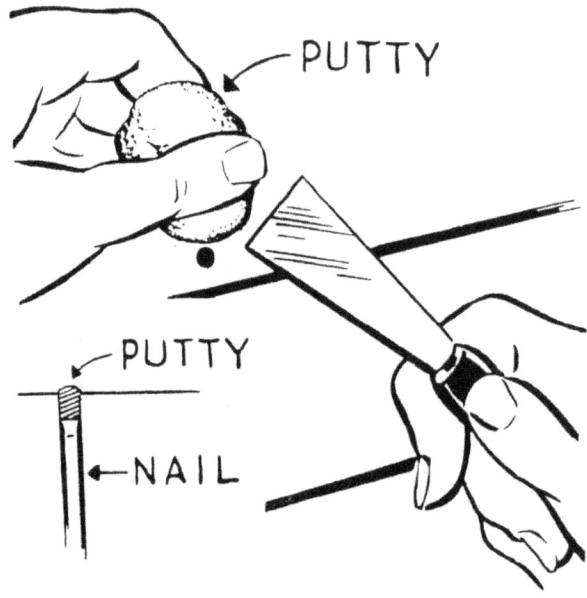

Figure 50. Puttying.

Notes

putty knife, applying sufficient pressure to completely fill the void. Tool face glazing approximately 1/16" short of sight line to allow paint to overlap onto glass. (See Figures 51 and 52.)

5.5.4 Channel Glazing. For bead or channel glazing, apply a generous amount of the compound to the fixed (stationary) side and the bottom of the channel. Place nonporous resilient spacer shims (such as vinyl floor tile) at points around the perimeter of the channel to position glass and prevent squeezing out of compound (keep spacer shims below edge of channel). Press glass into place until intimate contact with spacer shims is made. Spread compound on removable bead and gently press into place. Insert spacer shims between glass and removable bead (opposite spacer shims on fixed side of the channel) and apply pressure to removable bead until intimate contact with spacer shims is made. Fasten bead in place and strip excess compound. When glazing compound has attained a surface skin, apply paint, slightly overlapping the sight line. (See Figures 51 and 52.)

5.6 Patching Materials. Cracks, holes and crevices in masonry, plaster, wallboard and wood are filled with patching material. It is supplied either ready for use or as a dry powder to which water is added before use. There are a variety of types depending on the surface and its conditions.

5.6.1 Patching Plaster. This is used for repairing large areas in plaster. It is similar to ordinary plaster except that it hardens quickly. It is supplied as a powder.

5.6.2 Spackle. Spackling compound is used to fill cracks and small holes in plaster and wallboard. It is very easy to work with

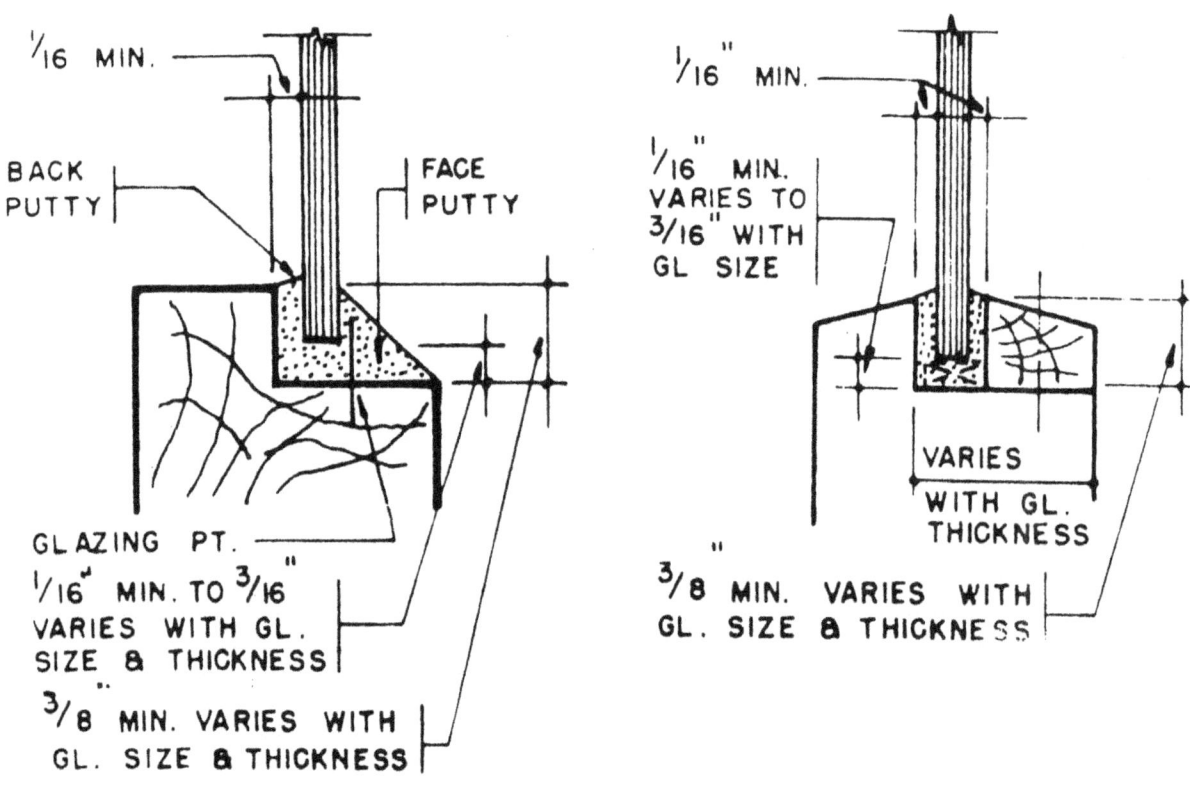

Face Glazing　　　　　　　　*Channel Glazing*

Figure 51. Glazing — Wood Frames.

and sands very well after it hardens. It is supplied both as a paste and as a powder.

5.6.3 Joint Cement. This is used primarily to seal the joints between wallboards. It can also be used to repair large cracks. It is supplied as a powder and is used in conjunction with perforated tape which gives it added strength. (See Figure 53.)

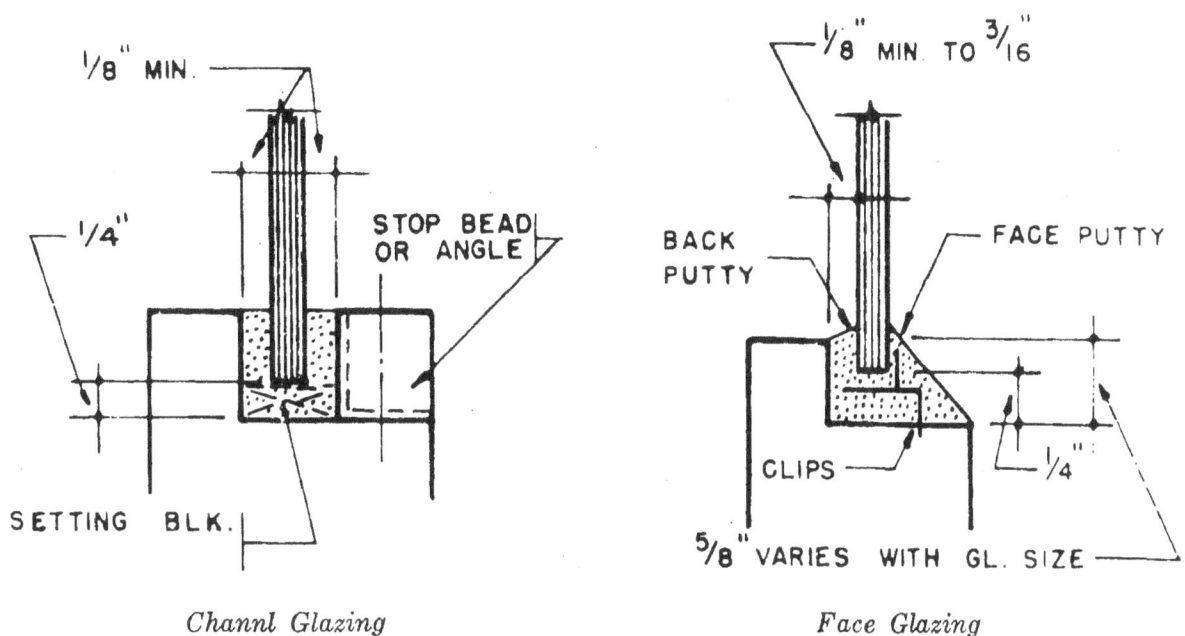

Channl Glazing *Face Glazing*

Figure 52. Glazing — Metal Frames.

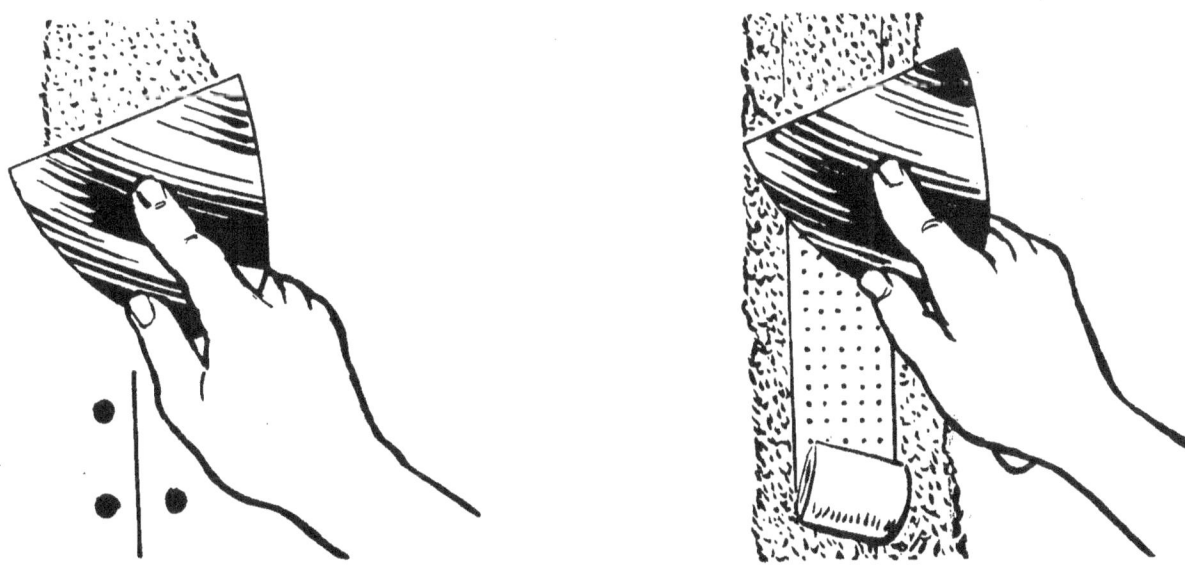

Covering joint between pieces of wallboard with perforated tape. Left. Filling joint and covering nail heads. Right. Embedding tape in cement.

Figure 53. Applying Joint Cement.

5.6.4 Portland Cement Grout. This is used to repair cracks in concrete and masonry. Hydrated lime is often added to slow up its cure time and lengthen its working life.

5.6.5 Plastic Wood. Plastic wood is a filler suitable for such repair work as filling gouges and nail holes. It is also used for building up and filling in wood patterns and joiner work. It is applied in a manner similar to putty. Sand plastic wood smooth after it has completely dried before applying paint.

5.6.6 Application of Patching Materials. When using any of the above patching materials (except plastic wood) on masonry, plaster, or wallboard, the crack should first be opened with a putty knife or wall scraper so that weak material is removed and the patching compound can be forced in completely. Dampen these areas with clear water and apply the compound with a putty knife or trowel depending on the size of the hole. Level and smooth off the surface allowing it to be slightly convex to allow for shrinkage. Follow manufacturer's instructions explicitly if they are available. None of these materials requires attention during drying, except for the Portland cement grout which should be kept damp at least one, and preferably two or three days for optimum cure. When the surface is dry and hard, sand it (except Portland cement) until it is smooth and level with the surrounding area.

SECTION 6 — PAINT APPLICATION

4.6.1 General. The most common methods of applying paint are by brush, roller and spray. Dip and flow coat methods are also used but the mechanics of application limit their use to shop work. Of the three designed for field use, brushing is the slowest method, rolling is much faster, and spraying is usually the fastest of all. The choice of method is based on many additional factors such as environment, type of substrate, type of coating to be applied, appearance of finish desired and skill of personnel involved in the operation.

4.6.1.1 Environment. General surroundings may prohibit the use of spray application because of possible fire hazards or potential damage from overspray. Typical of these are parking lots and open storage areas. Adjacent areas, not to be coated, must be masked when spraying is performed. This results in loss of time and, if extensive, may offset the advantage of the rapidity of spraying operations.

4.6.1.2 Type of Surface. Roller coating is most efficient on large flat surfaces. Corners, edges and odd shapes, however, must be brushed. Spraying also is most suitable for large surfaces, except that it can also be used for round or irregular shapes. Brushing is ideal for small surfaces or for cutting in corners and edges. Dip and flow coat methods are suitable for volume production painting of small items in the shop.

4.6.1.3 Type Of Coating. Rapid drying, lacquer type products, e.g., vinyls, should be sprayed. Application of such products by brush or roller may be extremely difficult especially in warm weather or outdoors on breezy days.

4.6.1.4 Appearance Of Finish. Coatings applied by brush may leave brush marks in the dried film; rolling leaves a stippled effect, while spraying yields the smoothest finish, if done properly.

4.6.1.5 Skill Of Painting Personnel. Personnel require the least amount of training to use rollers, and the most training to use spray equipment. The degree of training and experience of personnel will influence the selection of the application method.

4.6.2 Basic Application Procedures. To obtain optimum performance from a coating, there are certain basic application procedures which must be followed, regardless of the type of equipment selected for applying the paint. Cleaned, pretreated surfaces must be first-coated within the specific time limits established. It is essential that surface and ambient temperatures are between 50°F and 90°F for water-thinned coatings, and 45°F to 95°F for other coatings, unless the manufacturer specifies otherwise. The paint material should be maintained at a temperature of 65°F to 85°F at all times. Paint is not to be applied when the temperature is expected to drop to freezing before the paint has dried. Wind velocity should be below 15 miles per hour and relative humidity below 80%. Masonry surfaces that are damp (not wet) may be painted with latex or cementitious paints. Otherwise, the surface must be completely dry before painting. Paints should be applied at recommended spreading rates. When successive coats of the same paint are used, each coat should be tinted differently to aid in determining proper application and to assure complete coverage. Sufficient time must be allowed for each coat to dry thoroughly before topcoating. Allow the final coat to dry for as long as is practical before service is resumed.

6.3 Brush Application.

6.3.1 Equipment. Brushes, as any other tools, must be of first quality and maintained in perfect working condition at all times. Brushes are identified, first, by the type of bristle used. Brushes are made with either natural, synthetic or mixed bristles. Chinese hog bristles represent the finest of the natural bristles because of their length, durability and resiliency. Hog bristle has one unique characteristic in that the bristle end forks out like a tree branch. This "flagging" permits more paint to be carried on the brush and leaves finer brush marks on the applied coating which flow together more readily resulting in a smoother finish. Horsehair bristles are used in cheap brushes and are a very unsatisfactory substitute. The ends do not flag, the bristles quickly become limp, they hold far less paint and do not spread it as well. Brush marks left in the applied coating tend to be coarse and do not level out as smoothly. Some brushes contain a mixture of hog bristle and horsehair, and their quality depends upon the percentage of each type used. Animal hair is utilized in very fine brushes for special purposes. Badger hair, for example, produces a particularly good varnish brush. Squirrel and sable are ideal for striping, lining, lettering and free-hand art brushes. Of the synthetics, nylon is by far the most common. By artificially "exploding" the ends and kinking the fibres, manufacturers have increased the paint load nylon can carry, and have reduced the coarseness of brush marks. Nylon is steadily replacing hog bristle because of the difficulties in importing the latter. Nylon is almost always superior to horsehair. The very fact that nylon is a synthetic makes it unsuitable for applying lacquer, shellac, many creosote products and some other coatings that would soften or dissolve the bristles. Because water does not cause any appreciable swelling of nylon bristles, they are especially recommended for use with latex paints. Brushes are further identified by types, that is, the variety of shapes and sizes as are required for specific painting jobs. Types can be classified as follows: (See Figures 54 and 55.)

a. Wall Brushes: Flat, square-edged brushes ranging in widths from 3" to 6" and used for painting large, continuous surfaces, either interior or exterior.

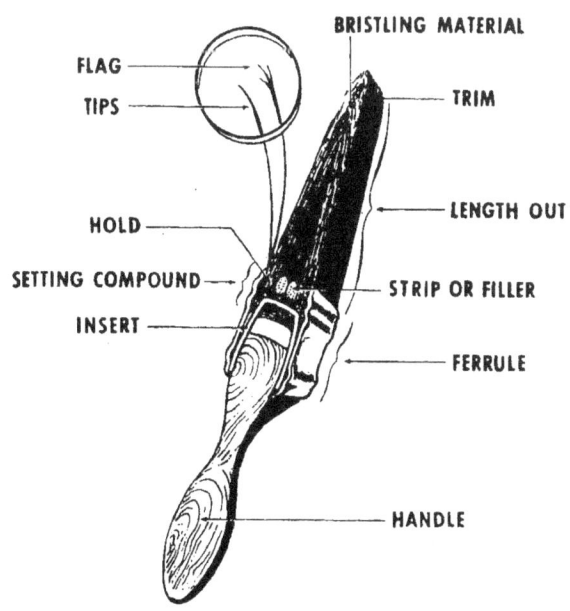

Figure 54. Typical Paint Brush.

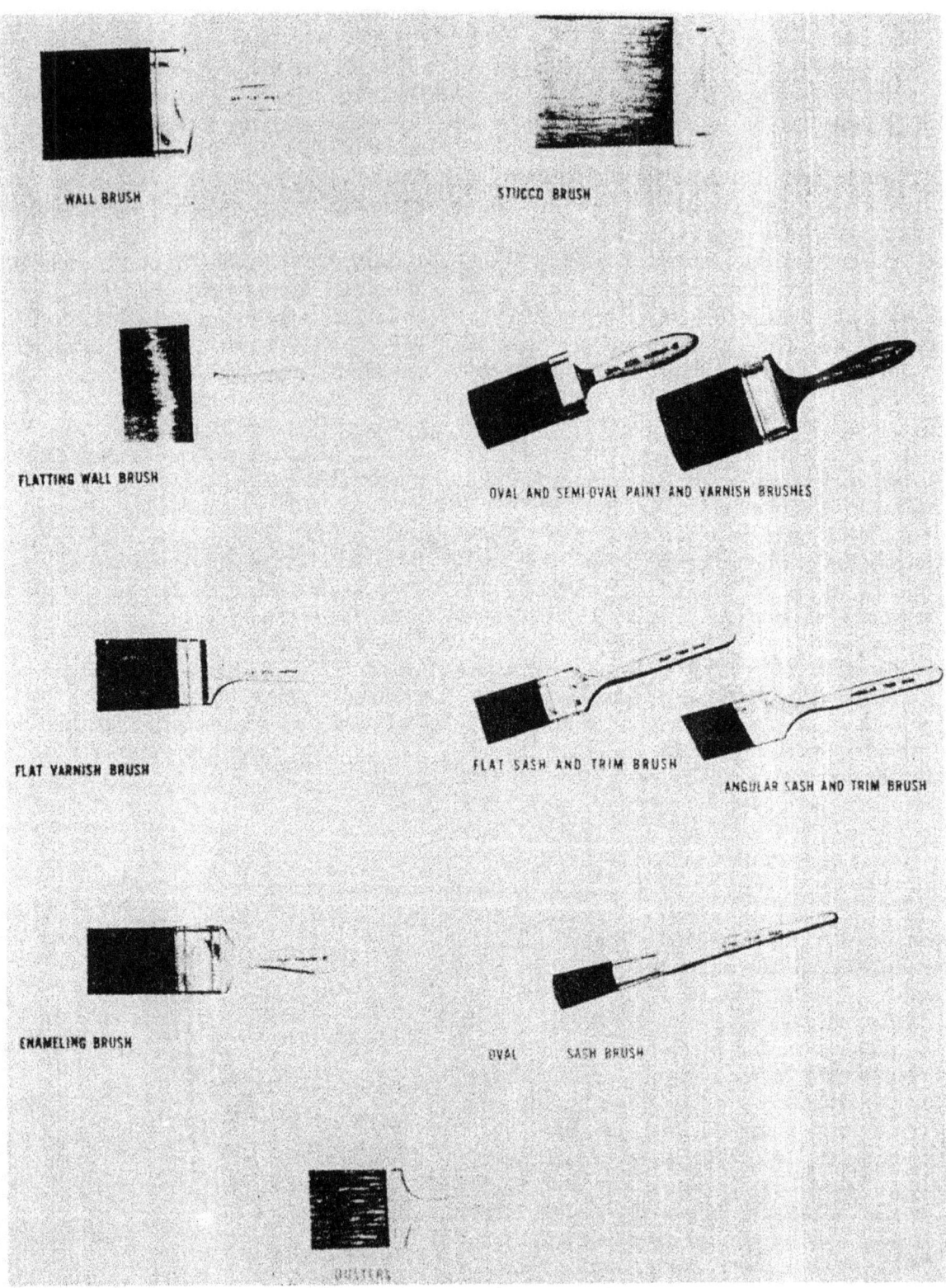

Figure 55. Types of Brushes.

b. *Sash and Trim Brushes:* Available in four shapes, flat square-edged, flat angle-edged, round and oval. These brushes range in width from 1½" to 3" or diameters of ½" to 2" and are used for painting window frames, sash, narrow boards, also interior and exterior trim surfaces. For fine-line painting, the edge of the brush is often chisel-shaped to make precise edging easier to accomplish.

c. *Enameling and Varnish Brushes:* Flat square-edged or chisel-edged brushes available in widths from 2" to 3". The select, fine bristles are comparatively shorter in length to cause relatively high viscosity gloss finishes to lay down in a smooth, even film.

d. *Stucco and Masonry Brushes:* These have the general appearance of flat wall brushes and are available in widths ranging from 5" to 6". Bristles can be of hog, other natural bristle or nylon; the latter is preferred for rough surfaces because of its resistance to abrasion.

Use the right size brush for the job. Avoid a brush that is too small or too large. The latter is particularly important. A large-area job does not necessarily go faster with an over-size brush. If the brush size is out of balance for the type of painting being done, the user tends to apply the coating at an uneven rate, general workmanship declines, and the applicator actually tires faster because of the extra output required per stroke. Synthetic fibre brushes are ready to use when received. The performance of natural bristle brushes is very much improved by a previous 48 hour soak in linseed oil followed by a thorough cleaning in mineral spirits. This process makes the bristles more flexible and serves to swell the bristles in the ferrule of the brush resulting in a better grip so that fewer bristles are apt to work loose when the brush is used.

6.3.2 Application. Dip the brush into the paint up to one-half of the bristle length, then withdraw and tap against the inside of the bucket to remove excess paint. (See Figure 56.) Hold the brush at an angle of 45° to the work. (See Figure 57.) Make several light strokes in the area to be painted; this will transfer much of the paint to the surface. Then spread the paint evenly and uniformly. Do not bear down on the brush. When one section of the surface is painted, adjacent areas should be painted so that the brush strokes are completed by sweeping the brush into the wet edge of the paint previously applied to the first section. This helps to eliminate lap marks and provides a more even coating. Finally, cross-brush lightly to smooth the painted surface and eliminate

Paint brush bristles should not be dipped into the paint more than half the length of the bristles.

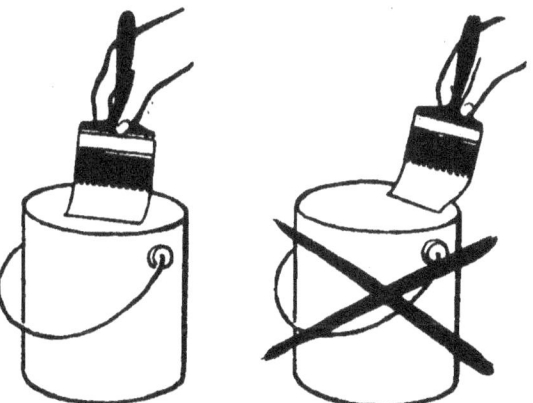

Excess paint should be removed from brush by gently tapping against side of can as shown at left, and NOT by wiping brush across top of can as shown at the right.

Figure 56. Loading a Paint Brush.

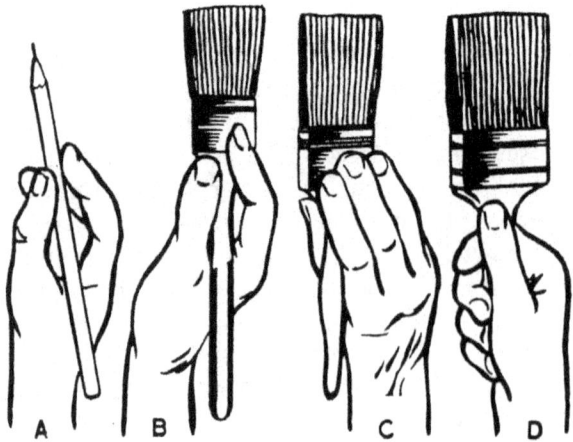

A, B. Grasping brush with pencil grip. C. Grip used for painting walls and floors. D. Simple grip with all fingers around brush handle, suitable for use when painting ceilings.

Figure 57. Holding a Paint Brush.

brush or sag marks. Very fast-drying finishes will not permit much brushing and crosslapping. In such cases the paint should be applied, spread rapidly and then allowed to dry undisturbed. To go back over such paint will only cause a piling up of the coating. Start major work on topmost area first, such as the ceiling of a room, then work downward, painting walls down to the floor. Begin painting at a corner or other logical vertical division. Cover only that area which can be easily reached without moving the ladder. Work downward painting progressive sections to the floor or ground level, then start at the top of the adjacent area and work down again. Paint trim, doors, windows or similar areas after walls and ceilings or other major surfaces are completed. A possible exception would be painting jobs where scaffolding is required. In such instances, paint both the major surface and any trim in the section as the scaffolding is moved along from area to area. When painting clapboards, mouldings or other surfaces with narrow leading or indented edges and other similar areas, paint these first and then paint the surrounding continuous surfaces. Corners and edges are always painted so that the stroke is completed by sweeping off the corner or edge. Avoid poking the brush into corners or crevices. Instead, use the edge of the brush and twist it slightly if necessary to cover rough surfaces.

6.4 Roller Application.

6.4.1 Equipment. A paint roller consists of a cylindrical sleeve or cover which slips on to a rotatable cage to which a handle is attached. (See Figure 58.) The cover may be 1½" to 2¼" inside diameter, and usually 3", 4", 7" and 9" in length. Special rollers are available in lengths from 1½" to 18". Proper roller application depends on the selection of the specific fabric and the thickness of fabric (nap length) based on the type of paint used and the smoothness or roughness of the surface to be painted. Special rollers are used for painting pipes, fences and other hard-to-reach areas. (See Figures 59 and 60.) The fabrics generally used are as follows:

a. Lambs Wool (pelt): This is the most solvent resistant type of material used and is available in nap lengths up to 1¼". It is recommended for synthetic finishes for application on semi-smooth and rough surfaces. It mats badly in water, and is not recommended for water paints.

b. Mohair: This is made primarily of Angora hair. It also is solvent resistant and is supplied in 3/16 and 1/4 inch nap length. It is recommended for synthetic enamels and

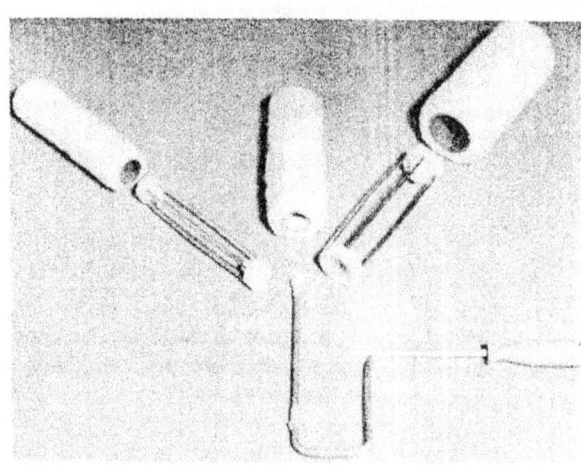

Figure 58. Parts of a Roller.

for use on smooth surfaces. It can be used with water paints also.

c. Dynel: This is a modified acrylic fibre which has excellent resistance to water. It is best for application of conventional water paints and solvent paints, except those which contain strong solvents, such as ketones. It is available in all nap lengths from ¼″ to 1¼″.

d. Dacron: This is a synthetic fibre which is somewhat softer than Dynel. It is best suited for exterior oil or latex paints. It is available in nap lengths from 5/16″ to ½″.

e. Rayon: This fabric is not recommended because of the poor results generally obtained from its use. Furthermore, rayon mats badly in water.

Table No. 8 can be used as a guide for choosing the proper roller cover.

6.4.2 Application. Pour the pre-mixed paint into the tray to about one-half of the depth of the tray. Immerse the roller completely, then roll it back and forth along the ramp to fill the cover completely and remove any excess paint. As an alternative to using the tray, place a specially designed galvanized wire screen into a five gallon can of the paint. This screen attaches to the can and remains at the correct angle for loading and spreading paint on the roller. (See Figures 61, 62.) The first load of paint on a roller should be worked out on newspaper to remove entrapped air from the roller cover. It is then ready for application. As the roller is passed over a surface, thousands of tiny fibres continually compress and expand, metering out the coating and wetting the surface. This is in sharp contrast to other application methods that depend upon the skill

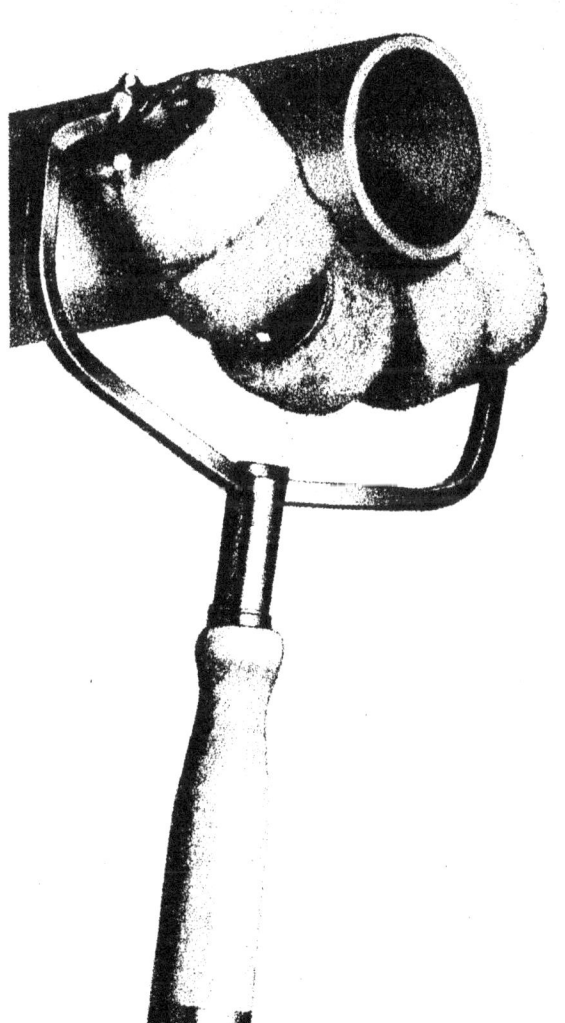

Figure 59. Pipe Roller.

Figure 60. Fence Roller.

Table 8. ROLLER SELECTION GUIDE

Type of Paint	Smooth (1)	Type of Surface Semi-smooth (2)	Rough (3)
Aluminum	C	A	A
Enamel or Semigloss (Alkyd)	A or B	A	
Enamel undercoat	A or B	A	
Epoxy coatings	B or D	D	D
Exterior House Paint:			
Latex for wood	C	A	
Latex for masonry	A	A	A
Oil or alkyd—wood	C	A	
Oil or alkyd—masonry	A	A	A
Floor enamel—all types	A or B	A	
Interior Wall paint:			
Alkyd or oil	A	A or D	A
Latex	A	A	A
Masonry sealer	B	A or D	A or D
Metal primers	A	A or D	
Varnish—all types	A or B		

Roller Cover Key*		Nap Length (inches)	
A—Dynel (modified acrylic)	¼–⅜	⅜–¾	1–1¼
B—Mohair	3/16–¼		
C—Dacron polyester	¼–⅜	½	
D—Lambswool pelt	¼–⅜	½–¾	1–1¼

(1) Smooth Surface: hardboard, smooth metal, smooth plaster, drywall, etc.

(2) Semi-smooth Surface: sand finished plaster and drywall, light stucco, blasted metal, semi-smooth masonry.

(3) Rough Surface: concrete or cinder block, brick, heavy stucco, wire fence.

* Comprehensive product standards do not exist in the Paint Roller Industry. Roller covers vary significantly in performance between manufacturers and most manufacturers have more than one quality level in the same generic class. This table is based on field experience with first line products of one manufacturer.

Figure 61. Roller and Tray.

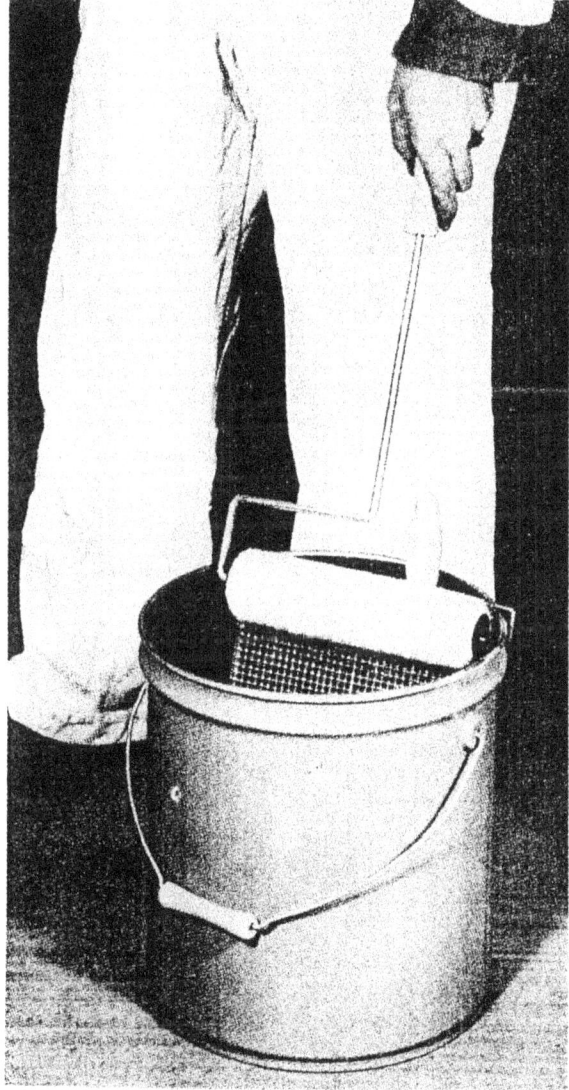

Figure 62. Roller and Wire Screen Attachment to Can.

and technique of the painter. The uniformity of application by roller is less susceptible to variance in painter ability than other methods. Basic rules must still be followed. Always trim around ceilings, mouldings, etc., before rolling the major wall or ceiling surfaces. Then roll as close as possible to maintain the same texture. Trimming is usually done with a 3 inch wall brush. Always roll paint onto the surface, working from the dry area into the just-painted area. Never roll completely in the same or one direction. Don't roll too fast and avoid spinning the roller at the end of the stroke. Always feather out final strokes to pick up any excess paint on the surface. This is accomplished by rolling the final stroke out with minimal pressure.

6.5 Spray Application.

6.5.1 Equipment. Spray equipment is available in four general types. (See Figures 63 and 64.)

a. Conventional Spray: The coating material is placed in a closed container, called a pot. The introduction of pressurized air from a compressor forces the material through a hose to the spray gun. (See Figures 65, 66.) The gun is also connected to a separate air hose. At the gun, the material is atomized by the air supplied through the central openings in the air cap (within the gun). Other air outlets on the outer ridges of the air cap shape the pattern of the material as it leaves the gun for the surface to be coated. This is the cheapest and most common spray technique but it tends to create excessive overspray because of the high ratio of air to paint used. Small jobs are sprayed with guns which can be attached to a quart paint container from which the paint is fed to the gun either by pressure or vacuum. (See Figure 67.)

b. Airless Spray: In this method, coatings are sprayed by the use of hydraulic pressure alone. The equipment is similar to conventional spray except that the compressor operates a hydraulic pump. Atomization of the material is accomplished by forcing the material through a specially shaped orifice at between 1500 and 3000 pounds per square inch. These pressures produce a high-speed stream of coating at the orifice. The high rate of speed plus the release of pressure causes atomization without compressed air; thus there is no air turbulence to deflect the paint (the cause of overspray in the conventional method). The absence of air also reduces rebounding of the paint in crevices and corners, thus providing more uniform coverage. Airless spraying usually permits the use of products with a higher viscosity. Thus less thinners are required and better film build is obtained and production is increased. The need for just a single hose leading into the gun makes it lighter to handle and less fatiguing. The lack of overspray offers still two other advantages; cleanup is usually easier and masking is minimized. Considerable caution must be exercised because of the high pressures required.

c. Hot Spray: The hot spray technique can be adapted to either conventional or airless spray painting, but is most often used with the former. The paint tank and hose are heated to raise the paint temperature to 130°F–180°F. Introducing heat lowers paint viscosity thereby reducing the quantity of

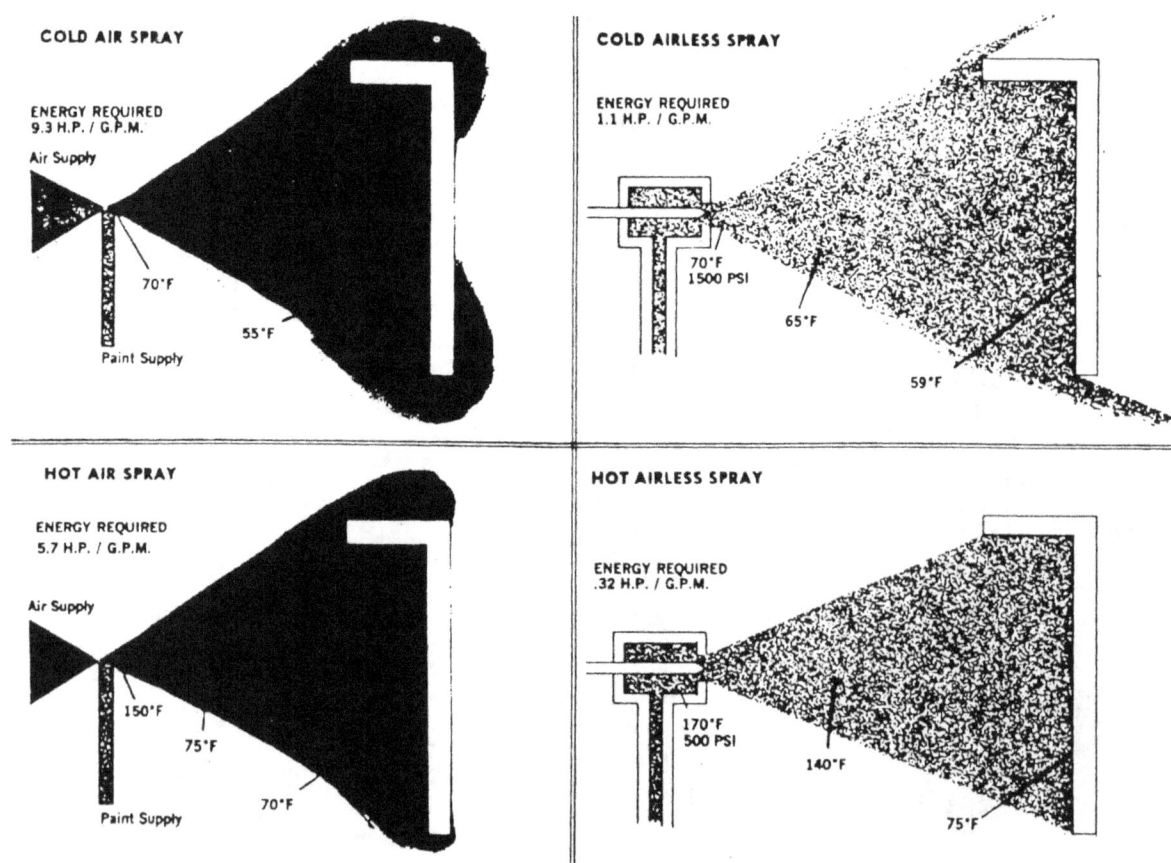

Dark Spots Are Paint Particles.

Figure 63. Basic Types of Spray.

solvent needed. The resultant coating has higher solids and will produce greater film thickness per coat. Heat also allows for use of lower pressure thus reducing overspray and rebounding. Applying the coating hot at the gun allows for more uniform application at low environmental temperatures.

Only materials specially formulated for hot spray application can be used.

6.5.2 Application. Most materials that can be brushed or rolled can be sprayed. Exceptions include very thick or stringy materials, some textured materials and some rubber-base coatings. Control of the spray

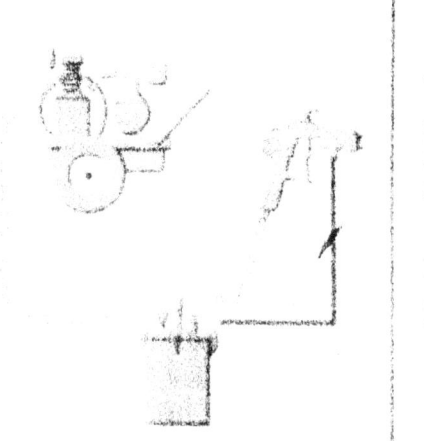
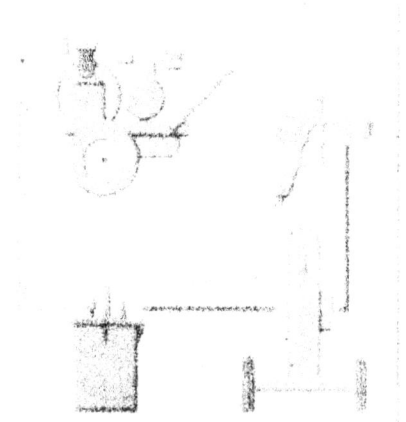

A—Conventional Spray

This is the most commonly used type of spray equipment. It employs compressed air to perform two vital functions: first, to atomize the paint at the nozzle of the gun and second, to feed the paint under pressure from the supply tank, pump or cup to the gun nozzle. This type of system is the most simple and versatile of all spraying outfits. Wide use of this type of system over the past forty years has led to the development and refinement of guns, nozzles, regulating devices and paint supply units for practically every conceivable type of coating material and painting problem. As a result, heavy mastics, highly abrasive coatings and water thin liquids can now be sprayed by this method with equal ease. Conventional spray also provides more selectivity of spray pattern size, degree of atomization and wetness of the coat than other methods and therefore is the most practical solution where these factors are important to the results of the job.

B—Hot Spray

This method is primarily a modified form of conventional spray. It is comprised of the same elements of equipment even to the cap and tip of the gun, however, the difference lies in the addition of a heating unit which offers several benefits under certain operational conditions. With most organic paints which become more fluid at elevated temperatures (100° to 180°), the hot spray system is capable of applying higher solid content paints. This in turn produces heavier coats and reduces shrinkage during drying. With heated paint better atomization is accomplished with lower air pressure and at the same time overspray is greatly reduced. This method also permits painting when atmospheric temperatures are well below the usual 60° to 70° minimum. Better flowout is attained and pinholing common to certain paints is effectively overcome by hot spray.

C—Airless Spray

In an airless system the spray is created by the forcing of paint through a restricted orifice at very high pressure. Atomization of the paint occurs without the use of air jets, thus the name airless spray. Liquid pressures of 1500 p.s.i. and higher are developed in special air or electric operated high pressure pumps and delivered to the gun through a single hose line.

This system provides a very rapid means of covering large surfaces with wide angle spray without over-spray mist or rebound. The single small diameter hose line makes gun handling easy. The spray produced has a full wet pattern for quick film build, but requires extra care in lapping and stroking to avoid excessive coverage that would result in runs, sags and wrinkles.

Figure 64. Types of Spray Equipment.

operation requires control over the following variables:

a. Viscosity Of The Paint: It must be low enough to permit proper atomization but high enough to apply without running or sagging. Generally, a trial and error approach is required.

b. Pot Pressures: This determines the *amount* of material forced through the nozzle. It is controlled at the air regulator or at the gun.

c. Atomizing Pressures: This is the air pressure supplied to the gun to atomize the material and produce a uniform wet film. Too much pressure here will cause excessive overspray or a dry spray. Too little pressure produces a speckled or dimpled effect.

d. Air Cap On Spray Gun: This controls the amount and distribution of air mixed with the coating at the gun. The amount of air and air pressure controls atomization while the distribution of the air determines the shape of the spray pattern.

e. Material Orifice (nozzle): The size of this opening controls the amount of material that can be passed through the gun.

f. Air and Material Controls On Gun: These are for rough adjustment of amount delivered. (See Figures 66, 67.)

Adjust paint viscosity only when necessary and then according to manufacturer's instructions. Excessive thinning results in needless overspray, excessive runs and sags, poor hiding and inferior surface protection.

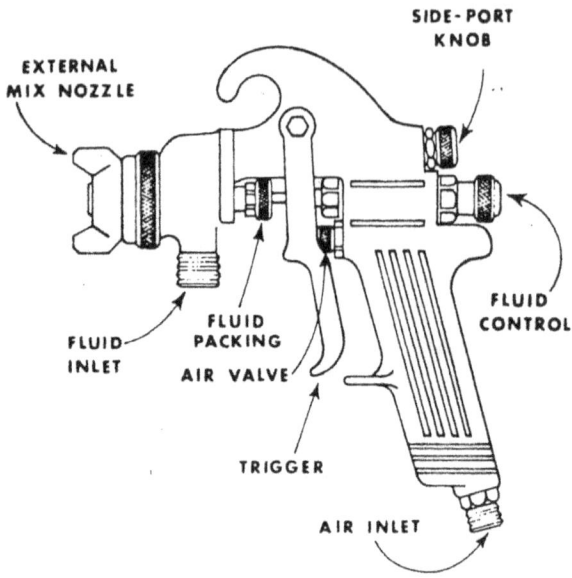

Figure 65. Modern Production Spray Gun.

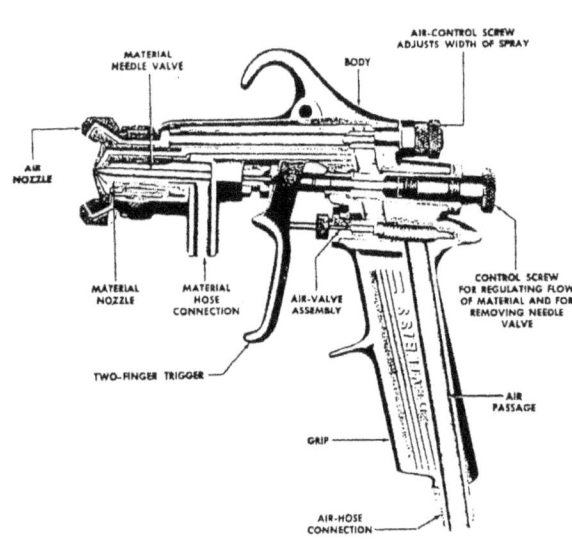

Figure 66. Spray Gun — Cross-Section.

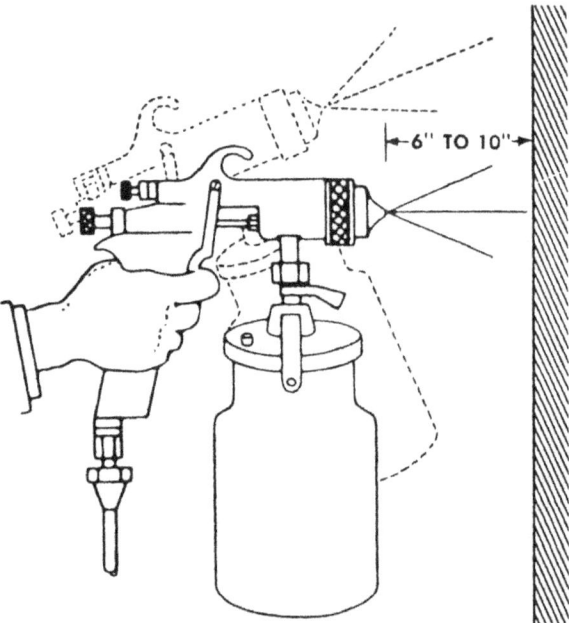

Figure 67. Spray Gun Held Perpendicular to Surface to Prevent Uneven Deposit of Paint.

During application, use the lowest material and air pressures that result in a quality finish with good flow out. Material pressure is best adjusted starting at the point where a solid stream of paint will flow out about 24" from the gun with the atomization air turned off. When the material is heavy or viscous, when the fluid hose is extra long, or when a more rapid rate of application is required, it will be necessary to increase the material hose pressure. In this case, it will be necessary to also increase the air pressure since it is important to maintain a proper ratio of material pressure to atomizing air pressure. At a temperature of 70°F. with a material hose length of 25 feet, the following air pressures are suggested for initial settings:

(Pounds)

Lacquers 40–45
Enamels 35
Alkyd Flats 25–30

There is no set rule for spray gun pressures because they will vary with the nozzle used, the paint used and surface to be coated. Use the minimum pressure necessary to reduce overspray. Adjusting the spray pattern requires that the spray width adjustment screw be turned clockwise for a round pattern and counter-clockwise for a fan pattern. Turn the material control screw clockwise to increase the flow. As the width of the pattern is increased, increase the flow of the paint to maintain the same coverage over the wider area. Keep the spray gun 6" to 10" from the surface being coated. Holding the gun too far away causes "dusting", in which the paint solvent evaporates in mid-air and the coating hits the surface in a nearly dry state. Tilting the gun causes the paint to be more heavily applied in one area than another of the spray pattern. Use a free-arm motion and feather out at the end of the stroke by pulling the gun trigger after beginning the stroke and releasing it before the stroke is completed. When spraying corners, stop 1" or 2" short of the corner. Then hold the gun so as to sweep up and down along the edge of the corner and hit both sides at the same time. (See Figures 67 thru 73.)

6.5.3 Problems. Problems which may occur during spraying and their solutions are shown in Figure 74.

6.6 Paint Mitt Application. The paint mitt is a mitten made of lambskin with the wool exposed and lined to prevent paint leaking through to the user's hand. It is excellent for painting small pipes, railings, wrought iron and similar surfaces. (See Figures 75 and 76.)

6.7 Cleanup. It is absolutely essential that all the tools and equipment be cleaned thoroughly immediately after use before the paint materials have a chance to get hard. Remove as much paint as possible, then clean thoroughly with a compatible solvent. Clean two or three times in fresh solvent until no paint is noticeable. Then wipe clean and dry. With good care, all tools and equipment will last much longer and will always be in prime condition for use. After cleaning, wash all brushes with mild detergent and warm water; rinse in clear water, then twirl to get rid of excess water, comb bristles straight with a metal comb, and place in brush-keepers or wrap in paper and allow to dry flat. (See Figures 77 through 80.) Also wash cleaned rollers in mild detergent and water. Rinse in clear water and twirl to get rid of excess. (Spinners are available which hold the brush or roller cover.) Then stand on end to dry. When dry, cover to keep clean. Spray equipment should be cleaned thoroughly by placing clean solvent in pots and passing it through hoses and guns. When

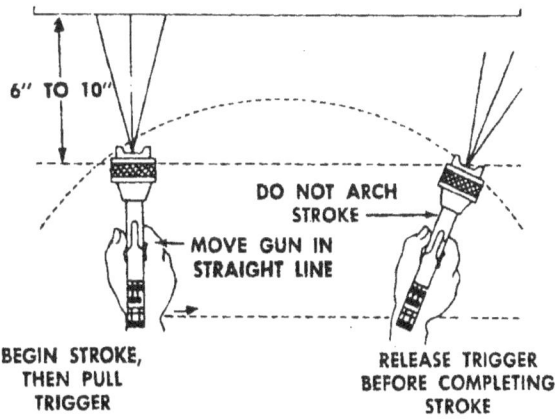

Figure 68. Proper Spray-Gun Stroke.

clean, empty, wipe clean and dry. Clean pots separately. Use extreme care when cleaning airless spray guns inasmuch as the high pressures used are hazardous, especially when the spray head is removed. (See Figure 74.)

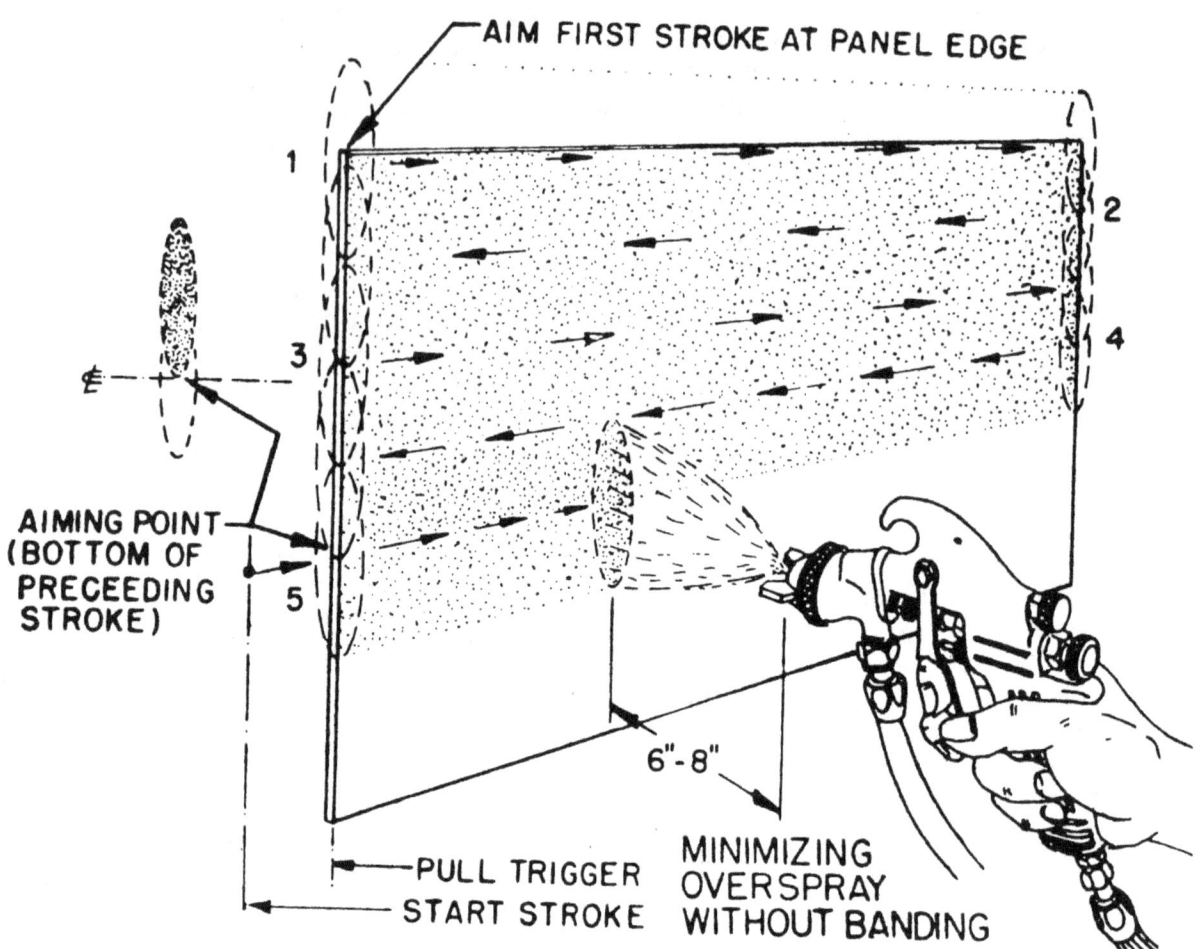

Figure 69. Spraying Large Flat Areas.

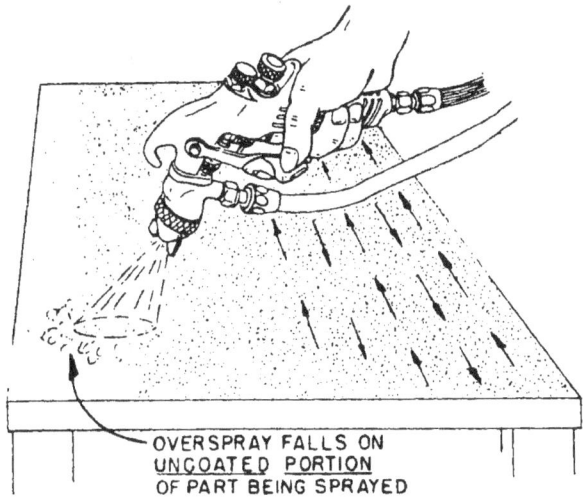

Figure 70. Spraying Horizontal Surfaces.

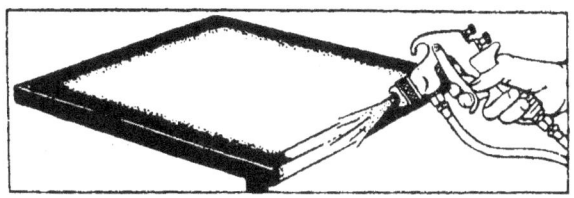

Figure 72. Spraying Edges and Corners.

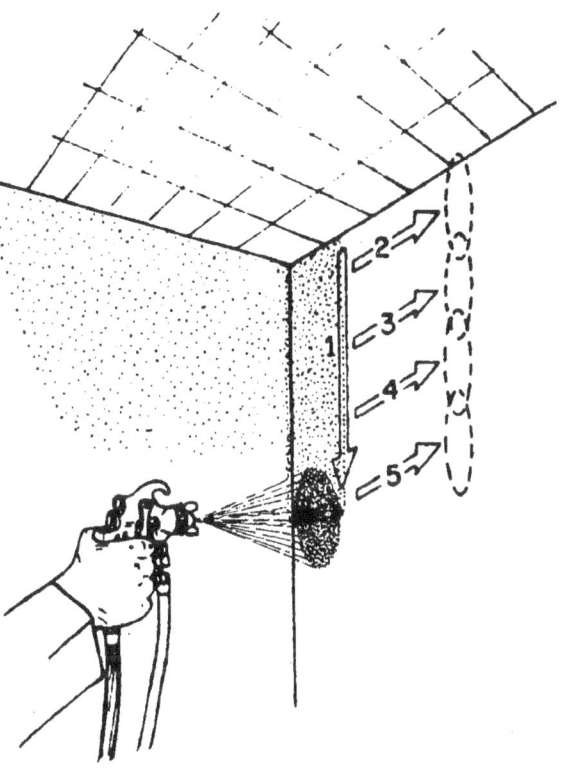

Figure 73. Painting Interior Corners.

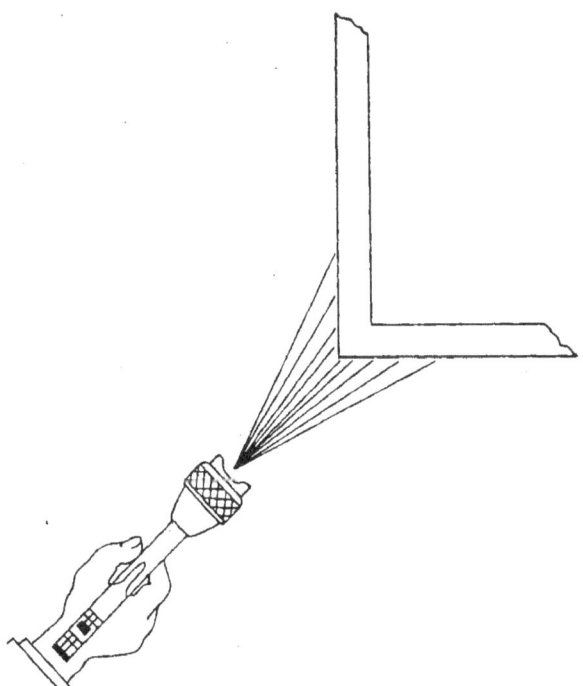

Figure 71. Spraying Corners.

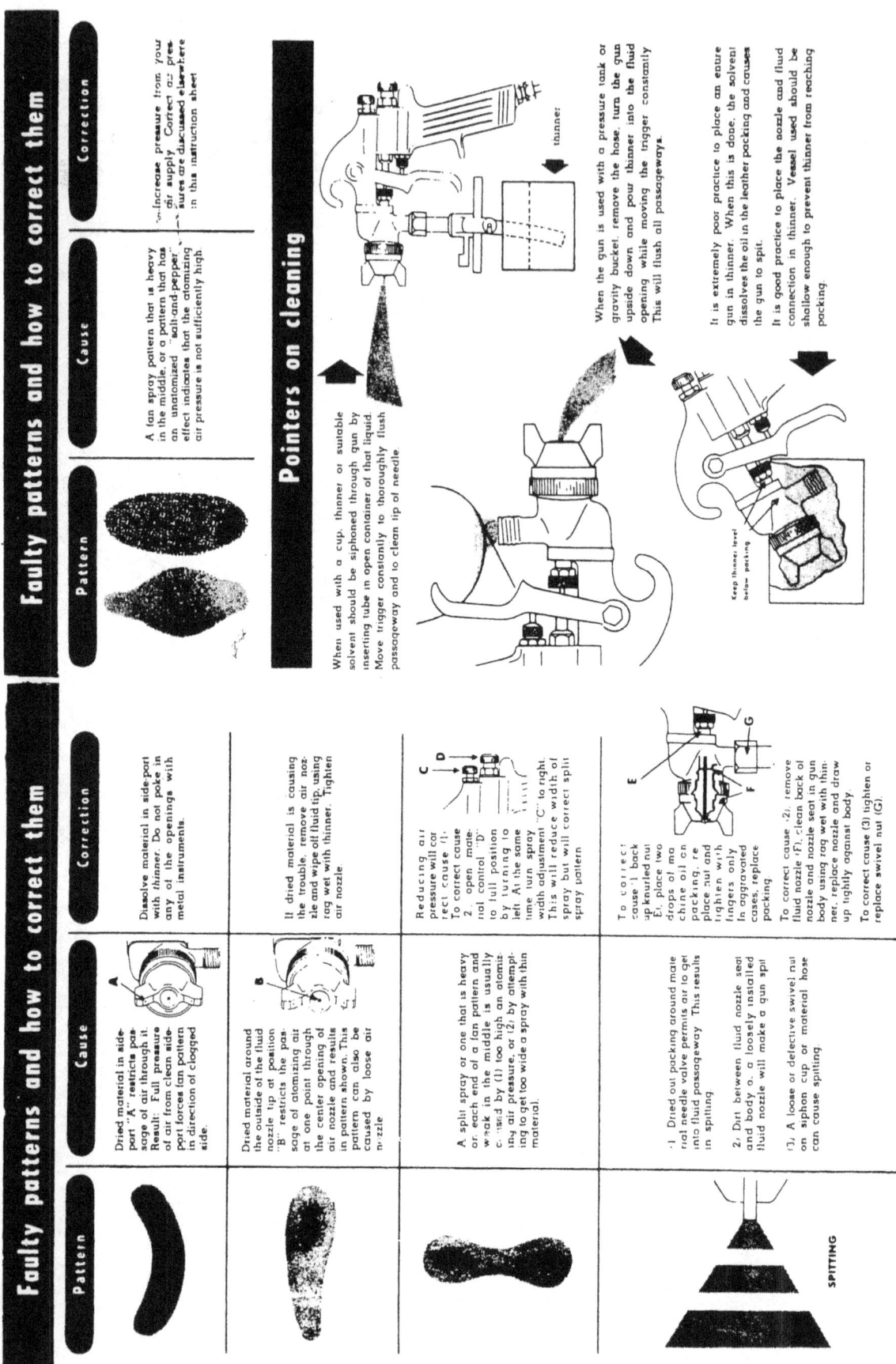

Figure 74. Spray Gun Adjustments and Cleaning.

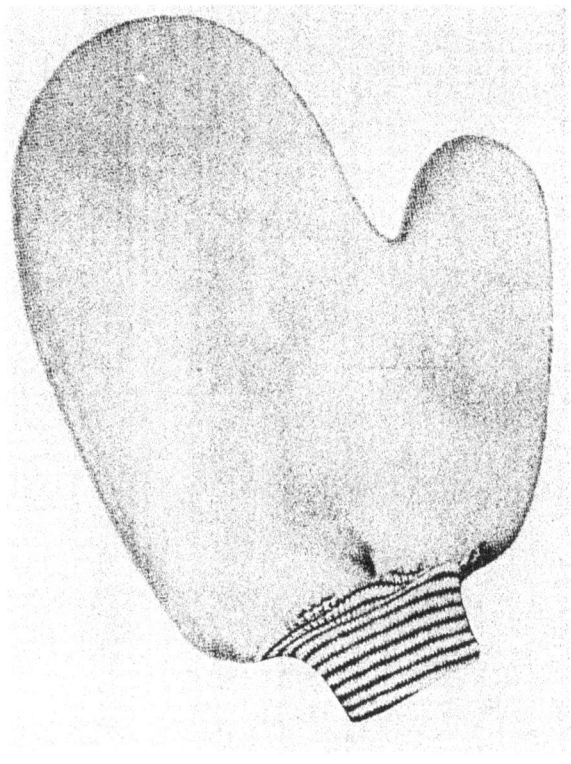

Figure 75. Paint Mitt.

Figure 76. Paint Mitt in Use.

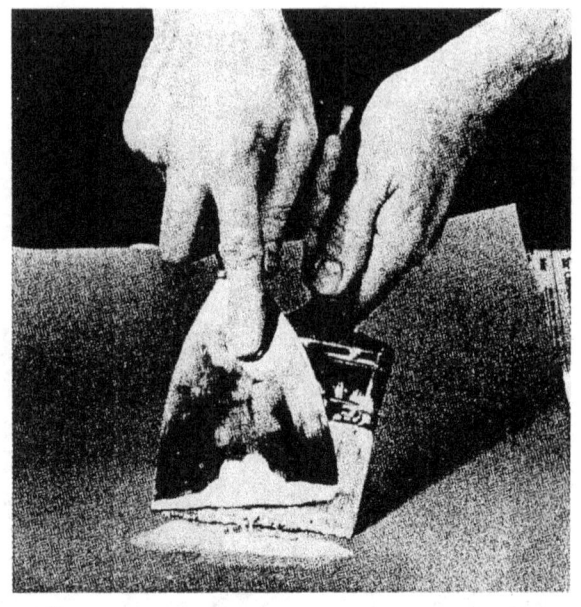

Figure 77.   Remove Excess Paint.

Figure 79.   Twirl Brush After Cleaning.

Figure 78.   Clean Brush Until No Paint Is Noticeable.

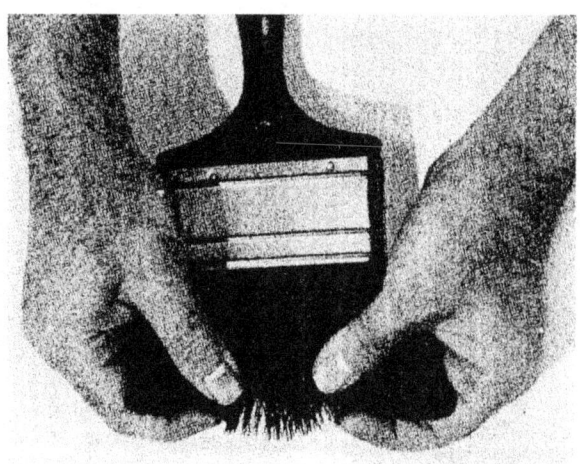

Figure 80.   Brush Should Be Completely Free of Paint.

GLOSSARY OF PAINTING TERMS

TABLE OF CONTENTS

	Page
Abrasive ... Bituminous Coating	A-1
Blast Angle ... Drier	A-2
Drift (Overspray) ... Furane Resins	A-3
Galvanized Steel ... Mandrel Test	A-4
Masking ... Polymerization	A-5
Polyvinyl Acetate (PVAc) ... Solvency	A-6
Solvent ... Vinyl Resins	A-7
Viscosity ... Zinc Yellow	A-8

GLOSSARY OF PAINTING TERMS

Painting operations employ terms that are peculiar to this field and, as such, may require some explanation or definition. This glossary is designed to provide the reader with some basic understanding of terms commonly used in painting and thus eliminate possible misunderstandings resulting from conflicting interpretations of terms and improve communication between all persons involved in the painting operation.

A

abrasive—the agent used for abrasive blast cleaning; for example, sand, grit, steel shot, etc.
absorption—process of soaking up, or assimilation of one substance by another.
accelerator—catalyst; a material which accelerates the hardening of certain coatings.
acetone—a fast evaporating, highly flammable solvent.
acoustic paint—paint which absorbs or deadens sound.
acrylic resin—a clear resin derived from polymerized esters of acrylic acid and methacrylic acid.
activator—catalyst or curing agent; accelerator.
adhesion—bonding strength, the attraction of a coating to the surface to which it is applied.
absorption—process of attraction to a surface; attachment; the retention of foreign molecules on the surface of a substance.
adulteration—the addition of unwanted materials.
agglomeration—formation of masses or aggregates of pigments; not dispersed.
air adjusting valve—spray gun valve controlling input air.
air bubble—bubble in paint film caused by entrapped air.
air cap (or air nozzle)—perforated housing for atomizing air at head of spray gun.
air drying—drying by oxidation or evaporation by simple exposure to air.
air entrapment—inclusion of air bubbles in paint film.
air hose—hose of air supply quality, usually red.
air jet (blast cleaning)—type of blast cleaning gun in which the abrasive is conveyed to the gun by partial vacuum.
airless spraying—spraying using hydraulic pressure to atomize the paint.
air manifold—common air supply chamber for several lines.
air transformer—device for controlled reduction in air pressure.
air valve—control valve in air line system.
air volume—quantity of air in cubic feet (usually per minute) at atmospheric pressure.
alcohol—a flammable solvent; alcohols commonly used in painting are ethyl alcohol (ethanol) and methyl alcohol (methanol, wood alcohol).
aliphatic hydrocarbons—flammable solvents of low solvent power, usually derived from petroleum.
alkali—caustic, such as sodium hydroxide, lye, etc.
alkyd resins—resins prepared from polyhydric alcohols and polybasic acids.
alligatoring—surface imperfections of paint having the appearance of alligator hide.
ambient temperature—room temperature or temperature of surroundings.
American gallon—231 cubic inches.
amides—curing agent combined with epoxy resins.
amines—curing agent combined with epoxy resins.
anchor pattern—profile of a surface, usually attained by blasting.
angle blasting—blast cleaning at angles less than 90 degrees.
angle of degree (airless spray cap)—orifice angle; controls width of spray, pattern angle.
anhydrous—dry, free of water in any form.
applicator—one who applies; tool for applying.
arcing—swinging spray gun away from the work.
aromatic hydrocarbons—strong solvents such as benzene, toluene, xylene.
asphalt—residue from petroleum refining; also a natural complex hydrocarbon.
atomize—break stream into small particles.

B

baking finish—product requiring heat cure.
banding—identifying with strips of tape.
barrier coating—shielding or blocking coating or film.
binder—resin; drying oil; latex emulsion; film former; vehicle.
bituminous coating—coal tar or asphalt based coating.

blast angle—angle of nozzle with reference to surface; also angle of particle propelled from rotating blast cleaning wheel with reference to surface.
blast cleaning—cleaning with propelled abrasives.
bleaching—removing color.
bleeder gun—a spray gun with no air valve; trigger controls fluid flow only.
bleeding—penetration of color from the underlying surface.
blisters—bubbles in dry or partially-dry paint film.
blooming—whitening; moisture blush; blushing.
blow-back (spray term)—rebound of atomized sprayed material.
blushing—whitening and loss of gloss due to moisture or improper solvent balance.
body—viscosity; middle or under coat; to thicken.
boilers (solvent)—solvents of particular evaporation rate.
bonding—adhesion
bounce-back—spray rebound similar to blow-back.
boxing—mixing by pouring back and forth from one container to another.
bridging—forming a skin over a depression.
bright blast—white blast; See 4.4.2.4.
brittleness—degree of resistance to cracking, breaking or bending.
broadcast—to sprinkle solid particles on a surface.
bronze tools—non-sparking tools; used when fire hazards are particularly acute.
bronzing—formation of metallic sheen on a paint film.
brushability—ability to be brushed.
brush-off blast—lowest blast cleaning standard; see 4.4.2.4.
bubbling—a term used to describe the appearance of blisters on the surface while a coating is being applied.

C

caking—hard settling of pigment from paint.
camouflage—the art or system for deception or concealment.
catalyst—accelerator; curing agent; promoter.
cat-eye—hole or holiday shaped like a cat's eye; cratering.
chalking—powdering of surface.
checking—formation of slight breaks in the film that do not penetrate to the underlying surface.
chipping—(1) cleaning steel using special hammers.
—(2) type of paint failure.
chlorinated rubber—a particular film former used as a binder, made by chlorinating natural rubber.
cleaner—(1) detergent, alkali, acid or other cleaning material; usually water or steam borne.
(2) solvent for cleaning paint equipment.
coal tar pitch—black residue remaining after coal tar is distilled.
coal tar-epoxy paint—paint in which binder or vehicle is a combination of coal tar with epoxy resin.
coatings—surface coverings; paints; barriers.
coat of paint—layer of dry paint resulting from a single wet application.

cobwebbing—a spider web effect caused by premature drying.
cohesion—property of holding self together.
cold-checking—checking caused by low temperatures.
cold-cracking—cracking occuring at low temperatures.
color-fast—non-fading.
color retention—ability to retain original color.
commercial blast—see 4.4.2.4.
compatibility—ability to mix with or adhere properly to other components or substances.
composition—analysis; make-up.
conditioner—see surface conditioner.
continuity—degree of being intact or pore free.
copolymer—large molecule resulting from simultaneous polymerization of different monomers.
copper sulfate test (for mill scale)—copper color indicates absence of mill scale when steel is swabbed with 5 to 10 per cent solution.
corrosion—oxidation; deterioration due to interaction with environment.
cracking—splitting, disintegration of paint by breaks through film to substrate.
cratering—formation of holes or deep depressions in paint film.
crawling—shrinking of paint to form uneven surface shortly after application.
crazing—development of non-uniform surface appearance of myriad tiny scales or cracks.
creepage—see crawling.
cross-linking—a particular method by which chemicals unite to form films.
cross-spray—spraying first in one direction and then at right angles.
curing—setting up; hardening.
curing agent—hardener; promoter.
curtaining—sagging.
curtains—sags having appearance of drapes.
cycling (of pump)—interval between strokes.

D

deadman valve—shut-off valve at blast nozzle, operated by remote control.
decorative painting—painting for appearance.
degreaser—chemical solution (compound) for grease removal.
delamination—separation of layers of paint films.
density—weight per unit volume.
detergent—cleaning agent.
dew point—temperature at which moisture condenses.
diluents—see thinners.
discoloration—color change.
dispersion—suspension of one substance in another.
distensibility—ability to be stretched.
distillation—purification or separation by volatilizing and condensing.
doctor blade—knife applicator of fixed film thickness.
double regulation—regulation of both pot and gun air pressure.
drier—chemical which promotes oxidation or drying of paint.

A-3

drift (overspray)—spray loss.
drop (scaffold)—one vertical descent of the scaffold.
drop cloth—protective cover.
dry film thickness—depth of applied coating when dry, expressed in mils (1/1000 in.).
dry spray—overspray or bounce back; sand finish due to spray particle being partially dried before reaching the surface.
drying oil—an oil which hardens in air.
drying time—time interval between application and a specified condition of dryness.
dry to handle—time interval between application and ability to be picked up without damage.
dry to recoat—time interval between application and ability to receive next coat satisfactorily.
dry to touch—time interval between application and ability to be touched lightly (tack-free time).
dulling—loss of gloss or sheen.

E

edging—striping.
efflorescence—deposit of soluble white salts on surface of brick and other masonry.
eggshell—between semi-gloss and flat.
elasticity—degree of recovery from stretching.
electrostatice spray—spraying in which electric charge attracts paint to surface.
emulsion paint—water-thinned paint with an emulsified oil and/or resin or latex vehicle.
enamel—a paint which is characterized by an ability to form an especially smooth film.
epoxy resins—film formers usually made from bisphenol A and epichlorohydrin.
epoxy amine—amine cured epoxy resin.
epoxy ester—epoxy modified oil; single package epoxy.
erosion—wearing away of paint films to expose the substrate or undercoat.
estimate—compute; calculated cost of a job.
etch—surface preparation of metal by chemical means.
evaporation rate—rate at which a solvent evaporates.
evaporation rate, final—time interval for complete evaporation of all solvents.
evaporation rate, initial—time interval during which low boiling solvent evaporates completely.
explosive limits—a range of the ratio of solvent vapor to air in which the mixture will explode if ignited. Below the lower or above the higher exposive limit, the mixture is too lean or too rich to explode. The critical ratio runs from about one to twelve per cent of solvent vapor by volume at atomospheric pressure.
extender—pigment which can contribute specific properties to paint, generally low in cost.
extension gun—pole gun.
external mix—spray equipment in which fluid and air join outside of aircap.

F

fading—reduction in brightness of color.
fallout (spray)—overspray
fanning (spray gun technique)—arcing; moving the spray gun away from the work.
fan pattern—geometry or shape of spray pattern.
feather edge—tapered edge.
feathering—(1) triggering a gun at the end of each stroke; (2) tapering edge.
Federal specifications—Government specifications for products, components and/or performance.
ferrous—iron containing.
field painting—painting at the job site.
filler—extender; bulking agent; inert pigment.
film build—dry thickness characteristics per coat.
film-former—a substance which forms a skin or membrane when dried from a liquid state.
film integrity—degree of continuity of film.
film thickness—depth of applied coating, expressed in mils (1/1000 in.).
film thickness gauge—device for measuring film thickness; both wet and dry gauges are available.
filter—strainer; purifier.
fineness of grind—measure of particle size or roughness of liquid paint; degree of dispersion of pigment in the binder.
fingers (airless spray)—broken airless spray pattern.
fire-retardant paint—a paint which will delay flaming or over-heating of substrate.
fish eye—see cratering.
flaking—disintegration in small pieces or flakes; see scaling.
flammability—measure of ease of catching fire; ability to burn.
flame cleaning—method of surface preparation of steel using flame.
flash point—the lowest temperature at which a given flammable material will flash if a flame or spark is present.
flatting—loss of gloss in coating film.
flexibility—ability to be bent without damage.
floating—separation of pigment colors on surface.
flooding—see floating.
flow—a measure of self leveling.
fluid adjusting screw—a screw on a spray gun which controls the amount of fluid entering the gun.
fluid flow—a measure of flow through a gun with atomizing air shut off.
fluid hose—specially designed hose for paint materials; usually black.
fluid nozzle—fluid tip with orifice; in a broader sense it means needle and tip combination.
fluid tip—orifice in gun into which needle is seated.
foaming—frothing.
fogging—misting.
forced drying—acceleration of drying by increasing the temperature above ambient temperature using an oven, infra red lamp or other heat source.
fungicide—a substance poisonous to fungi; retards or prevents fungi growth.
furane resins—dark chemical resistant resins made from furfuryl alcohol, furfural, and phenol.

G

galvanized steel—steel plated in a molten bath of zinc.

gas checking—fine checking; wrinkling, frosting under certain drying conditions; said to be caused by rapid oxygen absorption or by impurities in the air.

gel—a jelly-like substance.

gelling (gelation)—conversion of a liquid to a gel state.

glazing (puttying)—setting glass.

gloss—shininess; lustre; ability to reflect in mirror direction.

gloss retention—ability to retain original gloss.

grain—surface appearance, usually of wood.

gray blast cleaning—commercial blast. See 4.4.2.4.

grind gauge—instrument for measuring degree of pigment dispersion in liquid paint. Hegman is a common proprietary instrument.

grit—an abrasive obtained from slag and various other materials.

ground wire—a wire attached to dissipate electrostatic charge in airless spraying.

guide coat—a coat similar in composition to the finish or color coat, but of a different color to help obtain complete coverage.

gun distance—space between tip of gun and work.

H

hardener—curing agent; promoter; catalyst.

hardness—the degree to which a material will withstand pressure without deformation or scratching.

hazing—clouding.

heavy centered pattern—spray pattern having most paint in center, less at edges.

hiding power—ability to obscure underlying surface.

★**high boiling solvent**—solvent with a high boiling point such as diacetone alcohol or cellosolve acetate.

high build—producing thick dry films per coat.

high flash naphtha—aromatic solvent having a high flash point, (min. 113°F, 45°C).

hold out—ability (or property) to prevent soaking into substrate.

holiday—pinhole; skip; discontinuity; void.

holiday detector—device for detection of pinholes or holidays. See spark testing.

hot spray—spraying material heated to reduce viscosity.

humidity—measure of moisture content; relative humidity is the ratio of the quantity of water vapor in the air compared to the greatest amount possible at the given temperature. Saturated air is said to have a humidity of 100 per cent.

hydraulic spraying—spraying by hydraulic pressure. (See airless spraying.)

I

incompatibility—inability to mix with or adhere to another material.

indictor (pH) paper—a vegetable dyed paper indicating relative acidity or basicity (alkalinity).

inert pigment—a non-reactive pigment.

inflammability—measure of ease of catching fire; ability to burn; use of the word flammability is preferred to inflammability due to the possibile misinterpretation of the prefix "in" as a negative.

inhibitive pigment—one which retards the corrosion process.

inorganic coatings—those employing inorganic binders or vehicles.

intermediate coat—middle coat; guide coat.

internal mix—a spray gun in which the fluid and air are combined before they leave the gun.

intumesce—to form a voluminous char on ignition; foaming or swelling when exposed to flame.

iron phosphate coating—conversion coating; chemical deposit.

isocyanate resins—urethane resins.

K

KB (Kauri-Butanol) Value—measure of solvent power.

ketones—flammable organic solvents; commonly used ketones are acetone; methyl ethyl ketone (MEK); and methyl isobutyl ketone (MIBK).

Krebs Units (K.U.)—arbitrary units of viscosity.

L

lacquers—coatings which dry by evaporation of the solvent.

laitance—milky white deposit on new concrete.

laminar scale—rust formation in heavy layers.

latex—rubber like; a common binder for emulsion (water) paints; there are natural and synthetic latexes.

leafing—orientation of pigment flakes in horizontal planes.

leveling—flowing out to films of uniform thickness; tendency of brush marks to disappear.

lifting—softening and raising of an undercoat by application of a top coat.

livering—formation of curds or gelling.

long oil varnish—varnish with a high ratio of oil to resin; a resin having a large quantity of oil cooked per 100 pounds of resin (25 gallons or more per 100 pounds of resin).

★**low boiling solvent**—solvent with a low boiling point such as acetone or methyl alcohol.

low pressure spraying—conventional air spraying.

M

MAC (maximum allowable concentration)—maximum concentration of solvent vapor in parts per million parts of air in which a worker may work eight consecutive hours without an air fed mask; the lower the MAC number, the more toxic the solvent.

maintenance painting—(1) repair painting; any painting after the initial paint job; in a broader sense it includes painting of items installed during maintenance; (2) all painting except that done solely for aesthetics.

mandrel test—a physical bending test for adhesion and flexibility.

masking—covering areas not to be painted.
mastic—a heavy bodied high build coating.
(MEK) methyl ethyl ketone—a strong flammable organic solvent.
(MIBK) methyl isobutyl ketone—a strong flammable organic solvent.
mil—one one-thousandth of an inch; .001"; 1/1000 in.
mildew—fungus, mold.
mildewcide—substance poisonous to mildew; prevents or retards growth of mildew.
mild steel—structural steel; SAE 1020.
mill scale—oxide layer formed on steel by hot rolling.
mineral spirits—aliphatic hydrocarbon solvent.
miscible—capable of mixing or blending uniformly.
misses—holidays; skips; voids.
mist-coat—thin tack coat; thin adhesive coat.
moisture and oil separator—trap on air compressor or in air lines.
mottling—speckling; a nonuniform paint color.
mud-cracking—irregular cracking of dried film, as in a dried mud puddle.
multicolor finishes—speckled finishes; paints containing flecks of colors different from the base color.
MVT (moisture vapor transmission)—moisture vapor transmission rate through a known membrane.

N

naphtha—flamable aliphatic hydrocarbon solvent.
near-white blast cleaning—see 4.4.2.4.
needle (spray gun)—fluid metering pin.
neoprene—a rubber-like film former based on the polymerization of chloroprene.
non-drying oil—one which will not oxidize in air.
non-ferrous—containing no iron.
non-flammable—incombustible, will not burn.
non-toxic—not poisonous.
non-volatile—solid; non-evaporating; the portion of a paint left after the solvent evaporates.

O

oil color—coloring (pigment or dye) dispersed in oil.
oil length—gallons of oil reacted with 100 pounds of resin.
oleoresinous—film former containing oil and resin.
opacity—hiding power.
orange peel—dimpled appearance of dry film; resembling an orange peel.
organic—containing carbon compounds.
organosol—film former containing resin plasticizer and solvent.
orifice—opening; hole.
overatomized—dispersed too finely by use of excessive atomizing air pressure.
overcoat—second coat; top coat.
overlap—portion (width) of fresh paint covered by next layer.
overspray—sprayed paint which did not hit target; waste.

P

PVAc—see polyvinyl acetate.
PVC—see polyvinyl chloride or pigment volume concentration.
paint—all coating materials used in painting.
paint failure—the loss of usefulness of the paint coating.
paint heater—device for lowering viscosity of paint by heating.
paint program—comprehensive painting plan.
paint project—single paint job.
paint system—the complete number and type of coats comprising a paint job. In a broader sense, surface preparation, pre-treatments, dry film thickness, and manner of application are included in the definition of a paint system.
painting—all operations required to use paints properly.
painting materials—all materials required to adequately paint a surface.
pass (spray)—motion of the spray gun in one direction only.
passive defense—blending of colors to make structures less conspicuous.
pattern length—length of spray pattern.
pattern width—width of a spray pattern at vertical center.
peeling—failure in which paint curls or otherwise strips from substrate.
perm—unit of permeance; grains of water vapor per hour per square foot per inch of mercury—water vapor pressure difference.
phenolic resins—particular group of film formers; resins made from phenols and aldehydes.
phosphatize—form a thin inert phosphate coating on surface usually by treatment with phosphoric acid or other phosphate compound.
phthalic resins—a particular group of film formers; alkyd resins.
pH value—measure of acidity or alkalinity; pH 7 is neutral; the pH values of acids are less than 7, and of alkalis (bases) greater than 7.
pickling—a dipping process for cleaning steel and other metals; the pickling agent is usually an acid.
pigment grind—dispersion of pigment in a liquid vehicle.
pigments—solid coloring agents.
pigment volume concentration (PVC)—percent by volume occupied by pigment in dry film.
pitting—formation of small, usually shallow depressions or cavities.
pin-holing—formation of small holes through the entire thickness of coating; see cratering.
plasticizer—a paint ingredient which imparts flexibility.
plastisol—film former containing resin and plasticizer with no solvents.
pock marks—pits; craters.
pole-gun—spray gun equipped with an extension tube.
polymer—a large molecule formed by polymerization.
polymerization—chemical reaction in which small molecules combine to form large molecules.

polyvinyl acetate (PVAc)—a synthetic resin used extensively in emulsion (water) paints; produced by the polymerization of vinyl acetate.

polyvinyl chloride (PVC)—a synthetic resin used in solvent type coatings produced by the polymerization of vinyl chloride.

porosity—degree of integrity or continuity.

pot-life—time interval after mixing of reactive components during which liquid material is usable with no difficulty.

pressure balance—in spray painting, relationship of pot pressure to atomizing air pressure.

pressure drop—loss in pressure due usually to length or diameter of line or hose.

pressure feed—fluid flow caused by application of air or hydraulic pressure to paint.

pressure feed paint tank (pressure pot)—fluid container in which fluid flow is caused by air pressure.

pretreatment—chemical alteration of the surface to make it suitable for painting.

preventive maintenance painting—period touch-up painting or application of full coats of paint before deterioration starts.

prime coat—first coat on a substrate.

primer—material used for prime coat; usually a rust-inhibitive coating when used over ferrous metals.

production rate (sq. ft./day)—measurement of surface area cleaned or coated in one working day by one man.

profile—surface contour of a blast-cleaned surface as viewed from the edge; cross section of the surface.

profile depth—average distance between top of peaks and bottom of valleys on the surface.

proprietary—available on open market under brand name.

protective life—interval of time during which a paint system protects substrate from deterioration.

pump ratio—multiplier of input pressure to indicate output pressure; ratio of air piston area to fluid piston area.

R

reaching (spray gun)—extending spray stroke too far.

rebound—paint spray bounce back. See bounce back.

recoat time—time interval needed between application of successive coats.

red label—flammable or explosive materials with flash points below 80°F. (26.7°C).

reducer—a material which lowers viscosity but is not necessarily a solvent for the particular film-former; thinner.

reflectance—degree of light reflection.

repainting—a complete painting operation including surface preparation.

repair of surfaces—all procedures required to return the surface to a satisfactory condition for painting.

resin—a material, natural or synthetic, contained in varnishes, lacquers and paints; the film former.

respirator—safety breathing mask.

rise—height.

roller coating—the act of painting with a roller; the material used for roller painting.

round pattern—circular spray pattern.

runs—curtains; sags.

rust—corroded iron; red iron-oxide deposited on metal; also other metal oxides formed by corrosion.

rust bloom—discoloration indicating the beginning of rusting.

S

safety valve—pressure release valve preset to be released when pressure exceeds a safe operating limit.

sandblast—blast cleaning using sand as an abrasive.

sandy finish—a surface condition having the appearance of sandpaper; may result from overspray.

saponify—convert to soap.

scale—rust occurring in thin layers.

scaler—a hand cleaning chisel.

scaling—process of removing scale.

seal coating—coating used to prevent excessive absorption of the first coat of paint by the substrate; a primer.

sealer—a low viscosity (thin) liquid sometimes applied on wood, plaster, gypsum board, or masonry.

seeding—formulation of small agglomerates.

separation—division into components or layers by natural causes.

settling—caking; sediment.

shade—degree of color in a tint.

shelf-life—maximum interval in which a material may be stored and still be in usable condition.

shop coat—coating applied in fabricating shop.

short oil varnish—a varnish prepared by cooking a relatively small quantity of oil with 100 pounds of resin, quick drying; brittle; less than 25 gallons of oil per 100 pounds of resin.

shot blasting—blast cleaning using steel shot as the abrasive.

shrinkage—decrease in volume on drying.

silicate paints—those employing silicates as binders; used primarily in inorganic zinc rich coating.

silicone resins—a particular group of film formers; used in water-repellent and high-temperature paints; organo-silicon polymers.

silking—a surface defect characterized by parallel hair-like striations in coated films.

skinning—formation of a solid membrane on top of a liquid.

skips—holidays; misses; uncoated area; voids.

slow drying—requiring 24 hours or longer before recoating is possible.

solids—non-volatile portion of paint.

solids by volume—percentage of total volume occupied by non-volatiles.

solubility—degree to which a substance may be dissolved.

solution—a liquid in which a substance is dissolved.

solvency—measure of ability to dissolve.

solvent—a liquid in which another substance may be dissolved.

solvent balance—ratio of amounts of different solvents in a mixture of solvents.

solvent pop—blistering caused by entrapped solvent.

solvent release—ability to permit solvent to evaporate.

solvent wash—cleaning with solvent.

spalling—the cracking, breaking or splintering of materials, usually due to heat or freezing.

spark testing—detection of holidays (flaws). Using a special spark testing tool. See holiday detector.

spark-proof tools—bronze beryllium tools.

spar varnish—a varnish for exterior surfaces.

specular gloss—mirror-like reflectance.

spray cap—front enclosure of spray gun equipped with atomizing air holes.

spray head—combination of needle, tip, and air cap.

spray pattern—configuration of spray with gun held steady.

spreading rate—area covered by a unit volume of coating frequently expressed as square feet per gallon.

SSPC—Steel Structures Painting Council

steam clean—a cleaning process using live steam.

streaks—a surface defect characterized by essentially parallel lines of different colors or shades.

stroke (spray)—a single pass with a spray gun in one direction.

styrene-butadiene resin—a copolymer of styrene and butadiene.

substrate—basic surface.

suction feed (sandblaster)—one in which the abrasive is syphoned to the nozzle.

suction feed (spray gun)—one in which the fluid is syphoned to the spray head.

surface conditioner—preparatory coating applied to chalked, painted masonry surface for bonding chalk to under surface.

surface preparation—all operations necessary to prepare a surface to receive a coating of paint.

surfacer—a paint used to smooth the surface before finish coats are applied.

sweating—condensing moisture on a surface.

T

tack—degree of stickiness.

tail line—short piece of blast hose smaller than the main hose to permit better maneuverability.

tails (airless spray)—finger-like spray pattern.

tank white—good hiding, self-cleaning white paint for exterior metal surfaces.

tapered pattern—elliptical shaped spray pattern; a spray pattern with converging lines.

tape test—a particular type of adhesion test.

test pattern—spray pattern used in adjusting spray gun.

thermoplastic—becomes mobile or softens under heat.

thermosetting—becomes rigid under heat and cannot be remelted.

thinners—volatile organic liquids for reducing viscosity; solvents.

thixotropic—a gel which liquifies with agitation but gels again on standing.

through dry—ability of film to show no loosening, detachment, or evidence of distortion when the thumb, placed on film with maximum arm pressure, is turned through 90° in plane of film.

tie coat—intermediate coat used to bond different types of paint coats.

tint—a color produced by the mixture of white paint or pigment in a predominating amount with a non-white colored paint or pigment.

tone down—the process of reducing visual prominence of an installation by the application of external coatings; blending of overall color scheme with the surrounding environment.

tooth—profile; mechanical anchorage; surface roughness.

top coating—finish coat.

touch-up painting—spot repair painting usually conducted after initial painting.

toxic—poisonous.

toxicity—degree of poisonousness or harmfulness.

transition primer (block or barrier coat)—coating compatible with primer and with a finish coat, though the latter is not compatible with the primer.

triggering—intermittent squeezing and releasing of trigger.

two-component gun—one having two separate fluid sources leading to spray head, for spraying a coating and a catalyst simultaneously.

U

underatomized—not dispersed or broken up fine enough

unit cost—cost per given area.

urethane resins—a particular group of film formers, i.e. isocyanate resins.

useful life—the length of time a coating is expected to remain in service.

V

VM&P naphtha—varnish and paint manufacturers naphtha; a low power flammable hydrocarbon solvent.

vapor degreasing—a cleaning process utilizing condensing solvent as the cleaning agent.

vaporization—conversion from liquid or solid to gaseous state.

varnish—liquid composition of oil, resin thinners and driers, which converts to a transparent or translucent solid film after application as a coating.

vehicle—liquid carrier; binder; anything dissolved in the liquid portion of a paint is a part of the vehicle.

vinyl coating—one in which the major portion of the binder is of a vinyl resin.

vinyl copolymer—resins produced by copolymerizing vinyl monomers such as vinyl acetate and vinyl chloride.

vinyl resins—synthetic resins made from vinyl compounds such as vinyl acetate.

viscosity—a measure of fluidity.
viscosity cup—a device for measuring viscosity.
volatiles—fluids which evaporate rapidly.
volatile content—those materials which evaporate; usually expressed as a percentage.

W

washing—erosion of a paint film after rapid chalking.
wash primer—a thin rust-inhibiting paint which provides improved adhesion to subsequent coats.
water blasting—blast cleaning using high velocity water.
weld spatter—beads of metal left adjoining a weld.
wet edge—fluid boundary.
wet film gauge—device for measuring wet film thickness.
wet film thickness—thickness of liquid film immediately after application.
wet spray—spraying so that surface is covered with paint that has not started to dry.
wetting oils—products used to promote adhesion of applied coatings when all mill scale and rust cannot be removed.
white blast—see 4.4.2.4. blast cleaning to white metal.
wire brush—a hand cleaning tool comprised of bundles of wires; also the act of cleaning a surface with a wire brush, including power brushes.
wrinkling—a surface defect resembling the skin of a prune.
wrist action (spray gun)—swiveling of wrist without arcing forearm.

Y

yellowing—development of yellow color or cast, in whites, on aging.

Z

zinc phosphate coating—treatment used on steel to improve adhesion of coatings.
zinc silicate—inorganic zinc coating.
zinc yellow—commercial zinc chromate pigment.